THE STORY OF OSMASTON
BY ASHBOURNE

OSMASTON HISTORY GROUP

First published in Great Britain in 2018

A Commissioned Publication Printed and Published
on behalf of Osmaston History Group
by Moorleys Print & Publishing Ltd
23 Park Road, Ilkeston, Derbyshire DE7 5DA

Email : osmastonbook@outlook.com

Our grateful thanks to Foundation Derbyshire. Without their assistance "The Story of Osmaston By
Ashbourne" would not have been completed. Foundation Derbyshire is an independent local funder,
offering a wide variety of funding programmes to community and voluntary groups working across
Derby & Derbyshire. For further details see www.foundationderbyshire.org.

Funded by:
Foundation
Derbyshire

Acknowledgements

Many people have helped in the creation of this book, sometimes with advice, sometimes with information and many local people by way of sharing their personal memories, their ancestors' details and photographs and without whose contributions this book would not have been written.

Our grateful thanks are due to David & Dinah Archer, Dr David B H Barton, Andy Birch, Bob Bowden, Mrs Anne Clowes (nee Walker-Okeover), Mr Berkeley Cole, M⁻ K Davis, John & Margaret Dawson, Derbyshire Life, The Fielding family, Louie Goldberg, Mrs Betty Hardie (nee Stephens), The Highland Gathering Committee, Mrs Pat Holland, John Holmes, Sarah Le Marquand, Mrs Marsden, Norah Moody, Caroline Mummery, Mrs Oliver, Osmaston C of E Primary School, Osmaston & District W.I., Osmaston Wind Band, Mrs Anne Redfern (nee Morley), Tim Sadler, Jerry Shenton, Molly Silcock, Susan Silcock, Mrs Sue Smith & The Allsop Family, Sonya at Ashbourne Secretarial & Printing Services, Lt. Col & Mrs Charles Swabey, Mr John Teasdale, Mr & Mrs John Thorpe, Mrs Audrey Tomlinson (nee Normanshaw), Mrs Walker, Miss Jane Walker-Okeover, Sir Andrew Walker-Okeover, Mark Weston, Mr Winstanley, Charles Wright and Jack Wright. Also thanks to the staff at Derbyshire Records Office at Matlock and a big thank you for the assistance from Derby Local Studies Library. Also, the British Newspaper Archive www.britishnewspaperarchive.co.uk and the British Library Board.

We would like to say a special thank you to Paul and Tina of The Shoulder of Mutton for their help and support with our fund raising events over the last three years and a big thank you to everyone who has supported these events.

Introduction

THE STORY OF OSMASTON and the everyday story of country folk

Our book, "The Story of Osmaston By Ashbourne" is intended to show how the village of Osmaston was transformed from a small farming community into the characterful, mainly estate owned village it is today.

It highlights the impact of the arrival of a wealthy industrialist, Francis Wright, who built the vast Osmaston Manor and developed Osmaston into an estate village. It does not, however, concentrate solely on either the Wright family or the Walker-Okeover family who took over the estate and who lived there for 75 years. The Osmaston Estate continues under the ownership of the Walker-Okeover family today but, sadly, the Manor was demolished in the early 1960s.

The book is not intended to be a formal historical record but is written as a timescale of events and village life. Its aim is to record events, reminiscences, recollections and anecdotes before they disappear from local memory through a collection of photographs, newspaper cuttings and interviews with local families. The book mainly covers events over a period of 163 years to show the effect the outside world has had on Osmaston.   Throughout this period, the village joined together in showing their sorrow at funerals, both world wars and in celebrating weddings, births, jubilees, coronations, polo matches etc.

Whilst writing the book, we have all learnt something new, whether it be the boxing matches after polo, the war horses, motor cycle racing on the Manor drives, the grandeur of the balls held at the Manor or the generosity and kindness of the Wright's and Walker-Okeover families.

We are very proud of our heritage and hope that you too will discover something new, or memories will be revived, when you read our book.

Osmaston History Group
Maggie Silcock (Chair)
Gerald Parker
Keith Tucker
Ann Plant
Althea Devine

CONTENTS

Chapter 1. EARLY OSMASTON

Our story of Osmaston begins with a brief review of how the village developed over the years from very early times. We know that people have lived in the area from prehistoric times as they have left their mark on the local landscape in the form of ancient tumuli. Within Osmaston parish itself, there are three scheduled monuments which are tumuli. These are late Neolithic or early Bronze Age bowl barrows, i.e. mounds of earth and stone built over a burial site.

Tumulus close to Wyaston Road.
This late Neolithic or early Bronze Age (2500 to 1500 BCE) "bowl" barrow is one of a pair of barrows in this location. A third barrow lies to the east and others are located close by in Clifton and Wyaston parishes. They are all included in the Scheduled Monument Record.

Photograph Osmaston History Group

The road now known as Quilow was probably named after a field to the west of the village by the same name. This may suggest the location of a further barrow, or low e.g. Minninglow, Pea Low, Arbor Low.

6th-7th Century-A later Anglian burial mound (or Hleaw) was built nearby towards Wyaston showing that there were settlements in the area at this time.

1087-Domesday Record The earliest written mention of a village at Osmaston appeared in the Domesday Book of 1086 following a property survey carried out by the Normans. It was then known as Osmundestune. There is no mention of a church in the village at that time, although only churches generating tax were recorded. A church was mentioned at Shirley.

> "in Osmundestune Wallef and Ailet had 2 carucates of land assessed to the geld; land for 2 ploughs; 8 villeins and 4 bordars have 5 ploughs and 2 acres of meadow ; woodland for pannage 1 league in length and 1 league in width. In King Edward`s time worth £4- now worth 40 shillings. Elfin holds it".
> Domesday Book Series No.27 Philip Morgan

Osmundestune was later given to Henry de Ferrers, who held a large fief in more than a dozen counties. His main English manor was at Tutbury where, with his wife, he founded the Priory.

1100-At about this date, Henry de Ferrers gave permission, together with his son Nicholas de Brailsford, to pass the manor of Osmundestune to the Priory of Tutbury.

14th Century Moving on in time, the Priory of Tutbury made a survey of their property which recorded rents due to them from Osmaston. Their records state that despite Tutbury owning the manor of Osmaston and receiving 2/3rds of the tithes payable, they did not take responsibility for appointing a minister for the Chapel. This reference indicates that there was a Chapel in Osmaston before 1400. Local legend within the village claims that there was an early religious building at Osmaston which was known as the "wicker" church. In reality, this building would most likely have been a timber framed structure with wattle and daub.

1406-Chapel The Prior of Tutbury visited Brailsford on the 16th July 1406. Priory records of the visit also confirm the presence of an early chapel. "In the presence of Sir John Basset, Thomas Montgomery and other worthy parishioners, determined that John Wyggeston (Rector) was to be responsible for supplying a chaplain to celebrate in the chapel of Osmaston with an official warning of excommunication if he did not comply with the terms".

It is said that an early building was begun about 1400 and continued until building was finally completed in 1606 due to the "unrest in the country". Parish records from 1606 are held in Derbyshire Record Office. This Chapel was most probably built when the Kniveton family held the land.

1538-The manor of Osmaston was held by the Priory of Tutbury until the dissolution of the monasteries in 1538 by Henry V111. It was then given to the Kniveton family. Matthew Kniveton held it until his death in 1562.

LAND OWNERSHIP IN THE VILLAGE

1612-Knivetons. Documents in Derbyshire Record Office show that parcels of land in the village were sold off by William Kniveton to George & Homphrey Pegge in 1612 and 1613, *"to G. Pegge, R.Hurd, R. Hall and J. Prince, the holdings that they occupy plus parcels of enclosed land"*. This included land at Bellwell Shut, the site where Osmaston Manor was later built. Further sales in 1621 included *"parcels marked out for enclosure"* and *"60 acres of furze and heath"*.

1655-Meynells. Sir Andrew Kniveton, a supporter of Charles 1st, found himself in financial difficulty and sold the remainder of his land holding at Osmaston to Francis Meynell. This sale would have also included the title "Lordship of the Manor" of Osmaston. The majority of the land in the area had been enclosed by the middle of the 17th century, prior to the Enclosure Acts.

1735-Pegge Estates. A map in Derbyshire Record Office shows various parcels of village land were owned by the Reverend Samuel Pegge in 1735. Much of this land had been bought from Sir William Kniveton by George Pegge of Osmaston and his son Homphrey in scattered plots, located mainly on the western side of the parish. The land was enclosed before 1700.

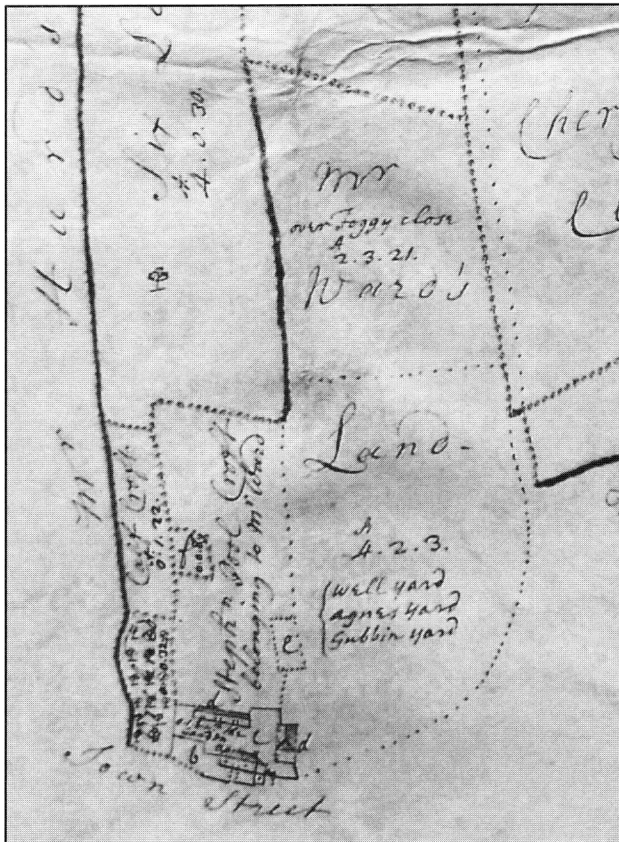

This map shows one small Pegge plot which was opposite the present church on "Town Street", now Moor Lane. Today, the village hall and school stand on part of this site. The uneven field opposite the current church still shows signs of a farm house and buildings which once stood there. Some of these buildings are shown on 1834 and 1838 maps.

The long vertical boundary, on the left of this map, today forms the edge of the village hall car park, with the public footpath following this line. The current school stands on what was then named "Stephen Pool Croft". The last traces of this pool can still be found behind the school site.
The Pegge families held the land until the 1790s.

Extract of Pegge Estate map of 1735 held by the Derbyshire Record Office ref D 741/1/2

1745-Army Troops. Part of the Jacobite army passed through Osmaston on the road to Derby. The village had grown up on one of the routes from Ashbourne south to Derby. The original route to Derby, passed along the current Moor Lane and along Madge Lane, now a green lane running east from the duck pond. This route lost its importance when the Derby-Ashbourne-Hurdlow turnpike was formed in 1773. It appears to have gone out of use by the mid-19th century but was still known as Derby Lane in the 1830s. On the west side was a medieval road to Tutbury.

OSMASTON CHURCH

In the 18th Century, it would seem that the Chapel was not always well supported by the church authorities. In 1726, the parishioners organised a petition regarding its neglect by the Rector of Brailsford. The petition appears to have had a positive outcome as changes were made. Lichfield Record Office holds a memorandum of an agreement and order "for the Rector's Curate at Shirley to serve also the cure at Osmaston".

From records in 1722 the following fees were charged :-	
Churching	4 pence
Registering	4 pence
Burial with coffin	1 shilling
Burial without coffin	6 pence
Marriage with Licence	5 shillings

Construction

There is no record of the building's construction but details of repair work from the Derbyshire Records Office suggest that it was made of brick and tile with a timber bell tower:

Expenses for maintaining the building and the churchyard:-
1795 £14-2s-6d was paid to the bricklayer plus £1-16s-16d for lime
1804 10s-0d for gravelling the church walks
1815 Paid to Mr Morley for 10 ridge tiles and 150 tiles and fetching the same 8s-3d
Paid for fetching 300 bricks and 150 tiles from Clifton 4s-0d
Paid Mr Ford for the bricks and tiles 18s-0d
Paid Mr Greatorex for his work £5-12s-0d
Paid Mr Roose's bill £3-7s-6d
Paid for soughing tiles and soughing the churchyard £1-7s-0d
1818 Paid to Thomas Oakden for tables in the singing loft 8s-0d

1666-Osmaston Church Charities

From as early as 1666, records of the local Pegge family Charity show that Osmaston church distributed bread every Sunday to the poor of Osmaston. Records for the year to March 1666 reflect an annual total of £5.4s.0d collected to buy 12 two penny loaves each week for distribution to six of the Ashbourne poor and six Osmaston poor. This practice continued as a tradition until the 1980s.

1800s OSMASTON VILLAGE LIFE

Maps and documents held in local Derbyshire Record Offices give us a good insight into the general working life of the village at this time. Farming was the main activity. Surviving Church Warden's accounts, together with the Vestry Minutes and the Overseers of the Poor accounts, also provide detail of life in the community in the latter part of the 18th and first half of the 19th centuries.

WEAVING

Hand loom weaving was well established at Osmaston by the late 18th century and gave work to both men and women. Overseer's accounts from 1800 to 1803 show that support was given specifically to the village weavers from 1800 when they were in need. The Overseer would buy materials to give to the weavers and paid them a daily or piece work rate for cloth woven in the weavers' own homes. Overseers, appointed annually, were responsible for collecting a poor rate to provide for the poor of the parish. The weaving industry nationally was affected by the growth of factories and from the economic downturn in the Napoleonic period. Although weaver cottages would have been scattered throughout the village, later census records (1841) describe two uninhabited properties in a now lost "Weavers Lane".

1800-1803 The following entries were found in the Overseers accounts for 1800 to 1803:

Paid for 6lbs Hurds* @ 12d	6 shillings
Paid for spinning	6 shillings
Paid Sarah Slater for weaving 48 yards of cloth	11shillings
Paid Fran Baker for weaving 24 yards of cloth	
Paid for 36lb of Hurds*	
Paid for 12lb of Flax	

*The reference to *Hurds* is to wool supplied by Robert Hurd who farmed at what is now known as Pond Farm. Other spinners and weavers receiving support from the overseers of the poor included:-

Betty Hodgkinson for weaving and warping 42 yards.	
William Yeomans for weaving and warping 58 yards	13 shillings and sixpence
Sarah Hodgkinson for one days` work with flax	
Martha Francis for washing and winding,	
John Hodgkinson, John Slater, John Wibberley, Edward Swindell and Mary Harris for spinning.	

Yarn made could be sold, with money received going to offset the cost of support. In 1802 £6 7s 6d was raised by the sale of yarn.

Support to weavers is recorded in the first decade of the 19th century. Both before and after this period, some of the weavers were receiving both financial assistance and coals in the winter from the overseer. It is likely that many of these weavers were fairly elderly.

1820-1830 The Directories for this period show that weaving in Osmaston had ceased.

1828-CHANGES TO ST MARTIN'S CHURCH

There were major changes after approval by the Consistory (i.e. Church) Court of Lichfield.

> "The north wall was taken down and placed 4 ½ feet further back with the new wall built 8 feet higher than the old. The wall on the south side has been raised about two feet, whereas a new gallery has been built extending from the west end of the church to the chancel against the north wall containing 5 pews".

Osmaston Church Drawn and etched by Alanjo Edwin Madelely, Derby 1844.

1830-At a Parish meeting, a rate of 5d in the pound "for the necessary expenses of the church" was set. Lewis's "Topographical List of Churches" of 1831 shows that these changes created forty three new "free sittings" and that £50 was granted towards the costs of work on the church.

LAND OWNERSHIP AT OSMASTON - JOHN BERESFORD'S WILL (1766-1834)

1834-Derbyshire Records Office holds an interesting map of Osmaston attached to a Beresford family will, (page 6). On the death of Mr John Beresford in 1834, the map was prepared to show areas of Osmaston, Shirley and Yeldersley held by the local Beresford family. The Beresford estate included 211 acres in Osmaston parish, 159 acres in Shirley parish and 187 acres in Yeldersley township.

John Beresford was an attorney who lived in Compton, Ashbourne (now Lloyds bank). He was the fourth of twelve children of Francis and Fanny Beresford of Ashbourne. Most of these children died young, leaving John and three sisters, Elizabeth, Judith and Selina.

The Beresford property in Osmaston, included Osmaston Cottage and the two fishponds, one of which had a boat house. John was influential in Osmaston, chairing Vestry meetings up to his death in 1834. It is believed that Osmaston Cottage, or The Fishing Cottage, was in fact the cottage now known as Park Cottage next to Home Farm.

A current photograph of Park Cottage but little has changed since it was built.

Photograph Osmaston History Group

In his will, the property was divided between his three sisters. Judith, who was un-married, was given property in Ashbourne for her lifetime, with the rest of the estate divided between Elizabeth and Selina. Elizabeth, the eldest sister, was the wife of John Wright of Butterley. Elizabeth died before John Beresford in 1833, which resulted in the real estate mentioned in the will passing to her "eldest surviving son, Francis Wright" who is mentioned in the will and is one of the two executors. Selina, the youngest sister, was married to the Reverend Samuel Martin, also of Butterley, who also inherited land in Osmaston. The coloured areas of the map on the following page shows the former Beresford land inherited by both Rev Martin and Francis Wright.

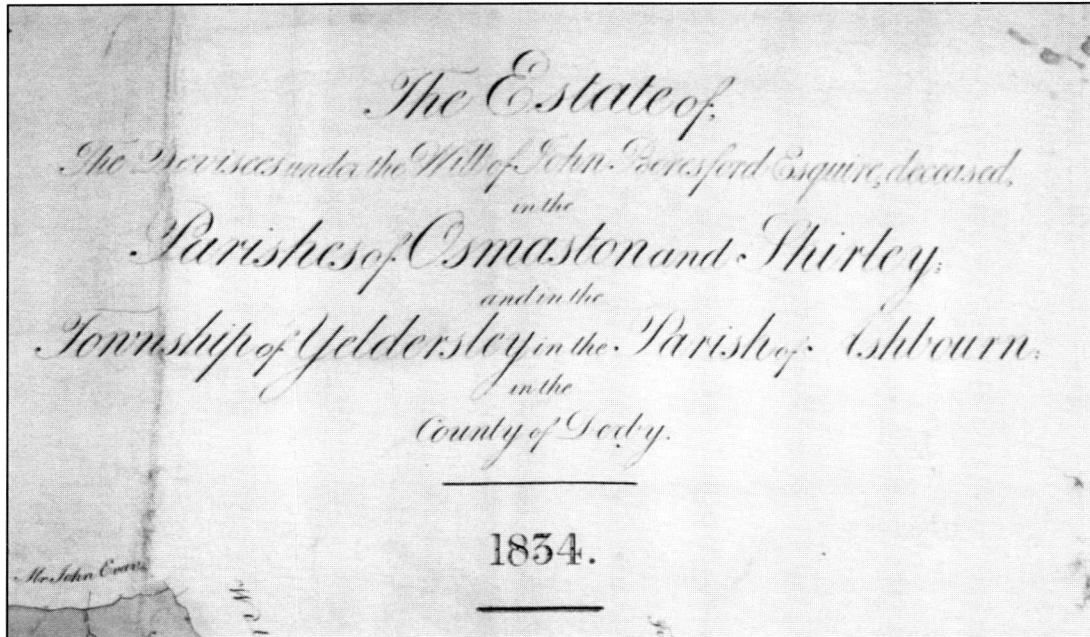

Beresford Will with Estate Map 1834 by J. Bennett of Tutbury   *D.R.O. Ref. D1849/8/1*

1836 - 1838 TITHE APPORTIONMENT ACT
Landownership Records

The Tithe Commissioners introduced parish surveys to establish who owned which land and who was liable to payment of tithes. Tithes were ancient taxes payable by land owners to the Rector. Osmaston's survey was made by J. Bennett of Tutbury and by 1838, the survey results were produced as a Tithe map, together with an Award Book detailing properties, their owners and tenants. A section of this detailed map, held at Derbyshire Records Office, on page 8, shows various parcels of land under different ownership, indicated by different colours and hatch markings.

This record gives a good snapshot of property ownership in the village before the arrival of Francis Wright who would build Osmaston Manor.

It recorded 370 acres arable land, 818 acres meadow or pasture, 10 acres woodland plus 23 acres of glebe land belonging to the Rectory. The Rector, the Reverend John Gardiner, was the owner of the tithes of both Osmaston and Brailsford. He didn't live in the area and was the vicar of the Octagon Church in Bath.

The whole Tithe Apportionment map (page 8) examined for Osmaston parish shows that the parish had parcels of land with 47 different owners. Land to the north west of the village inherited by the Reverend Samuel Martin, totalled about 96 acres. The rest of the former Beresford estate, from the 1834 will, 115 acres in Osmaston, land in Yeldersley and Shirley, was now owned by Francis Wright. His land in Shirley was the Shirley Common area, including Common Farm.

The following maps have been produced to show the land inherited from John Beresford's will and land ownership shown on the official 1838 Tithe records. The maps on the following pages have extracted details from the Tithe map to show ownership within the village by numbered tithe plots and is followed by a list of owners and occupiers.

Map Courtesy of Adrian Earp

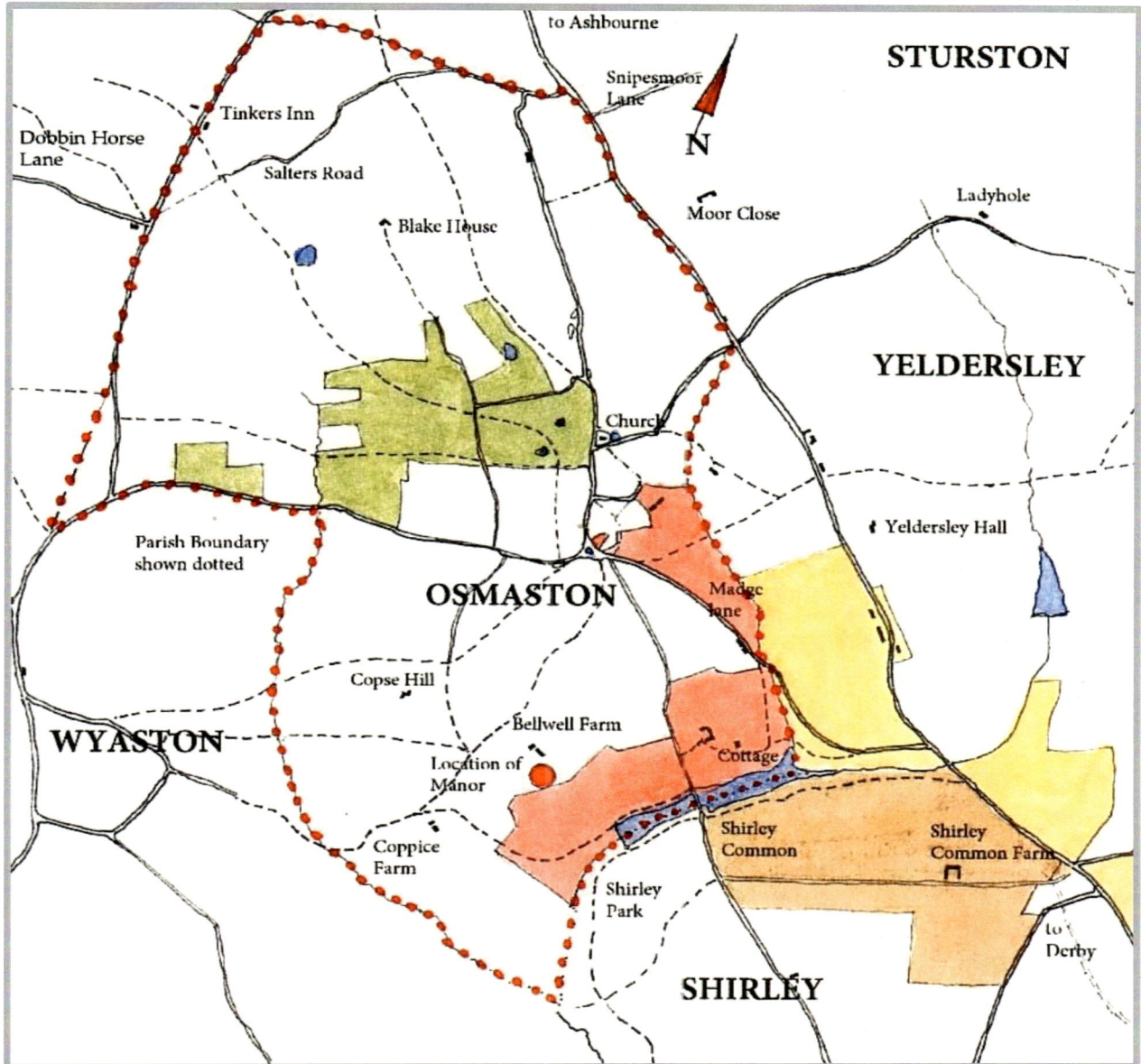

Map of Osmaston and surrounding area showing the property of the Beresford family in 1834 and coloured to show the ownership of this land as shown on the 1838 Tithe Map.

The Osmaston Parish boundary is shown as a red dotted line.

Land in Osmaston in the ownership of the Reverand Samuel Martin. He was married to Selina Beresford, the sister of Francis Wright's Mother, Elizabeth.

Land in Osmaston in the ownership of Francis Wright.
Land in Yeldersley in the ownership of Francis Wright (also owned Yeldersley Hollies).

Land in Shirley in the ownership of Francis Wright.

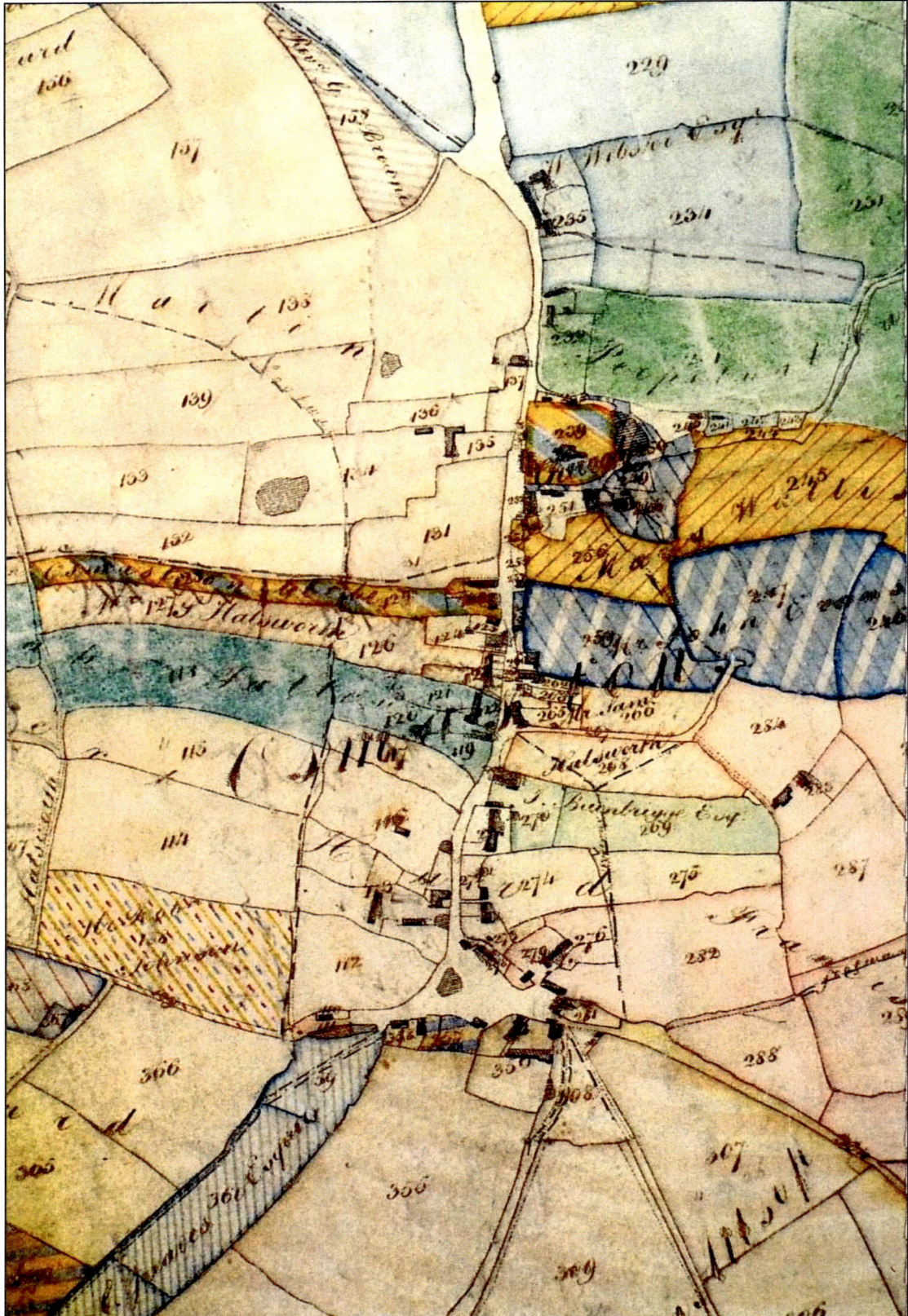

Osmaston : Section of the 1838 Tithe Apportionment Map by J. Bennett of Tutbury.

Derbyshire Record Office ref. D1849/8/2

Each colour or hatch marking shows a different owner - 47 in total within the parish.

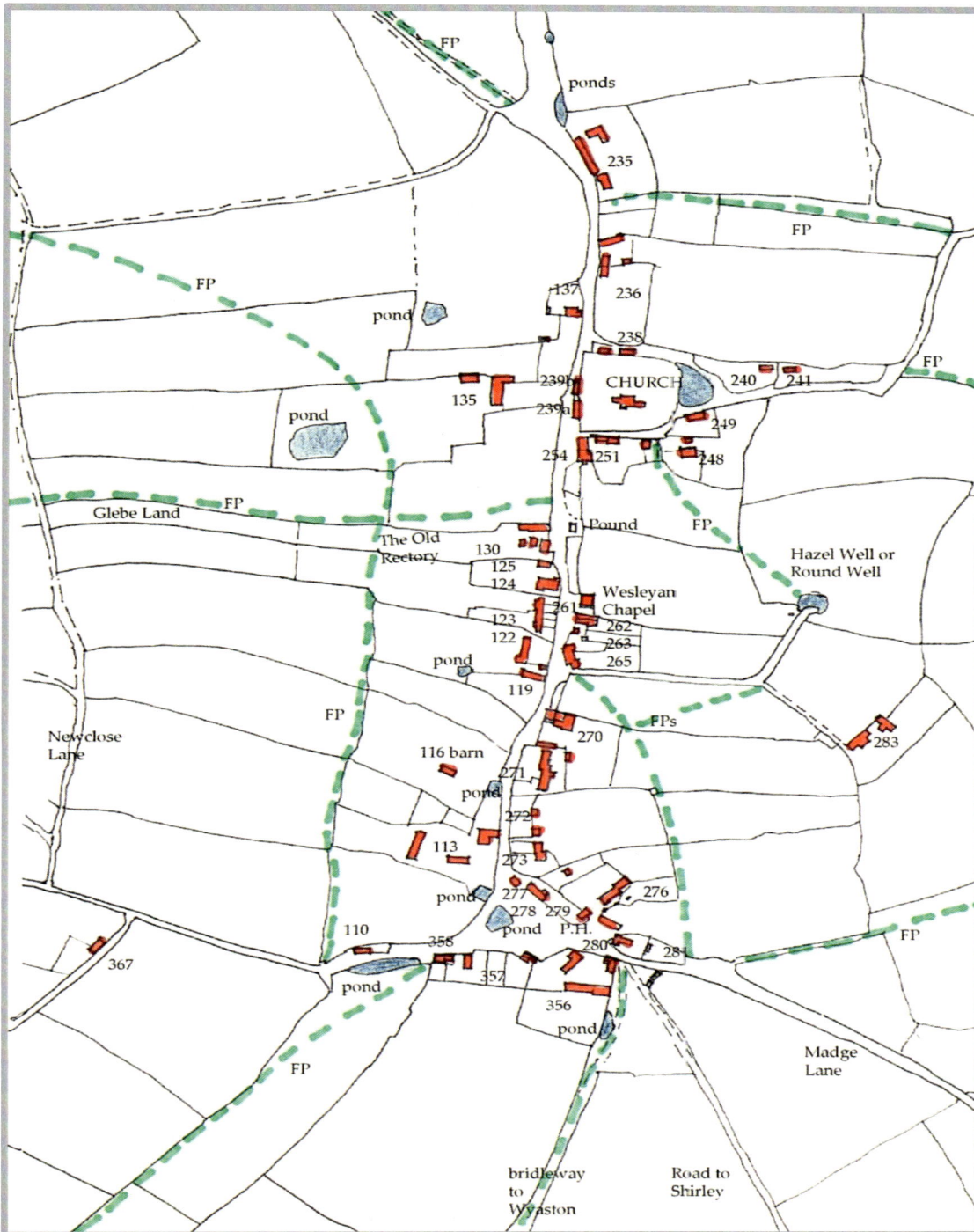

OSMASTON VILLAGE TAKEN FROM THE 1838 TITHE MAP, SHOWING BUILDINGS, FOOTPATHS AND PONDS.

In 1838, there were cottages close to the church, a Pound, a Wesleyan Chapel, several ponds and dwellings now demolished. The Shoulder of Mutton P.H. (number 279) was opposite the current village duck pond. The original Back Lane, (New Close Lane), ran on the western side of the village and indicates the original medieval structure of the village with strip plots. An "Old Manor House of Osmaston" is recorded by F Beresford Wright in a short family account of 1895 as a "barnlike building which stood at the present village entrance to the long lime avenue" – (number 356 on the above map).

9

OWNERS OF PROPERTIES IN OSMASTON VILLAGE - TAKEN FROM THE 1838 TITHE APPORTIONMENT MAP

The numbers run clockwise around road pattern from the top of the map and show 28 ownerships.

235	**Owner**. William Webster
	Occ. George Jackson farming
	127acres
	Part of Osmaston Glebe from 1862-74
236	**Owner**. Rev. Gervase Brown
	Occ. Joseph Wallis 23 acres
238	**Owner. Francis Wright**
	House & Garden (encroachment)
239b	**Owner/Occ**. John Kay
239a	**Owner/Occ**. John Wibberley
240	**Owner**. Joseph Smith
	Occ. Isaac Warner
241	**Owner**. Sarah Tatton
	Occ. James Hodgkinson
248	**Owner/Occ**. John Evans
249	**Owner**. John Evans
	Occ. Elizabeth Redfern
251	**Owner/Occ** William Wibberley
	House & Wheelwrights Shop
254	**Owner**. John Branston
	Occ. George Wibberley
261	**Owner/Occ** Joseph Greatorex
	Blacksmiths shop & Shoeing shed
262	**Owner**. Joseph Greatorex
	Occ. Susannah Edwards
264	**Owner/Occ** Joseph Greatorex sen.
265	**Owner/Occ**. Samuel Hallsworth
270	**Owner**. Joseph Bainbridge
	Occ. Joseph Greatorex jun
270a	**Owner**. Joseph Bainbridge
	Occ. Thomas Green
271	**Owner**. John Hellaby - cottages
	Occ. John Hudson
	Mary Frost
	Joseph Slater
	Joseph Pegg
	John Bainbridge
	William Plant
	John Francis
	Thomas Plant
273	**Owner**. Robert Hurds devisees
	Occ. Alice Johnson
276	**Owner. Francis Wright** - cottages
	Occ. Elizabeth Wibberley
	Robert Baines
	James Hodgkinson
	Mary Wheeldon
	Abraham Hodgkinson

277	**Owner/Occ** Sarah Hodgkinson
278	**Owner/Occ** Isaac Hodgkinson
279	**Owner. Francis Wright**
	The Shoulder of Mutton P.H.
	Occ. John Bestwick
280	**Owner**. William Brownson
	Occ. John Allcock
283	**Owner**. **Francis Wright**
	Occ. Joseph Greatorex – farming
	18 acres (now Hazelwell farm)
356	**Owner** Sar Gridon, Jos Eyre, Eliz Allsop
	Occ. Joseph Frost - farming 122 acres
357	**Owner**. William Oakden
	Occ. Herbert Baker- house & garden
358	**Owner** Sar Gridon, Jos Eyre, Eliz Allsop
	Occ. Joseph Frost - house & garden
110	**Owner/Occ**. William Tomlinson
113	**Owner**. Robert Hurds devisees
	Occ. John Collins - farming 81 acres
	(now Pond Farm)
119	Barn Occ . John Collins
367	Barn Occ, John Collins
122	**Owner**. Sarah Tattan
	Occ. Occ. John Kirkland –two houses
123	Owner. Samuel Hallsworth – cottages
	Occ. Ellen Plant
	Fanny Wheatley
	John Massey
	Charles Taylor - shoemaker
	James Onsley
	Berresford Adams
	William Palmer
124	**Owner/Occ**. William Murfin
125	**Owner/Occ**. Hannah Mellor
130	**Owner**. The Rector John Gardiner
	Occ. Henry Prince – farming 27 acres
	Known as Rectory House this is
	Glebe land at this time.
135	**Owner**. The Rev. Samuel Martin
	Occ. Thomas Sherwin - farmbuilding
	(the original house shown on the
	Pegge Estate map now demolished)
137	**Owner**. The Rev. Samuel Martin
	Occ. Thomas Sherwin - Farmhouse
	farming 92 acres.

Courtesy of Adrian Earp.

10

1838 FRANCIS WRIGHT ESTATE Many accounts of Osmaston generally suggest that Francis Wright had inherited the Osmaston estate from his mother, or purchased it from the Meynell family. It is likely that he may have purchased the title of Lordship of the Manor from the Meynells and he clearly inherited some land through his mother's family. John Beresford's will (1834 deceased) together with the Tithe records of 1838 show that Francis Wright owned only a part of Osmaston. To build Osmaston Manor on his preferred site, he needed to purchase the adjoining Bell Well Farm. This farm of 56 acres was owned by William and John Burnside, occupied by Joseph Cresswell and described as "old turf meadow" growing about 16 acres of wheat, oats, barley etc. More property was acquired by Wright over a long period of time.

1841

THE FIRST NATIONAL CENSUS OF HOUSEHOLDS This Census is important as it offers the last glimpse of the village before the development of Osmaston village and Osmaston Manor had any real impact. It provides details of the varied occupations of villagers which reflect the activities of a self-sufficient village like those throughout England.

The Wright family Francis and his family, having left Lenton, were now living in a property in Osmaston, most likely The Cottage, (now known as Park Cottage) where Francis could keep a close eye on proceedings at the Manor site. It is interesting to note that his son, Fitzherbert Wright, was born at Osmaston in 1841, yet a year later, his daughter Judith was born at Lenton.

Osmaston population- 271 people (119 male and 152 females) were living in 62 houses. This was an increase compared with 225 in 1801, but a decrease when compared with a recorded 289 in 1831 (Bagshaws Directory of Derbyshire). There were also fourteen farms, seven of which were named : Blake House, Tinkers Inn, Pastures, Copse Hill, Coppice, Bell Well and Rectory House.

Analysis by Occupation of Head of House

Farmer	19	Wheelwright	2
Labourer	17	Gardener	1
Independent	8	Coppersmith	1
Joiner	2	Writing Clerk	1
Charwoman	3	Blacksmith	1
Tailor	1	Chelsea pensioner	1
Lace maker	16	Horse keeper	1
Shoemaker	1	Gun maker	1
Washerwoman	3	Baker	1
Nurse	1	Beer seller	1
Widow	2	Gamekeeper	1

1841 Census – Lace Making
There were 16 females aged from 11 to 50 years, listed as "lace workers". The majority were in the 20-30 age range. This work was lace embroidery onto machine made net.
The Ashbourne area was heavily involved with this type of work with Ashbourne itself having over 80 such lace workers in 1841. There were no weavers recorded and one beer seller.

Many towns and villages in the East Midlands had lace machines at one time or another. In the 1840s most lace machines were small and worked by hand and could be located in houses or workshops. This carried on until the manufacture of machine-made lace in large purpose built factories.

Lace runners or embroiderers at work, c. 1843. Source: Charles Knight, The Pictorial Gallery of Arts. Volume 1 Useful Arts.

LICENSED PREMISES

1841-YELDERSLEY These premises are named on the later 1841 Tithe Map as The Running Horses on Painters Lane and are connected to Osmaston and to Yeldersley Hollies by footpaths.

The Derbyshire Directories (Greaves 1829: Bagshaws 1846 also refer to these). Located on the 18th Century turnpike it was a pick up/refreshment point. The 1841 Tithe map shows that adjoining the building, in front of the present row of cottages, was a pond where horses could be watered. The Running Horses also seems to have been a victim of declining traffic on the turnpike and closed around 1850. On the 1851 Census it appears to be a private house.

OSMASTON

The Derbyshire Record Office Quarter Sessions (1753-1823) show licenses granted together with the names of their guarantors.

These records show only one licensee for Osmaston throughout these years. No premises are named in these records but by 1800 other documents were referring to the "Shoulder of Mutton". However this has not always been sited at its present location. The Maps, shown on pages 8 and 9 clearly show that the Shoulder of Mutton was located in one of the thatch cottages, (now known as Elm Tree Cottage) near the pond. This was within the land that was inherited by Francis Wright. His puritan views almost certainly had a bearing on the moving of the Inn to its current building which was a former farm house on Moor Lane in the 1850s.

On the left corner is the village pub and opposite is the village water pump

Photograph Osmaston History Group

Recorded Innkeepers at the Shoulder of Mutton (situated by the duckpond in 1838)

1783- 1803	Hannah Swain
1804-1812	James Swain
1813-1821	William Toplis
1822-1824	Joseph Wallis
1825-1840	John Bestwick
1841-1843	William Lees (Beer seller)

It is also believed that Corner Cottage in Osmaston Village was also an Ale House called the New Inn, but no license was ever recorded, and this also applies to Tinkers Inn and Tinkers Inn Farm.

FRANCIS WRIGHT ACQUISITION OF OSMASTON LAND

Much of this will have been by private purchase. One of the early purchases will have been the Bell Well farm, for most of the Manor and outbuildings were built on this site and it was an integral part of Francis Wright's plans.

OSMASTON, NEAR ASHBORNE.

TO be SOLD or LET, all that substantial and convenient HOUSE, with the Stable, Barn, Dairy, and other requisite Outbuildings thereto belonging, all newly erected, now used as a FARM HOUSE and INN, and called " The Grange Inn," situate on the road side at Osmaston Grange, in the County of Derby; and also TEN CLOSES of PASTURE and ARABLE LAND adjoining to, and occupied with the said House, containing altogether about 28 Acres.

This Estate adjoins the Derby and Ashborne Turnpike Road, about one mile and a half from Ashborne; and, commanding extensive and varied views of the beautiful surrounding Scenery, presents an opportunity of purchasing or taking one of the most delightful sites for a Villa, in the County of Derby.

A considerable part of the purchase-money may remain on security of the premises.

The present Tenant will show the property; and for further information and treaty, apply to Mr. Robotham, Solicitor, Derby.

Derby, 12th September, 1850.

In 1850, the recently erected Grange Inn was put up for sale with 28 acres of farmland. It had probably been built to serve traffic on the Derby to Ashbourne Turnpike at about the time that The Running Horses at Painters Lane had closed. Although the name of the purchaser was not recorded by the newspaper, it was undoubtedly Francis Wright.

TO BE SOLD BY AUCTION,
By Mr. Hobson,

At the House of Mr. TOWNSEND, the Shoulder of Mutton Inn, Osmaston, on MONDAY, the 24th day of August next, at Five o'clock in the Afternoon, subject to such conditions as will be produced:

TWO Closes of Rich MEADOW LAND, lying together, in Osmaston, called *Range Flats*, containing about 4 Acres, in the occupation of Mr. Henry Prince, who will shew the same.

For further particulars apply to Mr. WISE, Solicitor, Ashborne.

30th July, 1846.

The occasional newspaper advertisement offered small parcels of land for sale and it would seem likely that these were all added to the Wright estate.

THE BAGSHAW DIRECTORY OF 1846

The Directory shows that Osmaston was still a Chapelry of Brailsford and that the land was principally used for grazing. The Lord of the Manor is shown as Francis Wright. It notes that *"weaving was formerly carried on in the village but by now has completely disappeared"* and that *"the Methodists have a neat brick chapel"*.

This chapel was still referred to about ten years later but seems to have disappeared shortly after this time.

EARLY OSMASTON PROPERTY – HOME FARM AND WEATHER VANE

It is thought that Home Farm was built next to Park Cottage (where the Wright family were living) in the early 1840s and would have proved extremely useful to the family.

Photograph Osmaston History Group

Home Farm Weather Vane

Photograph Osmaston History Group

The Farm had 5 sleeping rooms, parlour, kitchen, cheese room, dairy and offices. There were Lofts and machine rooms with shafting from a 12ft over-shot water wheel, supplied from shoot and pipe, connected with the reservoir, so that much of the farm work was efficiently done, without expense, by water power.

(The above description was taken from the Estate details when the Manor was sold by John Osmaston)

Chapter 2.   ARRIVAL OF FRANCIS WRIGHT

FRANCIS WRIGHT (1806-1873)

The decision by Francis Wright to build Osmaston Manor would have a lasting effect on the village and the surrounding area.
 Much has been written on the life of Francis Wright and his move to Osmaston during the 1840s. He was the son of a banking family and was now an established, wealthy businessman when he built Osmaston Manor.

Courtesy of National Portrait Gallery

THE WRIGHT FAMILY BACKGROUND

John Wright Snr. was the son of Thomas Wright and Grandson of Ichabod Wright founder of a successful banking business in Nottingham.

1790-John Wright Snr., who was a banker and
Industrialist, joined the bank, with his cousin, also known as Ichabod, and also John Smith Wright.
1791-John Wright Snr. married Elizabeth Beresford, the daughter of his future business partner at Butterley, making Francis Beresford, a solicitor of Compton House, Ashbourne, his father-in-law. This is where his connection with Ashbourne began.   Following their marriage in 1791, they lived at Willoughby Hall, Nottingham. Their first born son, John Wright and four daughters were born at the Hall. John Wright Snr., then built Lenton Hall, now a university hall of residence at Nottingham University, designed by architect H I Stevens. It was here in 1806 that their second son Francis Wright, was born into what was a very wealthy family.
1795-John Smith Wright retired, leaving John Wright Snr. and Ichabod to run the bank which they named Wright & Co.

John Wright, whilst still running the Wright Bank, became involved with the Iron Industry through his father-in-law Francis Beresford:-

1790-Francis Beresford and Benjamin Outram had already formed Benjamin Outram and Co. who, whilst excavating for the Cromford Canal with William Jessop had discovered coal and ironstone. Francis Beresford provided financial assistance in purchasing Butterley Hall Estate etc.
1791/2- Around this time John Wright Snr. and William Jessop joined Francis Beresford and Outram in Benjamin Outram & Co.
1803-Beresford died and John Wright took up his shares.
1805-Outram died and one of Jessops sons (William) took over.
1807-The company was renamed the Butterley Company.

The Butterley Company became one of the largest British iron and engineering companies supplying railway engines, tracks and buildings. Locally, they supplied the Cromford and High Peak Railway (a winding engine for the latter still exists in working order at Middleton Top Engine House near Wirksworth). In the 1860s the company produced the iron for the structure of St Pancras railway station, which still bears the Butterley Company name on the girders.

DEATH OF JOHN WRIGHT'S ELDEST SON

1827-John Wright's eldest son, John Wright junior, married Cecilia Georgiana Byng while in Paris. She was the natural daughter of Admiral Hon. George Byng and was born in Madras, India as a British subject.

John died the following year, in Naples, Italy, leaving his widow and a seven month old daughter, Lucy, who would become a well-known, published authoress of religious poems.
Following the death of their son, John Wright senior wrote a new will which made provision for the support of his granddaughter, Lucy and notes their second son, Francis as the main beneficiary.

In 1829, at the age of 23, Francis Wright was also given his father's shares in the Butterley Company.

MARRIAGE OF FRANCIS WRIGHT

1830-Francis Wright married Selina Fitzherbert, the daughter of Sir Henry Fitzherbert of Tissington Hall making his connection with Derbyshire even stronger. They later moved into Lenton Hall, Nottingham with their children.
Francis provided the land for a church and school in Lenton and Henry Isaac Stevens, was the Architect.

EARLY 1840s-THE ARCHITECT & BUILDING PLANS FOR OSMASTON

Francis' arrival in Osmaston would change the appearance of the village. With previous experience of funding buildings and the family's previous experience of architect Henry Isaac Stevens, it was unsurprising that Francis Wright would again choose him to design a new Manor, church and school at Osmaston. Stevens had previously built many churches and public buildings. A house on such a grand scale as Osmaston Manor was something new.

A great deal of the village was also re-modelled at this time with many of the original cottages rebuilt. Village tenants and new-comers, would have welcomed the opportunity to move into newly built houses.

Stevens had been responsible for many buildings around Derbyshire, many of which are still standing and include Full Street Baths, Derby; St Alkmunds Church, Derby; St James Church, Shardlow; Melbourne Athenaeum; St George's Church, Ticknall.

More local to Osmaston, at the same time as Osmaston was under construction were the former TSB Bank, Church Street, Ashbourne (in 1842), Clifton Church (1845), Ashbourne workhouse, which became St Oswald's Hospital, now demolished and replaced by modern housing, St John's Church, Ashbourne (1869), The Parsonage in Ashbourne (1853), St. Peter's Church, Parwich (1872) and Callow Hall near Mappleton 1849-1852.

Henry Stevens was certainly a busy man during this period.

1843-The current School and Church were two of the first buildings undertaken as Francis Wright wanted his workmen to have a school for their children and somewhere for them to pray.

Education and religion were high on his list of priorities and once the Church was completed he would regularly inspect the congregation to establish any absentees.

BUILDING A SCHOOL - OSMASTON C OF E PRIMARY SCHOOL

Photograph Osmaston History Group

The School consisted of Headmaster's accommodation, a Reading Room and 2 classrooms for children from the ages of 5 to 14 years. The Headmaster was Mr. Frederick Lucas and a Post Office was run from the school by Mr Marshall who was the Post Master. It is still possible to see the words "Post Office" on one of the School window lintels.

Photograph Osmaston History Group

Photograph Osmaston History Group

Local newspapers provide accounts of the newly built school.

> "The School was also of modern erection, and present a unique appearance provided with such a "House of Prayer" the means of grace within reach of all, the teaching of a faithful Minister, the advantages of sound education and the care and protection of a kind and indulgent landlord, the inhabitants of Osmaston are blessed indeed." Derbyshire Advertiser of 20 7 1849

Francis Wright was one of the earliest and warmest supporters of the Prize System for Schools especially in his mining districts and he attended the Annual Distribution of Prizes offered to Schools and judged by Her Majesty's Inspectors.

1843-BUILDING A NEW CHURCH – ST.MARTIN'S

On April 6th 1843, an Osmaston Parish meeting reported:

"Leave to be given to Francis Wright to take down the present church and to build a new one according to the plans exhibited after a faculty has been obtained for that purpose. Mr Wright hereby engaged to rebuild the same on his own responsibility except the chancel for which the Rector is responsible".

By the end of May 1843, the old church had gone and work on the new structure commenced, to a design once again, from Henry Isaac Stevens, architect of Derby. It is of medieval Gothic influence, and was the first church in Derbyshire built in this style. The cornerstone for the new church was laid by Francis & Selina Wright and their children.

Photograph
Osmaston
History
Group

At a meeting held on March 27th 1845, with the building of the new church nearly finished, the Archdeacon appointed Francis Wright as the Vicar's warden, replacing Henry Prince, who had carried out this elected role for a number of years.

Copy of original notes of Parish Meeting:

Osmaston Mar 27 1845
At a meeting held according to notice to appoint Churchwardens for this Township.

It was agreed that Francis Wright Esq should be appointed by the Archdeacon and that Mr John Townshend should be appointed by the Parish as Churchwardens for the ensuing year :-
The Churchwardens accounts were .... when it appeared that there was
A balance in hand of 3.8.1/4.

A Church rate was proposed for the ensuing year of 1 ½ to ...£
George ....
F Wright
Joseph Allsop(Snr)
John Townshend
Edward Bestwick
Joseph Frost
Henry Prince
Joseph Allsop

Design

St Martin's Church is medieval in form and contains a number of notable design features including the high-pitched roofs of both the nave and chancel, the tall four-square west tower, the side aisles, structural buttresses and stone tracery to the windows.

The current font is of Roche Abbey stone with lotus flowers carved around the bowl.

The tower houses a clock made by John Whitehurst, the third, of Whitehurst's of Derby. The clock is a double-framed type and bears a cartouche signed by John Whitehurst in 1845. It was wound manually each week by the church verger who climbed 42 steps up a stone spiral staircase in the bell tower.

1845-the tower had a peal of five bells (a sixth bell was installed in 1914). Most church bells have cast-in inscriptions, more usually, a one line quotation plus the name of the bell founder and donor of the bell. The tenor bell at St Martin's has the following long inscription :-

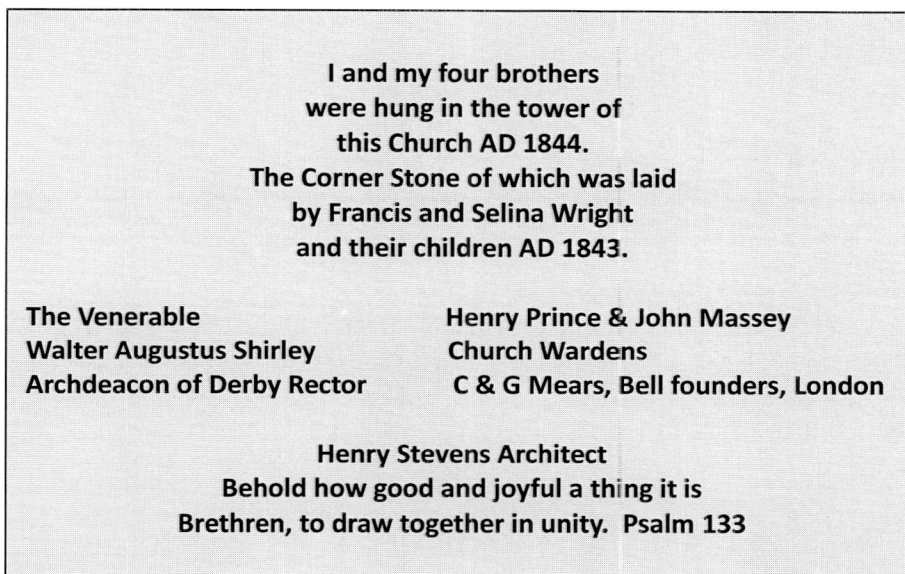

> **I and my four brothers**
> **were hung in the tower of**
> **this Church AD 1844.**
> **The Corner Stone of which was laid**
> **by Francis and Selina Wright**
> **and their children AD 1843.**
>
> **The Venerable**   **Henry Prince & John Massey**
> **Walter Augustus Shirley**   **Church Wardens**
> **Archdeacon of Derby Rector**   **C & G Mears, Bell founders, London**
>
> **Henry Stevens Architect**
> **Behold how good and joyful a thing it is**
> **Brethren, to draw together in unity. Psalm 133**

The Church opened in June 1845 at a total building cost of approximately £8000. It would appear that Bishop Walter Augustus Shirley, Archdeacon of Derby (1797 - 1847) also made a contribution to the cost of the rebuild. The Church was said to be one of Stevens' best churches and showed his ability as a church designer.

During the completion celebrations a Mr. Robert Trivett, who was playing his fiddle on the tower, fell and unfortunately died.

1845-Change to Coat of Arms-Francis Wright's father was granted a Coat of Arms in 1825 for the Wright Family with a Unicorn's head. A change was made for Francis in 1845. His Crest had 3 spearheads and the Unicorn's head. The motto attached read "AD REM", which translates "pertinent" or "to the purpose". The Unicorn's head became a symbol of the Butterley Company.

In 1847-Osmaston was constituted as an independent parish.

In 1849 a newspaper article in the Derbyshire Advertiser of 20th July reported a find which was attributed to a former church building. The current location of a stone bearing this inscription is not known.

"In the wall of the church of Osmaston, which was removed to make way for the present structure- near the pulpit, was a stone bearing this inscription, " A.D. CCCCCC", and said to have been part of the original and earliest building. But the use of A.D. was not adopted before the days of the Venerable Bede, who first used it in his history of the Saxons, about 700."

Church Charities

It has been a tradition for many centuries for the gentry to provide provision for the poor within their parish and local landowners in Osmaston continued this distribution. There are surviving records of "The Osmaston Church Charity" dating from 1926 to 1983. The charity operated for centuries before this surviving record. The record (DRO ref.D2723/R/1/176) shows that there were incomes from three charities to support villagers. These were the Gospel Greave, the Pegge family and Kniveton family charities. The first entry of 1926 states there was an annual income of £8-14s– 0d which was distributed as monetary payment to various villagers together with a loaf of bread.

The Vicar and the Church Wardens were the Trustees overseeing the accounts from the various benefactors over the years. In 1953, the ancient tradition of distributing bread was stopped with payments in cash continuing. From 1971 to 1981, the total payments distributed amounted to £8.70 per year and were paid out as £1 payments to several individuals. In 1982 the total was £7.70 and in 1983, £9.70. Most took the form of £1 annual payments to individuals to continue the tradition.

PREPARATIONS BEGIN FOR BUILDING OSMASTON MANOR

It is thought that the Blacksmiths Forge and Saw Mill were some of the first buildings to be constructed, at roughly the same time, and in close proximity to each other on the current bridleway from Osmaston to Shirley.

Osmaston Saw Mill-(photograph Osmaston History Group taken from the rear)

Early Blacksmiths were William Selby and John Tomlinson. Gerald Parker recalls that in the 1930s the Blacksmith was Mr Joe Hogston, and in the 1960s it was Tom Sutton. In the 1970s it was his son, Graham Sutton who made the horseshoe seat located by the village duck pond. This was one of the last items to be made at the forge. Opposite the Blacksmiths forge is a cart shed which still exists and it is also likely that a Wheelwright was also nearby.

The Sawmill had a huge overshot water wheel which would have pumped water to the building works and driven the saws for cutting wood etc.

Photograph Osmaston History Group

A recent photograph of Osmaston Saw Mill Water Wheel.   The Building remains virtually unchanged to this day.

The following is taken from a lecture by H I Stevens at the Ordinary General Meeting of the Royal Institute of British Architects on Monday April 28th 1851.

"An excellent and copious supply of water was secured before any portion of the house was erected.

A water wheel, fixed in a mill house near the lower ponds, whenever the power is not required for sawing or other purposes, works three pumps, which supply by iron pipes, a larger reservoir placed at such a level that the water from it rises by its own pressure to the highest roof. This throws up a much larger quantity of water than is required for ordinary purposes.

Another wheel (supplied from a large cast iron tank in connection with the storage reservoir) which is fixed at the side of the stable wall and furnished with proper shafts and gearing, turns the kitchen jack and various appliances for abridging labour in the wash house, laundry, dairy and stables.

Building sites are not always so favourable as at Osmaston for the supply of water but in many instances which have come under my own observation, due advantage has not been taken of the natural facilities in this respect".

1846-BUILDING WORK COMMENCES ON OSMASTON MANOR The first stone was laid on 22nd May with the overall construction of the Manor taking about three years to complete. The limestone used to build or clad the house came from a local source at Kniveton. Dressed by the stone masons it was laid on a very thin mortar course.

Ashover gritstone, from Stanton Moor, was used for the window and door dressings, quoins, mullions, balustrades etc. and were dressed by skilled masons, probably on site, though the more complex pieces were most likely dressed in the quarry and transported to site.

A Weighbridge was constructed in the village and each load of stone, steel, sand, timber etc. would have been weighed and recorded before entering the manor site. It is thought to have been built outside of the Shoulder of Mutton Public House.

New Village Residents

There would have been large numbers of stone masons working, not only in the quarries at Kniveton but also on site at Osmaston and it is likely that there was an almost constant procession of horses and carts bringing materials to the Manor site from all directions. We must suppose that temporary accommodation was built on site to house some of the itinerant labour force, though it is interesting to note that many lodged in the village itself and several had moved in to occupy village properties.

1851-Census Records show the following people from the building trade at Osmaston at the time of the census. It can reasonably be assumed, that most were working on completing the Manor. A comparison with the occupations shown by the 1841 census (page 11) indicates the impact of the building work on the existing village.

Householders		Lodgers	
William Walker	Engineer	Michael Wooley	Carpenter
Joseph Woolley	Joiner	William Goodwin	Joiner
George Skinner	Joiner	William Kidd	Joiner
James Wilson	Joiner	Robert Trivett	Joiner
William Peet	Joiner	William Stevenson	Joiner
William Wibberley	Carpenter	Joseph Brown	Joiner
Thomas Richie	Carpenter	Thomas Myot	Joiner
James Dyer	Plasterer	M Leak	Marble Mason
William Davy	Stone Mason	George Kirby	Marble Mason
Frederick Hibb	Stone Mason		
Adam Boyce	Stone Mason		
Henry Dix	Plasterer		
Charles Baillie	Clerk of Works, Surveyor		

Building Innovations

The Manor was one of the country's very first buildings to use an iron frame construction. Owning a family foundry at Butterley would certainly have been helpful in this and Francis took full advantage of facilities at his disposal. He originally planned a house with traditional pitched tiled roofs but with Stevens' input, an innovative design was used to provide a flat roof outline which was more pleasing to the eye and could also be used as a terrace.

This decision meant that traditional flues and chimney stacks would have interrupted the design and an alternative method of heating and ventilating smoke had to be devised to remove the need for chimneys.

Early Etching by Bemrose & Son– The Manor was built without chimneys

A Smoke Tunnel Stevens therefore adopted the "Sylvester principal" which involved every fireplace, about 40 of them, having flues that went downwards! A complicated system, the flues from all fireplaces and boilers connected, through various junctions, into a huge underground horizontal brick lined shaft that formed a tunnel. It travelled at a slight incline some 600 feet under the house and all the way to the centre of the walled garden behind the house.

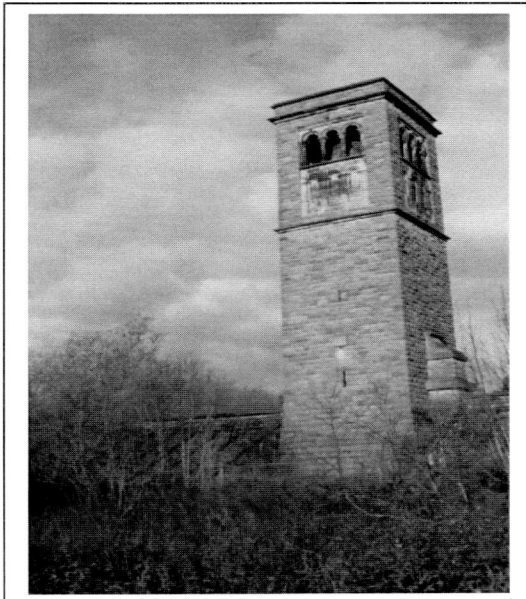

This smoke tunnel led to a **stone tower**, pictured here, in the same stone, originally 150 feet tall, 21 feet square at the base and 17 feet square at the top. It was lined with a round cast iron flue, some eight feet in diameter. A spiral, cast iron staircase was built in a gap between the flue and the tower walls. Two huge coal boilers were installed in its base where the smoke tunnel and the vertical tower met. These boilers heated the tower to create an updraft which drew smoke from all fireplaces, along the smoke tunnel and up the vertical tower into the sky. The boilers also heated the glass houses in the walled kitchen garden and also the walls themselves via large cast iron pipes running inside the hollow walls. The tops of the walls had cast iron cappings and flaps that could be opened or closed to regulate the temperature of lean-to glasshouses built along the walls.

Photograph Osmaston History Group

Despite its innovative design and huge installation costs, the system never operated successfully and within a few years the "Sylvester principal" was abandoned and would be replaced by a traditional system of flues and chimneys and the smoke tower was reduced in height and used as an observatory tower.

House fittings-Hot water was supplied to the house by more boilers installed under a brew-house built at the rear of the kitchen courtyard. This hot water was used to supply baths, heat a conservatory and keep a large upstairs plunge bath water warm. A fresh air shaft in the form of a further tower some 63 feet tall, was built next to the kitchen which drew in air to feed the various heating boilers.

A GUIDED TOUR OF THE HOUSE

The most comprehensive description of Osmaston Manor, on its completion, comes from an article in The Derbyshire Advertiser of July 20th 1849 and is reproduced in almost its entirety here. It provides a walking tour of the house. The article has been divided into headings to enable selective reading and is also punctuated by later recollections of living at the Manor by Miss Anne and Miss Jane Walker-Okeover.

External Description-*"On approaching the Mansion, the spectator is struck with the magnitude and stability which the building presents, the sombre hue of the dark blue limestone of which the walls are composed, contrasting agreeably with the light appearance of the gritstone forming the doorways, windows and all the moulded and ornamental parts of the building. The east side of the Mansion occupies an elevation of 333 feet in length, the right wing of which is the front of the drawing room and the library, the entrance to the former from off the terrace will be by a flight of stone steps, right and left, which land in the centre, the landing to be guarded by a balustrade. The doorway is circular headed and on each side of it is a window, two panes in height. The front windows of the drawing room and the library, together with those of the rooms over them are square bays while those at the end are canted bay windows, very large and projecting the width of two panes from the face of the building. The oriel or compass window immediately over the entrance to the drawing room is beautiful in design and elegant in detail. This window forms one of the chief ornamental features in the exterior of the building and is equally cheerful in the interior. The front part of this wing comprises the drawing room and the library, with the great hall, the length of the two former rooms and lighted by a window at each end."*

Osmaston Manor-Aerial Exterior View with chimneys *Photograph courtesy of Sir Andrew Walker-Okeover Bt.*

Arcade and Gallery:

"We now come to the front of the arcade, which, with the wing we have been describing and the conservatory (not yet erected) will form a quadrangle. The arcade is 150 feet in length, composed of blank arches. Above is a gallery of the same dimensions, the roof of which is flat and is surmounted by a bold parapet perforated with circular headed mullions,…. In fine weather this gallery will form a delightful promenade. Each extremity of the arcade is terminated by a square tower, from the four pillars of which spring a groined arch. The tower at the southern extremity is for the reception of the clock, which will have two faces, under a bold projecting cornice, which is surmounted by a parapet perforated round the four sides so as to form these very appropriate words "WORK WHILE IT IS DAY".

Photograph Courtesy of Sir Andrew Walker-Okeover Bt.

The remainder is the main building, part of which over the breakfast room and chapel and dining rooms, is three storeys high, the roof of it is flat, covered with large slates, 6 feet by 3, and 1 ¼ inches in thickness; it overlooks the remainder of the building and is guarded by a long unbroken line of parapet, the large stone letters of which form the words "THE WORKS OF OUR HANDS ARE VANITY BUT WHATSOEVER GOD DOETH IT SHALL BE FOR EVER".

Outside Main Entrance:

"The other part of the quadrangle comprises the entrance to the great hall and end of the drawing room, under a portico of three arches. ….

Passing by the site for the conservatory and a side entrance to the riding school which we leave to the right, we reach the west side and by a large archway enter the stable court, which is 100 feet long and 66 in width. The floors of the chambers over the stables are supported by metal beams, which project a distance of 12 feet into the court yard and form the support for a covering of slate and glass.

*The side opposite to the archway entrance is nearly 100 feet in length and entirely taken up with **coach houses**, the doors of which are to slide between the metal pillars which support the floors above. To the right is the **tennis court** and **riding school**, which is entered by a large doorway. It is 54 feet long by 30 feet wide and 27 in height. The roof, by which it is lighted, is composed of seven pairs of cast iron principles, with pitch pine boarding and a covering of slate and glass. It has been varnished and presents a light and elegant appearance. Part of the other end of the court and the remaining side are taken up by stables for 17 horses, fitted up in a substantial manner. The back entrance to the house is situated in the courtyard which is 80 feet long by 54 feet wide, in which also is the entrance to the engine house, brew house, bake house, wash house and other conveniences."*

GROUND FLOOR PLAN OF THE MANOR

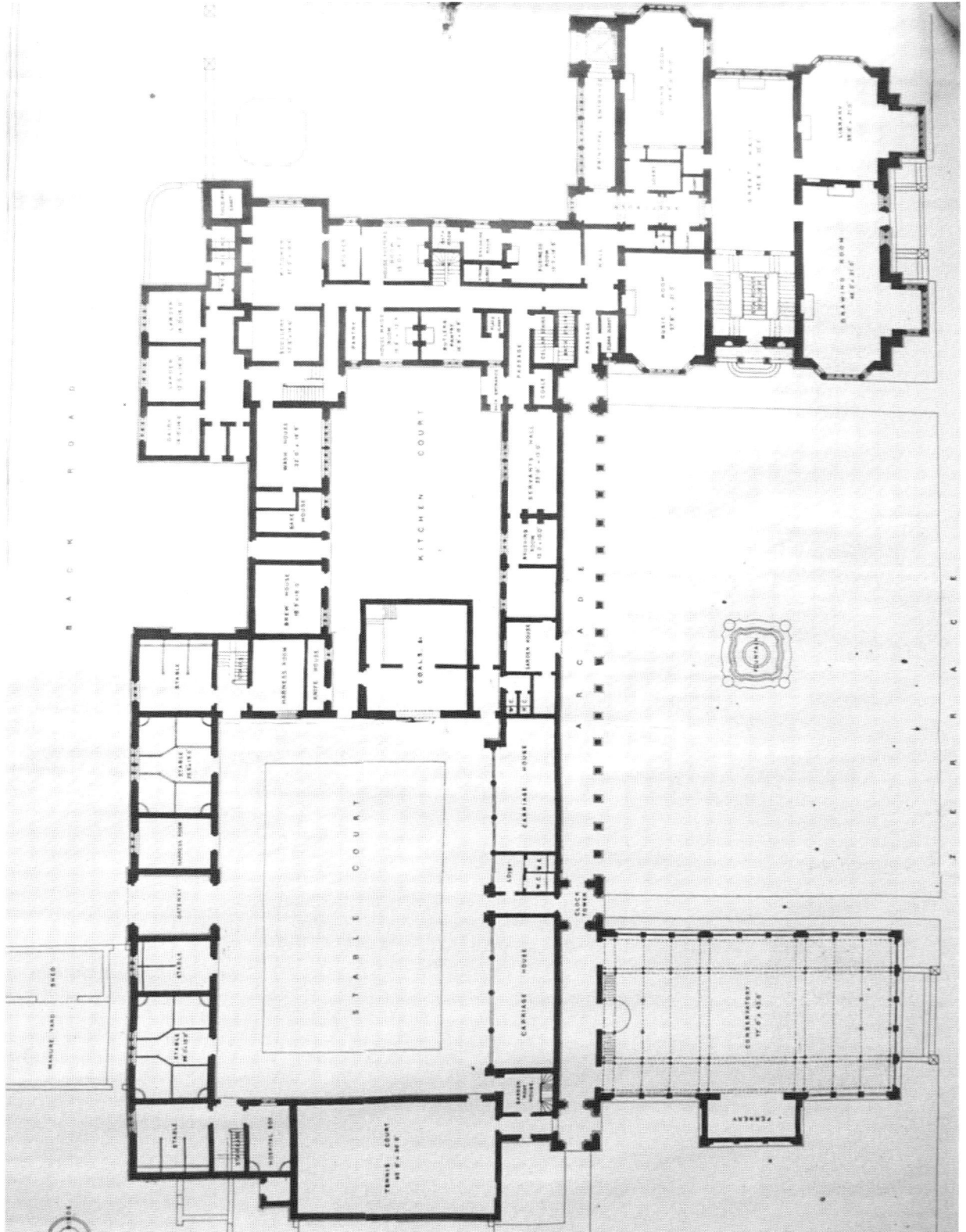

Plan Osmaston History Group

Interior Description-"*We pass by the exterior of the kitchen, housekeeper's room, Mr Wright's business room and come to the carriage entrance, access to the Mansion being gained by a large arched doorway. The arch is groined and to the left is a niche for the reception of a statue. We next join the corridor, the first part of which is about 42 feet in length and lighted by a circular-headed window, 12 panes in width; the ceiling is divided into panels and surrounded by a cornice; the upper part of the walls are also panelled and finished in marble cement. The floor is laid with rich encaustic tiles, disposed in bold and effective figures, the prevailing colours being black, red and blue and are from the manufactory of Messrs Minton of Stoke.*"

"From the stone porch the big oak front door opens into a marble hall which runs the full length of the house to a glass door leading out to the arcade" Memoirs Miss Jane Walker-Okeover

An internal Corridor
Photograph courtesy of Sir Andrew Walker-Okeover Bt.

"*At a right angle we now enter the second corridor. The floor is a continuation of the preceding one and the ceiling which is circular, is divided into compartments and these again sub-divided into panels. The design of this corridor is elegant and the design and execution so near an approximation as to be scarcely distinguished from statuary marble – the effect of the whole is evidently what was intended cheerful and splendid.*"

The lobby inside this door contains a metal table which is heated by hot water and during dinner is used as a hot plate for dishes and food as the kitchen must have been nearly 100 yds. away.......the walls were covered in embossed leather and furniture was carved natural oak, the table seating 24.
Memoirs Miss Jane Walker-Okeover

Dining Room

Photograph courtesy of Sir Andrew Walker Okeover Bt.

From the corridor we enter the dining room, which is 40 feet long, 21 ½ feet wide and 16 ½ feet in height. "The ceiling is divided into raised and moulded panels by horizontal and transverse beams, which are moulded; at the foot of the cornice and projecting slightly from the face of the wall there is also one height of framed panelling, the bottom edge of which is moulded; it has a large bay window at the end and a small one at the side."

"The windows are fitted up with oak sashes and frames; the sashes that are hung slide through the transoms, one sheet only of plate glass being in each sash, which with the frame, is let go far into the stone as to show a very small margin of woodwork and thus give to the window an extremely neat and compact appearance.

A doorway will lead out of the corridor into the great hall, which is 73 feet in length by 22 feet wide and lighted at each end by two very large windows. From the hall, access is gained to the dining room and library, both of which, together with the hall and rooms over them, are yet in an unfinished state."

The Library

Photograph courtesy of Sir Andrew Walker-Okeover Bt.

Ceiling detail, furnishings and fireplace details.

Date unknown.

Photograph Courtesy of Sir Andrew Walker-Okeover Bt.

"Under the floor was a very big water tank for use in case of fire. The walls were hung with hessian and covered by 3 tapestries."   Memoirs Miss Jane Walker-Okeover

"The best staircase at the South West end of the hall is to be of oak; the first flight will start from the centre of the floor and will land under the large window; it then ascends right and left, going up the opposite sides of the wall until it again meets on the landing, which is immediately over where the first flight commenced."

Photograph Courtesy Osmaston History Group

Breakfast Room and Chapel- *"We next enter the breakfast room and chapel, size 30 feet by 21 ½ feet; the doorway is fitted up with oak framed linings, architraves and a massive double margin oak door, which we take to be a sample of the fitting up to be followed throughout the main building. The window is similar to the one described in the dining room; the ceiling is covered and divided by bold projecting ribs into compartments and again into panels, the ribs following the sweep of the cove terminate on the top of the cornice, which projects and forms a circular support, below which trusses will be fixed. The chimney pieces in this and the dining room are only temporary construction of stone. Nearly opposite is Mr Wright's business room, dressing room and bathroom; the windows are fitted up with boring shutters, which, with the doors and other principal finishings are of oak.*

A large pair of oak folding sash doors, with circular headed fanlight forms the communication between the house and the arcade, ... From off the first landing of the second staircase a door leads to the long gallery over the arcade, along the side of which is a range of bedrooms. Another flight lands on the chamber storey. We pass Mr Wright's bedroom to the left and ascending three steps, enter the passage in which is situated Mrs Wright's boudoir, the size of which is 27 feet by 21 ½ feet. It has a large bay window, similar to the one in the Chapel, directly over which it stands. The ceiling is ornamented with rich flowing scroll work with large angle pieces and an enriched cornice. The chimney piece, a very handsome one with the Lewis quartoize style, is of veined marble. The front of the fireplace which is of enamelled china decorated with groups of flowers springing from vases at the sides and top presents an altogether and chaste appearance. The door and all the fittings of the room are of Spanish chestnut which is varnished.
Before leaving this room we cannot but express our admiration of the beautiful recesses formed by the bay windows, which when furnished with wide benches and having the window as a rest for the arm,....."

Bedrooms, School Room and Nursery-"*The other rooms situated along this passage are bedrooms and at the other end is the **school room**, from the window of which a splendid view is obtained; this is about 25 feet by 21 ½ feet and is fitted up in chestnut; it also has a dado 2 ½ feet high round the room. The storey above in which is the **nursery**, is similar in arrangement and fitted up with deal and like all the other suites of rooms contains a **water closet** and **bathroom**. The top storey of the house contains three bedrooms and a glass door leads to the large flat roof, around which is a parapet, which has been described*".

Bedrooms continued

"There were 6 double and 4 single bedrooms with 5 bathrooms in this main part of the house. Hot water was not always forthcoming. One marvellous bath had a hooded end with brass taps labelled hot, cold, shower and wave".

The windows (of the nursery) were barred to stop children falling out. A door opened onto the flat slate roof where we played."
Memoirs Miss Jane Walker-Okeover

Servants' Quarters-"*On entering the long passage, the walls of which, together with those of the kitchen, servants hall to which it leads, are all finished with clean pressed brickwork, the angles being canted and the joints finished with white putty, the skirting is slate, and the bells, 49 in number, are hung on one side of this passage. From it, we ascend the staircase to the men servants' bedrooms, ten in number, each room having a fireplace. There is also a water closet and bathroom with a plentiful supply of water. Directly above this are the women servants' bedrooms, similar in arrangement and convenience to the men's, the staircase to them being in a different part of the house.*"

Kitchen with the latest fittings – water wheel driven spit-"*The kitchen is a fine lofty room, lighted with a large window, the casement of which, as well as of all the other parts of the offices, are iron and brass; hung in the centre and can instantly be opened to any distance by a simple contrivance at the bottom. The kitchen-range occupies one side entirely; at each end are the hot plates and in the centre are the ovens, which, as well as the fireplaces, have sliding doors by which means the fires, when not required may be hid from view. A thermometer is inserted in the door for marking the exact heat of the oven and the spit is turned by the connecting machinery from a large water wheel; the plate warmer on the opposite side is a metal table, heated with hot water and surrounded with tinned sliding doors; a large copper is in the scullery and in the top of which they form a part are boiling and steaming apparatus of various sizes.*"

"When built all this was the very best in kitchen design but after the war, a nightmare."
Memoirs Miss Jane Walker-Okeover

Larders, Dairy and Washroom with Dolly and drying machine-"*Passing the larders, dairies, we reach the wash-house which is fitted up with every convenience, hot and cold rain water being obtained by taps. There is also worked by the machinery from the water wheel a dolly and a drying machine, which completely overcomes the disadvantage arising from wringing and also effects the drying very speedily, when starch or other material is to be left in, the quantity can be fixed with exactness, the machine being so arranged that the speed and therefore the effect can be regulated at pleasure from 200 to 2000 revolutions per minute and the time required for the operation is not more than five minutes. The laundry is over and is the same size as the wash house; it is ascended by a stone staircase*".

OSMASTON MANOR WAS EQUIPPED WITH THE LATEST INNOVATIONS

Innovations such as a hydraulic lift, spin driers, washing machines, rotisseries, dough kneading machines etc. powered by water and almost every room in the house artificially warmed, meant that Osmaston Manor was later given the title of "The Worlds most Technologically advanced House". Lord Armstrong's Cragside House, in Northumberland was renowned for its innovative equipment and use of water driven generators of electricity in 1878. Apart from the use of electricity following its construction, Osmaston was 20 years ahead of Cragside in the use of household equipment.

Cellars with Smoke Tunnel designed to remove the need for individual chimneys-
"Through the centre of the cellars, which are very extensive, passes the main smoke tunnel into which the smoke is conducted by flues from every part of the house. The smoke travels in the tunnel which is underground and 600 feet in length and then escapes by the smoke tower, … "
Cellar Railway and Hydraulic Lift to supply coal to each storey of the house-*"The next thing claiming attention in the cellars is the railway the length of which is about 300 feet, with curves, turntables; the coal for the supply of the house travels on this line until the coal lift is reached, the large box then being filled, it is raised by hydraulic power, four storeys in height supplying on its way each of the intermediate storeys."*

The following is taken from a lecture by H I Stevens at the Ordinary General Meeting of the Royal Institute of British Architects on Monday April 28th 1851.

"The coal-yard is placed in the centre of the stable and kitchen courts. It is however passed without notice in consequence of its being several feet below the court, on the same level as the passage leading to the stokery and communicating with the brew-house and cellars. On the inclined floor of this passage a tramway is laid with turning tables at the point of the angles. The tracks running on this way convey wine and malt liquor into the cellars and, by means of a hydraulic lift connected with it, coals or heavy goods are raised to the bedroom floors without the slightest interference with the staircases in the house. The principal lift rises to the height of 40 feet from the cellar floor and has a well or a cylinder of the same depth below, in which the plunger works. The machine was put in action by the introduction of water at the bottom, which, by its pressure forces the piston upwards. There is another lift connected with the scullery for the use of the kitchen officers. The boilers attached to the heating apparatus and supplying hot water to the baths and house generally are fixed immediately under the brew-house and the pipeage from them is intended to heat the conservatory also while a large plunge bath is rendered tepid from the same source".

Water Supply-*"Three pumps worked by a water wheel at the pond force the water up the hill into the reservoir, a distance of nearly half a mile, from which the house is supplied."*
"Water is conducted all over the house in pipes approximately four to five miles in length. In the cellars and under the dining room is the cistern into which the main water from every part of the house is conducted. It is capable of holding 30,000 gallons."
Cellars-*"The railway traverses the long passage, along each side of which are cellars and then turning to the left are the wine cellars, the appearance of the doors which clearly says "no admittance". In the construction of the cellars not less than one million two hundred thousand bricks were used and throughout the building for girders and other heavy castings there have been used upwards of 350 tons of cast iron."*
Fire Proof Construction-*"The building throughout is of fire-proof construction, the floors being supported by iron girders, with brick arches between."*

Construction Contractors-"*The Architect is Mr H I Stevens of Derby. The principal part of the works has been carried on by men in the employ of Mr Wright. The plastering has been done by Brookhouse of Derby and Bird of Ashby. The plumbing by Mr Crump of Derby. All under the superintendence of Mr Bailey, the Clerk of Works.*"

Ice House-Without the benefit of freezers, houses of this status, used ice houses to store ice for use in the kitchens. There is still evidence of one large Ice House where they would have collected ice in winter. It is likely there would have been another nearer the House. In a subsequent sales catalogue for the Manor, one is mentioned as an Ice Pit about 18ft in diameter and 12ft deep.

GARDEN TERRACES AND FOUNTAINS

Over time, the gardens fronting the house were terraced with fountains and garden furniture. The house, built on arable land growing oats and turnips, would eventually overlook newly formed parkland landscape. Earlier ponds were enhanced to develop the lakes that exist today. It is generally understood that Joseph Paxton gave advice on the glass houses and landscape design.

"*The pleasure grounds and gardens attached to the house are very extensive and are being laid out with consummate taste*".

Photograph Courtesy of Sir Andrew Walker-Okeover Bt.

Lakes-During the landscaping, alterations were made to the lakes. One of the lakes was used for ice skating and ice hockey and continued as such until the 1930s. Gerald Parker can remember it used as a skating rink then and recalls a skating party when the lake had coloured lights strung across it. Photograph courtesy of Sir Andrew Walker-Okeover Bt.

> **Fountains and water features** - Lecture by H I Stevens, architect 28th April 1851
>
> "The sawmill pumped water up to two reservoirs from about half a mile distant. One reservoir contained lake water which was used for the gardens, ponds and fountains, the other contained spring water pumped from a source under the sawmill. The water from both reservoirs was piped down to the Manor and gardens through cast iron pipes. A number of valve pits are dotted around in various locations where the flow of water could be controlled or diverted to different places as and when required.
>
> There were fountains, not only in the Manor gardens and conservatory but also in the village pond, a small pond below the Manor and massive water spout at the far end of the larger lake where another overshot waterwheel ran more pumps in addition to the ones in the sawmill. A water garden with a sunken grotto with a glass roof was also supplied from these pumps for their various ponds and waterfalls."

The larger reservoir was also used for washing and ordinary domestic use. With a bathing house, it would have been used for swimming and Gerald Parker, a member of the History Group, can remember a Mr. Oakden from the Lane End who became entangled in the weeds and drowned.

Manor Conservatory with specimen palms and ferns. A Fernery was built attached to the Conservatory Date unknown

Photograph Courtesy of Sir Andrew Walker-Okeover Bt.

The Keepers House

During the building of the Manor, other estate buildings were constructed. The Keeper's House, used by the gamekeeper, was described as a "Pretty Stone built and slated House in Swiss Style" in a sales catalogue for the estate. It had three rooms upstairs with two on the ground floor, an office and kennels. There was also a piggery.

Photograph Osmaston History Group

At a later date a new laundry building was constructed nearby and Keepers Cottage was used by the laundry staff and became known as Laundry Cottage.

1849-OFFICIAL OPENING OF THE HOUSE
A grand celebration was held for the workers.

"Several apartments in the Mansion being so far completed as to allow of the reception of Mr Wright and the members of his family, he proceeded to take possession on Wednesday last and to mark the event, gave a dinner to the whole of the men engaged at the works, his tenants and the labourers employed on the estate. The dinner took place at 2 o'clock in the spacious Riding School for 250 to 300 people. At 4 o'clock the wives and daughters of the guests, including almost the whole of the female portion of villagers, to the number of about 200, partook of tea in the riding school.

At about half past five, both men and women, together with a large number of visitors, in all about 500, assembled in the great hall to witness the presentation of a Bible and Common Prayer Book to Mr Wright and a silver ink stand to the Rev W B Hayne and to hear suitable addresses on the occasion."

Extract from Derbyshire Advertiser of the 20th July 1849

The celebrations were somewhat subdued as Mrs Selina Wright's sister had died.

Francis Wright, Selina and some of their children were now installed in Osmaston Manor. None of the children had been born in Osmaston Manor but 3 had been born at Osmaston, at possibly Park Cottage. Marcus who had been born in 1845 had sadly died in 1847. The Francis Wright family consisted of:-

John	b 21.06.1831	Radcliffe on Trent, Notts	d 01.11.1901	(age 70)
Henry	b 1833	Radcliffe on Trent, Notts	d 13.08.1880	(age 47)
Agnes	b 10.08.1834	Radcliffe on Trent, Notts	d 1857	(age 22)
Elizabeth	b 09.09.1835	Radcliffe on Trent, Notts	d 02.04.1909	(age 73)
Selina	b 24.09.1836	Larncote, Notts	d 1900	(age 63)
Francis	b 30.12.1837	Radcliffe on Trent, Notts	d 16.12.1911	(age 73)
Frances	b 06.02.1839	Lenton, Notts	d 16.02.1914	(age 75)
Mary	b 27.03.1840	Lenton, Notts	d 1920	(age 79)
Fitzherbert	b 26.06.1841	Osmaston	d 19.12.1910	(age 69)
Judith	b 16.11.1842	Lenton	d 23.03.1903	(age 60)
Marcus	b 12.05.1845	Osmaston	d 27.07.1847	(age 2)
Phillip	b 24.09.1846	Osmaston	d 27.04.1915	(age 68)

Francis Wright was a very religious man whose faith steered all aspects of his and his family's lives. During the construction of the Manor all workers were required to attend a weekly service every Wednesday in the Prayer Room as well as compulsory church attendance on Sunday for the workforce and tenants. Social functions would begin and end with prayers of forgiveness and thanks.

Despite Francis Wright's hard business head and his evangelising, he was also a genial host, opening his grand house up to numerous events from family weddings to village sports matches, gardening societies, religious groups, balls and hunting parties both inside and out on the lovely terraces overlooking the lakes. He also occasionally bestowed gifts on the poorer families and those in illness.

1849- John Wright (Francis Wright's father) died in Nottingham and Francis inherited from his Estate.

1850-Lord of the Manor Francis Wright was shown to hold the title of Lord of the Manor of Osmaston. As this did not result from land ownership, it is likely that he purchased this from the Meynell family. Glover's Directory of Derbyshire of 1827 shows that the Lordship of the Manor of Osmaston was then held by Mrs. Elizabeth Meynell of Bradley, although she did not in fact appear to own any land in the Parish. At a public auction held in Loughborough, Francis also purchased the Lordship of the Manor of Ashbourne for the sum of £1500. This purchase gave him rights over all tolls, fairs and markets in the town.

THE 1851 CENSUS

The Manor The census shows Francis and Selina sharing the Manor with five of their children – Selina (15), Francis (14), Mary (11), John (20) and Phillip (5) along with one butler, one housekeeper, one governess, one lady's maid, one nurse, one cook, one kitchen maid, two laundry maids, two housemaids, one dairyman, one footman, two grooms, one labourer, one under-gardener.

Village Shop-The Census shows a Shop in Osmaston with Eliza Coxon, then aged 61, as a "shopkeeper", helped by her sister Mary Bott. This shop was close to the Shoulder of Mutton on Moor Lane. The 1838 Tithe map shows Thomas Coxon as a baker with his wife Eliza in a small house attached to the farmhouse which became the pub.

Osmaston School - Census records show the Schoolmaster as Frederick Lucas and the Postmaster as Mr John Marshall who operated a Post Office at the School. Letters arrived from Derby at 7.30 am and were despatched at 5.30 pm. All letters were sent via Ashbourne which was also the nearest money order office. Mr & Mrs Moon who were the school caretakers moved into the School master's accommodation at the school and Mr Lucas moved to another property.

1852- COMING OF AGE OF JOHN WRIGHT HEIR TO OSMASTON

One of the first major events at the house was a banquet to celebrate the 21st birthday of their eldest son, John, on 27th June 1852. Some 400 to 500 family, friends, tenants and employees were entertained on the estate during the day with a feast and speeches for family and friends held in the Racquet Court. It was a formal event with one speech recounting that John and a brother had travelled through Europe with their tutor. In the evening, the workmen and labourers of the estate sat down to a lavish meal and an address from Francis and John Wright. The proceedings were concluded with prayers and the singing of the National Anthem. No alcohol was consumed, not even for the toast.

1855 At Osmaston Manor

Annual Meeting of the ladies Hibernian Female School Society. By the truly Christian hospitality of Francis Wright, Esq., we enjoyed the privilege of witnessing the happy scene of Thursday last where a large and highly respectable company had assembled to celebrate the anniversary of the Ashbourne Branch of the above society. Derbyshire Advertiser & Journal 20 4 1855

1856-Gardening Success Polypodium Piloselloides Natural History of Ferns British & Exotic Volume 1 by E J Lowe 1856 acknowledged Mr Henderson of Wentworth and Mr Lamb of Osmaston Manor for plants of this species.

1856-First-hand account of life at the Manor by a university friend

A memoir account written by Rev. John Barton who attended Cambridge University with Francis Wright, junior, of his visit to the Manor. This account is included courtesy of Dr David B.H. Barton, Barton Family History website, found at bartonhistory.wikispaces.com :-

"Then on another day during my visit that Easter, came a great gathering of friends and neighbours from all the countryside to hear of the work of some Irish Society for maintaining missionary work for Roman Catholics. The Great Hall was that day the place of meeting and friends assembled must have numbered some 130, all of whom remained afterwards to lunch. I remember going down with Frank through the kitchens and larders the day before and seeing the provision made for entertaining and hearing that besides 130 visitors to be provided for, upstairs there would be 80 Coachmen and footmen, also to have lunch in the Servants Hall. Such is a specimen of the way in which these dear people used influence and wealth for Christ".

1856-First-hand account of life at the Manor by a university friend continued...

"Then there was a large room, almost as long as the dining room, which was called the Prayer Room in which twice every day all that large household were gathered together – some 24 servants and often as many more visitors and friends. Nothing could have been more impressive than the way in which Mr Wright or, as it often was, Mrs Wright, conducted that service, there was such a reality about it all. Then there would be a run on The Cake, or a ramble through the Derbyshire lanes or an expedition to Dovedale, seven miles distant or a ramble through the woods. Nothing was lacking and made up a life of the most thorough enjoyment all sanctified by the feeling that the Master and Lord of all was present as the chief and honoured guest to help all with his presence." Courtesy of bartonhistory.wikispaces.com.

1857- Henry Wright (Son of Francis Wright) married Lucy Sophia Leslie Melville.

1857- Death of Agnes daughter of Mr & Mrs Wright Extract from Barton Family History website, bartonhistorywikispaces.com. Rev. J. Barton was visiting Osmaston Manor at this time.

Summer 1857 –"On my way northwards I was to spend a few days with Frank Wright at Osmaston. When I arrived there I found them in deep anxiety on account of the very serious illness of the eldest daughter, Agnes, a most beloved daughter and sister and one indeed it was a privilege to have known and loved. Her whole countenance betokening as it did the peace that reigned within and the unselfish thoughtfulness for the comfort of everyone.... Dear Agnes had been ill ever since the early spring with some internal ailment and on July 1st Henry told me that it was all over." Agnes was interred in the Family Vault in St Martin's Church. Rev J Barton

1858-DRINKING RULES AT THE SHOULDER OF MUTTON LICENSED PREMISES

The influence of Francis Wright's attitude to alcohol can be seen in an old notice recorded by a passing traveller and published in the Derbyshire Advertiser in November 1858:

A MODEL PUBLIC HOUSE

A correspondent writes- Sir, In my rambles this summer, while going from Bellion to Osmaston Manor , the residence of Mr Francis Wright, I passed through the village of Osmaston, and calling at the little public house in this place, was much amused to find on the wall of the parlour a list of rules framed, which appeared to me to be so original that I took the trouble to write off a copy of them, and should you think that they are worthy of insertion, they are at your disposal. The landlady of the house assured me that the regulations are strictly kept – if so I think we may call it a model public house.

RULES TO BE OBSERVED AT THIS HOUSE ON THE LORD`S DAY

1. *No Ale whatever to be drunk on the premises*
2. *Families may be supplied with ale to drink with their meals at home*

ON WEEK DAYS

1. *On no account to allow any oaths profane language or cards*
2. *No ale to be filled to anyone if he appears to have had enough or if he comes in having been drinking elsewhere.*
3. *Never to furnish more than two glasses of spirits at a time.*
4. *No ale to be filled after nine o`clock.*
5. *As this house is kept open for accommodation of travellers and those transacting business in the Parish, parties are not allowed to frequent this house for the mere purpose of drinking.*

NB. *It is particularly requested that everyone frequenting this house will to the utmost of his power,assist the landlord in maintaining the observance of the above rules, and preserving at all times peace and good order.*

1858- Village tenants in need are given assistance

"Through the kind liberality of Francis Wright, Esq., of Osmaston Manor, the poor widows and families of Osmaston and Shirley have been presented with a ton of coals each, and numerous poor persons of the above villages have been supplied with flannel and warm clothing,—an example well worthy of imitation".

Derbyshire Advertiser & Journal 19 2 1858

1859-A Double Wedding of Two Daughters – Extract from Barton Family History website, bartonhistorywikispaces.com by Rev. John Barton who attended the wedding.

"Two of Mr & Mrs Wright's daughters were to be married – the younger daughter Fanny (Frances) to our dear brother Frederic Wigram, and the elder daughter Elizabeth to Mr Bridges Plumptre. Frederic had won Fanny's heart during the previous summer whilst detained at the Manor…. And the marriage was a subject of great rejoicing to both families as it was to ourselves individually. The wedding was without exception the prettiest and most perfect in all respects that I was ever present at, or can expect to be again.

There is a practice in that part of Derbyshire known as the Tissington Well Dressings, consisting in the ornamentation of a board covered with a thick coat of wet clay with a tapestry formed out of the heads of freshly culled flowers, these being dibbed into the wet clay by means of a slate pencil and thus kept in position when the board is placed upright, while the moisture of the clay keeps them fresh. All sorts of coloured devices are made in this way- the different colours being represented by flowers of a corresponding hue. Such devices were introduced into the wedding festival decorations with grand effect, the most striking being a huge shield suspended over Mr Wright's chair at the luncheon table which was served in the racquet court on which were again quartered, also in colours, the arms of the two bridegrooms. Along the gallery at the end of the racket court ran a band of golden gauze on which stood out the purple daisies, looking like the richest gold and purple velvet…

About 80 people sat down for the wedding breakfast….."

Rev. J. Barton

1860-Exhibition of Flower Gardens and Pleasure Gardens at the Manor

WEDNESDAY, July 4th, 1860.

"The Exhibition will be open to subscribers to the society (and non-subscribers on payment of 2s. 6d.), at One o'clock; and to the public at Two o'clock, on payment of sixpence each; and after Four o'clock, to all persons tidily dressed, at threepence each. - Tickets for admittance to the Exhibition, the Flower Gardens, and Pleasure Grounds, may be had of the - Secretary, of Miss Hoon, and Messrs. HOBSON, Stationers, Ashbourne; at the School-rooms, Osmaston, Shirley, Edlaston, and Bradley; and on the day of exhibition at the Front Entrance, near the House, and the Carriage gate from Wyaston."

Derby Mercury 27 6 1860

1861 Census

School- The village School continued with a Richard Wilkes as a National Schoolmaster and his wife, Elizabeth Wilkes as Schoolmistress.

Shop- The village shop is shown as being in possession of a Bryan Wibberley as a "Shopkeeper" with his wife Elizabeth, daughter Martha and sons, Charles and John. At this time the shop and the postal service were separate undertakings. Bryan Wibberley died in 1874, he was described as a grocer and baker and his wife Elizabeth continued as a "Shopkeeper".

1861-Cricket Match at Village

A cricket match recorded between Osmaston and Ednaston, had the following teams:-

Osmaston		Ednaston		
F B Wright	S Thornby	W Boden	W H Sale	R Thomas
V Martin	W B Hall	J Richardson	C J Boden	
B Fitzherbert	W Fitzherbert	J Copestake	C A Wade	
C Watts-Russell	J Hall	H Boden	P Richardson	
G Richards	C Edwards	W F Ashton	C J Holden	

1862-Battle Drill at Osmaston

"The Butterley and Dove Valley Rifle Corps marched to Osmaston Manor to carry out Battalion drill and skirmishing in the grounds before an audience. Attacks took place from the woods and finished with a bayonet charge at the sawmill." Derby Mercury 8 10 1862

1862-The Colonial Church and Schools Society

"On Saturday last, October 4th, the masters and mistresses of the various schools, together with several Scripture readers employed by F. Wright, Esq., enjoyed their annual treat at Osmaston Manor. The weather proving beautiful nothing was wanting to render it a day of much enjoyment to the invited. Mr. Wright and his family, by their kindness and condescension, strove to make all happy; the time passed only too rapidly, and when it became necessary to return all united in cordially expressing their thanks to Mr. Wright for his generous hospitality."
Derby Mercury 8 10 1862

Also in that paper- "**Dove Valley Rifle Corps Band** A donation of £31 has been received from Francis Wright, Esq., of Osmaston Manor, since the closing of the amateur concert account."

1862–Marriage Francis Beresford Wright married Adeline Frances Henrietta Fitzherbert.

1863- Osmaston Reading Room Society held their first meeting in the School classrooms on 22nd April 1863 for the purpose of conversation. This society would hold meetings where lectures were given by visiting lecturers and artefacts were displayed and discussed. A nominal membership fee was charged annually.

1863-Marriage of Francis Wright's daughter. Mary Wright married Charles Douglas Fox, the son of Sir Charles Fox, a civil engineer who designed the Crystal Palace. Charles Douglas was senior partner of Douglas Fox and Partners. The Mersey Tunnel, designed by his father, was built by Charles Douglas as joint engineer to the Mersey Tunnel Co. as were the Snowdon Mountain Railway, and part of the Great Central Railway. He worked on several London early tube lines: the Great Northern, the Hampstead, linking Charing Cross, Golders Green and Highgate. He was joint engineer of the Railway, the first electric elevated city railway in the world.
Another of Francis Wright's daughters would also later marry into this family.

1864-Life at the Manor Rev. John Barton who had visited in 1856 as a friend of Francis Junior, returned to stay at the manor with his wife, Emily. Emily's memories of the Manor are provided courtesy of the Barton Family History website, found at bartonhistory.wikispaces.com:-

> "In June we went to Osmaston Manor together, near Derby, the home of the Wright family. It was a rare pleasure and privilege to breathe so Christ-like an atmosphere in so palatial residence. Our kind host himself took me all over the place, showing me everything (even to the mashing of potatoes!) was worked by machinery, turned by a stream!".

1865–Fitzherbert Wright married Charlotte Rudolphine Von Beckman.

1865-Trent College Francis Wright was a founder member and involved in the building of the College. According to some early records, Trent College was "designed as a boarding school for boys of the middle class; that is, for the sons of farmers and men of business, and of such professional men as are not able to meet the expenses of the great public schools". The school opened its doors to its first 53 students in 1868 and there is a large memorial to Francis Wright.

1867–Francis Wright was President of the Reading Room Society which continued to meet in the Reading Room provided for the village which served as a school room during the day within the School. Reading Rooms commonly provided newspapers.

> **1867 Osmaston Manor Garden Society.** "The first meeting of this society, established for the encouragement of all and good taste in gardens, and the cultivation of superior flowers, vegetables, and fruit, was held in the beautiful grounds of Francis Wright Esq., at Osmaston Manor on Thursday." Nottingham Guardian 12 7 1867

1868–The Butterley Co. was the largest producer of iron in the country and cast the massive arches forming the span of St Pancras Station. At the time, it was the largest unsupported structure in the world.

WRIGHT FAMILY WEDDINGS

1868-Philip Wright, married Alice Elizabeth Bury.

> ***1869-Wedding Of Selina Wright*** "On Wednesday, the 25th, the nuptials of Selina, third daughter of Francis Wright Esq. of Osmaston Manor, with Francis, second son of Sir Charles. Fox Knt., were celebrated at the village church of Osmaston... The Wedding Party left the Manor at 10.45 proceeding to church under numerous triumphal arches, erected by the villagers to whom great credit is due for their heartfelt wishes for the happiness of her who had so long lived amongst them.
>
> The entrance to the churchyard was surmounted by the texts "Guide me by Thy counsel...God is the Strength of my heart". The arms and initials of the bride and bridegroom, also furnished many pretty devices for the shields and banners – in fact there was not a single house that had not contributed something to the gay and festive appearance of the village. After the service – which was conducted by the Rev. Gerard Smith, assisted by the Rev. Henry Wright – a hymn composed for the occasion was heartily sung by the school children and congregation.
>
> After signing the register the happy pair proceeded to the carriage, the bride's path being thickly strewn with flowers by her Class at the Sunday School, the bells at the same time ringing out merrily.
>
> The Bridesmaids, six in number, in simple but effective dresses presented as fair a spectacle as mortal eye could wish to see. The wedding breakfast was held in the Racquet Court of the Manor which was ornamented with wreaths of evergreen texts, mottos etc. Their health was proposed by Douglas Fox, John Wright and the Bride's father, Mr Francis Wright before the Bride and Groom announced their speedy departure. Her sister Mary had already married into the Fox family." Derbyshire Advertiser & Journal 6 9 1869

1870s-MORE LAND ACQUIRED BY FRANCIS WRIGHT About this time, Francis made a large extension to his Osmaston estate. The Reverend Talbot A.L. Greaves, born at Mayfield Hall and Vicar of Melcombe Regis, Dorset, put estates previously owned by his father Dr. William Greaves, up for sale.

In Osmaston, this estate included Blake House, Tinkers Inn and Osmaston Pastures farms, plus parcels of land in Wyaston, Yeaveley and Shirley. It was auctioned in at least twelve lots and in 1870 an estate map was prepared by John Parkin, Land Agent and Surveyor, of Idrigdgehay.

Francis Wright bought the whole estate for the sum of £36,000, which added 181 acres in Osmaston, 194 in Wyaston, 38 in Yeaveley and 88 acres in Shirley. The deed of conveyance was dated 3rd April 1872.

Derbyshire Records Office Ref D7213/19

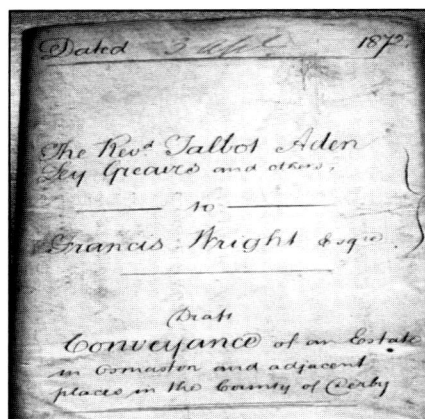

BLAKE HOUSE-This was part of the extensive Greave's estate bought by Francis Wright in 1872. It is a farm house probably built in the late 18th century.
The photograph was taken by a WAAF lady who was billeted on the airfield in WW2. It is a brick farm house with a parapetted front elevation, with unusually tall top storey windows.
The bay windows and porch would have been added in the 19th century.
Photograph circa 1940 Osmaston History Group

BY MR. HOBSON.

BLAKE HOUSE, NEAR ASHBORNE.

TO BE SOLD BY AUCTION,
By Mr. HOBSON,

At the Bell Inn, in Ashborne, on Saturday the 7th day of March next, at 4 o'clock in the afternoon, subject to such conditions as will be then produced;

A FREEHOLD ESTATE called BLAKE HOUSE, consisting of a neat sashed Brick Messuage, suitable for the residence of a genteel Family, and for a Hunting Seat, with the Lawn, Orchard, Gardens, Stables, Barns, Outbuildings, some of which might at a moderate expense be converted into Coach houses, and other Offices requisite for a Gentleman, and about Eighty Acres of arable, meadow and pasture Land lying compact and immediately adjoining the House, in possession of Mr. Benjamin Johnson.
    The Estate is situate in the parish of Osmaston, within 2 miles of Ashborne, and near to the turnpike road from thence to Derby, and to Shirley Park, and other Fox Covers where the Hounds frequently meet.
    There is also an entire Pew in Osmaston Church belonging to the Messuage.
    The Tenant will shew the Estate, and for further particulars apply personally, or by letters (post-paid) to W. WARD, Esq. Harvest Cottage, Sheffield, or Messrs. JOHNSON and WISE, Solicitors, Ashborne.
    Ashborne, 9th February, 1829.

The house is not shown on the early 18th century Pegge estate map. In 1829, the property was for sale as a *"neat sashed Brick Messuage suitable for a genteel family with potential for a hunting seat and conversion of buildings into Coach houses– together with a complete pew in the church"*.

The tenant was then Benjamin Johnson. It didn't sell and was again offered for sale or let.
In 1838, Tithe Apportionment records show, it was owned by William Greaves and occupied by George Sillitoe, farming 79 acres.

TENANTS AND HISTORY OF BLAKE HOUSE

Photographs of the Allsop family courtesy of Mrs S Smith
and also family history memoirs of the Allsop family

Thomas and Mary Elizabeth Allsop

Thomas Allsop was born at Yeldersley in 1816.
He married Mary Elizabeth Hunt-Maddox at
St. Peters Derby in 1838. In 1841 they were
living in the thatched cottage at Painters Lane
then owned by Francis Wright.

Thomas worked as a wheelwright at this
address.

By 1851 he had moved to Blake House as a
tenant of the Greaves estate and was then a
farmer of 126 acres.

By this time the couple had 4 children; Mary
Ellen, b 1839, Selina, b 1844; George, b 1847
& Fanny, b 1857. The House and land would
have been bought by Francis Wright. Thomas
remained at Blake House until his death in
1883.

His wife Mary had died in 1881. They are both
buried in St Martin's churchyard.

Fanny Allsop was the youngest of
the four children of Thomas and
Mary.

She married Isaac Grindey in 1883
and lived at Newton Grange. She
died in 1909 and is buried at
Tissington.

George Allsop was working as a
land steward at Powerstock
Dorset in 1881.

He married Elizabeth Spencer in
1882 and after returning to Blake
House in 1883 on the death of his
father, moved to Middlesbrough
before 1900.

He died in Sheffield 1928.

Fanny Allsop
1858-1909

George Allsop
1848-1928

Selina didn't marry and went to live with her sister Fanny at Newton Grange. She died in 1900 and is
buried at Osmaston. Mary Ellen married farmer, John Massey in 1870. They lived at Dalbury where she
died in 1909. A year after her death, her husband John Massey was murdered in his farm buildings at
Dalbury.

In the post war period, the house suffered significant roof problems and was reduced in height to
two storeys and rendered. The position of Blake House is indicated on the Map of Osmaston on Page
7.

FRANCIS WRIGHT'S ILL HEALTH

1873-Within 10 months of the extension of his estate in February 1873, Francis Wright became unwell during an inspection of building works at Derby Royal Infirmary, where he had been President of the Board and a benefactor. Having caught a severe chill, he returned to the Manor. A week later, he returned to work at Butterley where he once again was taken ill and returned home. He was attended by a Mr Goodwin of Ashbourne and Dr Ogle of Derby. His condition, however, deteriorated and he died at 8.30 pm on Monday 24th February. The cause of death was said to be "Bright's Disease", (degeneration of the kidneys) aggravated by exhaustion and a severe attack of bronchitis.

1873 OBITUARY

Many obituaries appeared in newspapers around the country. The following tribute is taken from The Derbyshire Advertiser of 28th February 1873:

"A deeply religious man, Francis' purse was never closed against an appeal for the building, beautifying and endowing of churches and schools. Amongst the more prominent institutions in which he took a lively interest and of some of which he was the local President, we may mention the Church Missionary Society, the British and Foreign Bible Society, the Church Pastoral Aid Society, The Religious Tract Society, The Colonial Church and School Society (whose meetings for several years have been held at Osmaston Manor), the Irish Church Mission, The Derby and Derbyshire Nursing Association, the Home for Penitent Females at Derby, the Society for Promoting Christianity amongst the Jews etc. etc. If he had any preference it was in favour of those societies which sought first the good of his own countrymen at home and abroad. Mr Wright was also Chairman of the Board of Directors of Trent College, Chairman of the Ashbourne Local Board and of the Ashbourne Bench of Magistrates. He qualified as a Magistrate in 1841 and the Lord Lieutenant appointed him a Deputy Lieutenant. He was a Magistrate for Nottinghamshire, a Deputy Lieutenant for that County, President of the County Church Pastoral Aid Society and one of the Committee of the Nottingham Town Mission. He had also served the office of High Sheriff for Nottinghamshire."

FUNERAL OF FRANCIS WRIGHT-The following newspaper entry describes, in much detail, the funeral procession and also the service in St Martin's Church, Osmaston. It provides a comprehensive picture of the formalities, etiquette and social order of a Victorian funeral of 1873. The funeral took place on a day of sleet and snow.

Funeral report of the late Francis Wright of Osmaston Manor taken from the Derbyshire Advertiser of March 7th 1873.

"No more impressive scene has ever been witnessed in this neighbourhood than that which attended the funeral of the late Francis Wright Esq, which took place at Osmaston, near Ashbourne on Saturday last. The high estimation in which the deceased gentleman was held by all classes and ranks of society and the more than love which was felt for him by those to whom he had at once been the loving master and tried friend, were in themselves sufficient to account for the very general and unmistakable display of affection and regard which was manifested for his memory on the mournful occasion.

The Manor, grand always and solemn in its vastness, had on Saturday an even more sombre aspect than usual and this characteristic intensified by that feeling of sadness and gloom which is always associated with the presence of the dead – was by no means lessened by the condition of the weather, which, throughout the day, was of the most inclement character.

Shortly after 10 o'clock the tenantry from Lenton and other parts of the Nottinghamshire estates, arrived in carriages from Derby station; and, from that time, the arrival of vehicles containing persons more or less intimately connected with the deceased, was continuous almost up to the time of the departure of the funeral cortège, when a detachment of Butterley officials, about 30 in number and consisting of foremen, agents and workmen, arrived, in time to take their appointed places in the procession to the Church. All these, as well as the tenantry from the Nottinghamshire and Derbyshire estates, the members of the household and others taking part in the procession, were provided with shoulder- scarves, hat-bands and gloves.

Engraved memorial cards, executed by Messrs Bemrose and accompanied by an appropriate paper entitled "Words of peace and consolation to those who have lost one dear to them" were distributed to all comers and many, doubtless, will be long treasured by their owners as mementos of him whose worth they were intended to commemorate. The card, which is headed with the coat of arms of the deceased, bears the following inscription:-

---

IN MEMORY OF

FRANCIS WRIGHT ESQUIRE

OF OSMASTON MANOR, DERBYSHIRE

Born December 21st 1806

Died February 24th 1873

"Whatsoever thy hand findeth to do, do it with thy might" - Eccles. ix.IO

"Whatsoever ye do in word or deed, do all in the name of the Lord Jesus, giving thanks to God

and the Father by Him" - Colos.iii.I7

"Who loved me and gave Himself for me" - Galat.ii.20

Cortege Leaving the Manor – Order of Procession

"Shortly before 1 o'clock, the body was lifted into the hearse (a plumeless one, with four horses) and the procession, marshalled by Mr J W Lister of Ashbourne, the Undertaker, departed for St Martin's Church."

The detail which follows provides an indication of the formality of funerals during the Victorian period and the order of procession.

PROCESSION
The Undertaker
First Carriage
Mr R D Goodwin and Dr Ogle, medical attendants

Second Carriage
The Rev W G Vernon and the Rev J W Reeve

Pall Bearers
Mr Hall, butler and Mr Marsden, engineer on the estate

Bearers	**Bearers**
E Williamson	G Charlesworth
J Hand	J Burton
G Goodall	M Woolley
Jas Smith	T Williamson

Pall Bearers

Mr Trivett, clerk of the works.   Mr McGibbon, bailiff

First Mourning Coach

Mr John Wright, Miss E A Wright, the Rev Henry and Mrs Wright

Second Mourning Coach

Mr F B Wright, Mrs F E Wigram, Mr & Mrs J B Plumptre

Third Mourning Coach

Mr and Mrs C D Fox, Mr and Mrs F Fox

Fourth Mourning Coach

Mr and Mrs Fitzherbert Wright, Mr Philip Wright, Mr Blaskett Botcherby

Fifth Mourning Coach

Col Fitzherbert and Sir John Alleyne Bart., Mr G Wright, Mr John Martin

Sixth Mourning Coach

Mr A Blackwood, Mr Chas Plumptre, the Rev H W Plumptre,

Mr R Ramsden, Mr M Martin, Major Martin, Miss Hamitt Gill

Private carriages in which were

Lord Scarsdale, the Hon E W K Coke, Sir Matthew Blakiston

Rowland Smith Esq. MP, Mr Kingdon, Miss Cox and Miss Harriet Gell

The private carriages of the following had been sent:-

The Misses Evans (Darley House)

Mr Harrison (Snelston), Mr Frank (Ashbourne Hall), the Rev E H Abney,

and Mrs Alderson (Wyaston)

Mr A Shrosbery, agent, Mr H W Hollis estate auditor

Mr Bean, underground manager and salesman, Butterley Works

Mr G Staley, chief cashier

Tenantry from Nottingham, Lenton, Lowdham and Osmaston

The Butterley Officials

Mr Twilley, Head Gamekeeper

The Gardeners and Servants

Mr Blood

Workmen and Cottagers

A detachment of County Police

Several members of the clergy join the procession and villagers line the route.

On the arrival of the procession at the village, the following clergy joined it – The Rev T W Bury, the Rev F Corfield, the Rev J G Croker, the Rev J T Werge, The Rev J Payne, the Rev H W Wood, the Rev H Greaves, the Rev C J Hamilton, the Rev C W Richards, the Rev T F Fenn, the Rev G Howard, the Rev J Teague, the Rev Ley Greaves and the Rev C F Powys.

"The appearance of the cortège as it passed through the grounds to the Church, which is about a mile distant from the house and in the direction of Ashbourne, was of a most mournful and impressive character. The long and melancholy train of mourners wending its way through the snow clad grounds, in the laying out of which the deceased gentleman had taken so much intelligent care – leaving behind it the great earthly Home which of his abundance he had reared, onwards to the village church, which his liberality had erected – formed a spectacle intensely painful in its suggestiveness. In everything there was sadness – sadness because each and all called into remembrance the memory of him to whose fertile conception and creative genius they owed their existence.

The great moving spirit which had planned and executed the various works which bear his impress – the mainspring of that complicated web, which, an abundance of wealth and a thorough knowledge of the best ways of disposing of it had here succeeded in weaving – was gone! Notwithstanding the miserable state of the weather and the drenching rain and sleet which were falling at the time, the villagers lined the route of procession through Osmaston and showed by their evident grief and sympathy for the bereaved family of the deceased, that they thoroughly appreciated the many improvements for good in their social and moral condition, which his philanthropic and watchful care had been the means of effecting.

On arriving at the entrance to the church-yard the corpse was met by the Rev Gerard Smith and the Rev W G Vernon, the past and present Vicars of Osmaston, the latter repeating the words of the beautiful text with which the Service of the Burial of the Dead is opened, "I am the resurrection and the life".......The coffin, which was covered with a heavy black velvet pall, bordered with white satin, upon which loving hands had placed a wreath of white camellias, was then placed on trestles immediately within the Church and the simple and touching Burial Service of the Church was proceeded with, the mourners being seated in the pews in the body of the Church, the children of the schools occupying the chancel. The Rev Gerard Smith read the first portion of the service, as well as the portion of Scripture appointed to be used on these occasions, taken from the fifteenth chapter of St Paul's first Epistle to the Corinthians. A hymn was then sung with much feeling, the mass of black-clad men, and their deep tones, giving it a peculiar power.

The Church (of which the pulpit, reading-desk and communion table were draped with black) is capable of accommodating about 400 persons and it was with some difficulty that the whole of those taking part in the funeral procession could find places in the sacred edifice. This was, however, done in perfect order and there was a total absence of that unseemly crushing which in too many instances, is the distinguishing feature of such occasions. Doubtless this was owing in great measure to the admirable forethought of those who had charge of the arrangements, and also to the efficient services of a detachment of police stationed in the churchyard under the direction of Superintendent Whieldon, of the Ashbourne district. Outside, a large concourse of villagers and others anxious to pay the last tribute of respect to their deceased friend and master, awaited the concluding portion of the ceremony which followed at the side of the vault, into which the coffin was ultimately lowered but which, of necessity, could only be witnessed by a few of the nearest and dearest friends of the deceased, who, amid signs of deepest sorrow, committed him to his last resting place "in sure and certain hope of the resurrection to eternal life.

The concluding portion of the service, at the vault side, was read by the Rev W G Vernon, who, prior to the separation of the mourners, delivered the following address "My dear Parishioners and Friends, we are now gathered round the last earthly dwelling-place of the builder of this beautiful temple. In him, we have all lost the kindest of friends and the most princely of benefactors. Our loss, however, is assuredly, his gain. Oh! Do not let the day pass without an earnest prayer ascending from every heart – for others, that God will minister comfort to those who so much need it; for ourselves, that the present, and all future ministers of this parish may be kept faithful ambassadors of Christ, as he so earnestly desired – that in this our temple, Sunday after Sunday, mourners may be comforted and sinners aroused, anxious inquirers directed, and saints built up and strengthened. And oh! Do let us all, young, middle-aged and old, pray as we never prayed before, that God will give us individually a large measure of His Holy Spirit; that we may daily "grow in grace and in knowledge of our Lord and Saviour Jesus Christ"; so that, after a life of faith and good works, our last end may be as peaceful as that of our kind friend and benefactor; and that, through the merits of the Saviour he loved and served, we, with him, may be dwellers together in that land of which St John tells us "I saw no temple therein, for the Lord God Almighty and the Lamb are the temple of it". God grant it to each one of us for Jesus Christ's sake. Amen"

"The vault in which the remains of the deceased gentleman are deposited is immediately underneath the chancel, which rests upon its arches; it consists of a spacious chamber, flanked on either side by a series of stone recesses; in the central one of which, on the left hand, the mortal remains of the deceased were placed. The vault, which we believe, was constructed under the direction of Mr Wright, when the Church was erected by himself, already contained four occupants, Mrs John Wright, the deceased wife of the present possessor of the Estate; Miss Agnes Wright, the eldest unmarried daughter of the deceased gentleman; an infant daughter of the Rev F E and Mrs Wigram (nee Wright) of Highfield Vicarage, Southampton, and Marcus Beresford, Mr Wright's youngest son.

The last sad offices to the dead having been paid, the funeral cortège wended its way back to the Manor. We should state that the coffin, which contained an oak shell in an inner coffin of lead, was of highly polished English Oak, with massive brass furniture and bore the following inscription:-

> FRANCIS WRIGHT
> Born Dec 21st 1806.   Died Feb 24th 1873

The undertaker was Mr J W Lister of Ashbourne and the hearse, mourning coaches and horses were jointly supplied by Mrs Wallis of The Green Man Hotel, Ashbourne Messrs W Wallis and Son of Derby. The former gentleman and Mr P Wallis of Derby efficiently performed the various duties they were called upon to discharge. (Mourning coaches were sent to represent families who were unable to attend the actual funeral).

The tenants and Butterley workmen from a distance, on their return to the Manor, partook of a cold collation, which was served in the Racket Court".

The plaque, which is on the roof apex of the School, was installed by estate tenants following the death of Francis Wright in appreciation of his gift.

Photograph Osmaston History Group

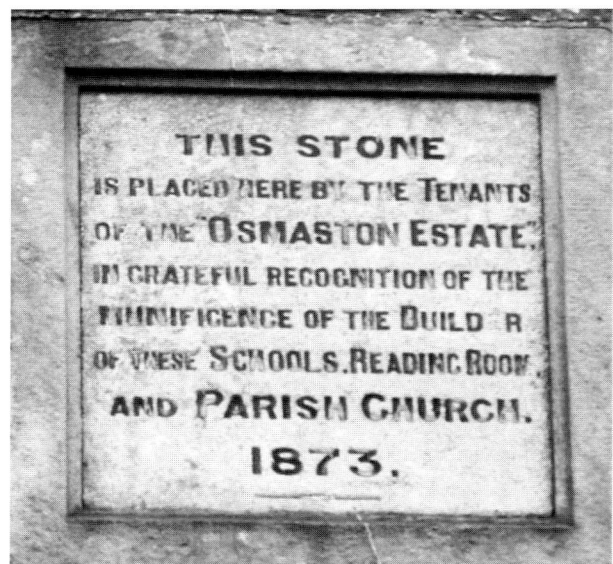

Following the passing of Francis Wright, the Manor and the Osmaston Estate were inherited by his eldest son, John Wright.

Chapter 3. THE FUTURE OF OSMASTON ESTATE

JOHN WRIGHT (1831 -1901)

1873-Following the death of his father, John Wright, as the eldest son inherited the Osmaston Estate and Manor. In addition to inheriting the estate, he received the sum of £125,000. He did not however, inherit any involvement in his father's Butterley business. It is unclear whether this was his choice or whether his father chose to exclude him. John was already married with a family.

EARLY LIFE-He was born in 1831 at Lenton Hall, Nottinghamshire. Before his 21st birthday, celebrated at Osmaston Manor, he had spent time travelling abroad with his brother accompanied by their tutor.

YELDERSLEY is included in the story of Osmaston as it has a long association with the village and the Wright and Walker families.   A brief account follows:-

1087-Yeldersley was mentioned in the Domesday Book as Gelderslei.

1600s an original Yeldersley Hall stood on an alternate site and was home of Catherine Pegge, a mistress of Charles II who bore him two sons.
The land originally belonged to the Meynell family of Bradley, but by the 17th century much of the land was owned by the Pegge family.
 A building remains on the site today.
Photograph Osmaston History Group

1631-The Yeldersley estate also owned Ladyhole House, of a similar period. In the will of John Lee, Ladyhole House was left to his daughter, Elizabeth. She was married to the son of Sir Thomas Gresley (Baronet) of Netherseal. They lived at Ladyhole House which remained with the Gresley family until 1837 when it passed to the Reverend William Nigel.

1700s-In the late 18th century, the Pegge estate was bought by Edmund Evans. The Evans family owned cotton mills at Darley Abbey and were also part of the Crompton and Evans bank in Derby.
1800-Evans built a new house close to the Ashbourne to Derby turnpike (now the A52) on Painters or Penters Lane as it was originally named. The original 17th century Hall then became a farmhouse. Postcard courtesy of Osmaston History Group

1824-When Edmund Evans died, Yeldersley House was left to his daughter Elizabeth, wife of John Harrison, an attorney, of nearby Snelston Hall. Yeldersley House was then leased out, usually for periods of ten years.

1831-A document at the DRO shows that Francis Hurt, the younger, had leased the house which then had a newly built lodge, gardener's cottage, pleasure grounds and fish ponds, at an annual rent of £130 for the 45 acres.

1841-Census shows the house as occupied by a Mrs Mundy.

1851 & 1861-Census records the Reverend Roger Vaughan with his wife and daughter. He was the "perpetual curate of Atlow". The census of 1861 shows him still in occupation, along with two female servants.

JOHN WRIGHT MARRIAGES AND CHILDREN

1853-John married Emily Sophia Plumptre in June and went on to have four children, Eleanor, Francis, Marcus and Emily.

1860-Emily Sophia died in April of this year. Following the early death of Emily, John took his children and travelled across Europe and the Middle East, travelling by cart in places.

1861-In December, John married a Florence Mary Rice and together they would have eleven further children: Rosamunde, Violet, Olive, Basil, Cecil, Bertram, Osmund, Lionel, John, Ulric and Arthur.

1862-Move to Yeldersley House-It is most likely that John and Florence moved into the house at about this time. All of their eleven children were born at Yeldersley.

Photograph courtesy of Charles Melville Wright of John Osmaston and his wife Florence with all his children

1868-It is unclear when the Wright family purchased the property. However, a letter dated 31st August 1868 to John Harrison of Snelston Hall (DRO. D157/MT/49), from a W.Bates, his agent at Snelston, stated that- "Mr Wright has made an offer of £6000 for the Yeldersley Estate".

This is most likely for the house and 45 acres. It would have been after the purchase of the property that John Wright was able to change the name to Yeldersley Hall.

1871-**Census**. The house was now shown as Yeldersley Hall with John Wright (later Osmaston) continuing to live there. He had a butler, a coachman, a groom, a page, and ten female servants. A gardener was living in the Lodge. The original old hall had become a farm house.

Local Involvement

John would become Deputy Lieutenant of Derbyshire and Justice of the Peace of both Derbyshire and Staffordshire. He shared his father's opposition of Ashbourne Shrovetide football and announced with others, that anyone trespassing on his land during any game would be prosecuted. John held the Lordships of the Manors of both Ashbourne and Osmaston.

JOHN WRIGHT AT OSMASTON MANOR

1873-Following the passing of his father, John Wright moved into the Manor and his mother, Selina, with his unmarried sister, Judith, moved into Yeldersley Hall with long-time butler, William Hall. Selina lived at Yeldersley until her death in 1889.

Over the next few years John built Gardener's Cottage in 1879 and enhanced the Manor gardens by adding a substantial rock garden and fernery. A description was published in Derbyshire Countryside in October 1936 by G Barton. "The simplicity of its construction is the secret of its beauty. Nothing is overdone and everything seems to be in its right place to produce a charming effect...."

"The rocks are nicely worn with age and stand out with boldness. Beneath these hardy ferns are a host of aquatic and moisture loving plants grown in the crevices down to the waters edge."

1876-Change of Family Name to Osmaston

John Wright changed his name by Deed Poll to Osmaston with effect from 8th September 1876. The local newspaper recorded:

"John Wright J.P. D.L. enrolled a deed poll in Chancery ....." "desirous of distinguishing by this means the main stem of the family from its collateral branches and of perpetuating in it the name of a place which is entirely his own". Derbyshire Advertiser and Journal 22 9 1876

Business Activities-With his newly acquired inheritance, John began investing in property and business. An unpublished booklet written by Henry Osmaston dated 10th June 2002 includes a letter written by Emily Osmaston, John's daughter to her half-brother, Arthur Osmaston. It gives an insight into John's business activities and the number of unfortunate investments made.

In 1878-21st Celebration at the Manor

"A gathering of some 200 guests were invited to the Manor to celebrate the 21st birthday of Francis Plumptre Osmaston, John's son from his first marriage. Tenants of Lenton and Langar were invited in addition to family and friends.

Having arrived by train at Derby, their arrival at Osmaston was delayed due to a huge thunderstorm with lightening striking and destroying the Manor flagpole and flag. Guests were given a guided tour of the Manor and walked freely in the gardens, sitting down to a meal in the Racquet Court during the afternoon.

Several speeches were made and gifts presented to Francis. His father made a thoughtful and profound speech reflecting on his own life, his travels abroad and his late father. There were frequent bouts of laughter during the speeches". Derbyshire Advertiser & Journal 9 8 1878

1880- Sad death of John's Brother "One of the saddest occurrences to record is that of the death by drowning in Lake Coniston, Cumberland, of the Rev. Henry Wright, second son of the late Francis Wright." Derbyshire Advertiser & Journal 20 8 1880.

This was a very sad time for John, in a very short space of time he had lost his wife, father and brother and life had changed considerably.

1880-Changes to Osmaston Village

By this date, changes continued to be made to the village. Cottages close to the church, the Wesleyan Chapel, and the Pound had been demolished.

1881-A New Vicarage and Carriage House were built on Church Lane.

Many other buildings had been rebuilt or had undergone substantial alterations. The Shoulder of Mutton Public House had moved to its present location. On the south side of the pond only one of the cottages remained at this time and the drive to the Manor had been built on a different alignment to the original bridle path.

1881-Census:

Osmaston Manor- The census record for this year shows that there were no members of the Osmaston family at the Manor. Just one person resided at the Manor, Thomas Williamson, who is described as an "usher". The property would remain empty for long periods.

The School-The Census also recorded that Mr Walter Beeby, a certified teacher, and his wife Charlotte Hanna had now taken over the School.

1881-Travel Book John Osmaston wrote and published a book on his early travels "Old Ali –Travels Long Ago".

1883-EXHIBITION OF PAINTINGS BY JOSEPH WRIGHT OF DERBY

An article in a book of notable paintings came to the Group's notice which suggested that the Osmaston family had owned paintings by internationally recognised Derbyshire artist, Joseph Wright. Derby Museum and Art Gallery subsequently confirmed that in 1883 they held an exhibition of work by the local artist. Their records show that John Osmaston lent Joseph Wright's now famous painting "The Orrery" to the gallery. His brother, Fitzherbert Wright provided Joseph Wright's "The Alchemist".

About 100 paintings and 80 sketches were displayed. An article in the local press of the day mentions "The Orrery" and says of "The Alchemist" that is was "in many respects the gem of the collection". Owners of paintings on loan were thanked. The paintings were returned and John Osmaston then offered "The Orrery" for sale without success. An appeal was made by Derby people for funds to buy the painting. Money was received and the painting was purchased by public subscription. It was then donated to Derby Gallery where, to this day, it takes pride of place in their Joseph Wright Gallery. (Derby Mercury advert for exhibition dated 14th March 1883 for the exhibition on 21st March 1883.)

Paintings from the Manor were previously shown in the Midland Counties Exhibition held in 1870 at Derby Drill Hall. A collection of minerals thought to have been started by Francis Wright was also given to Derby Museum, followed by additions thought to have been made by John Osmaston's brother, Francis Beresford Wright. Some of the collection remains at the museum.

With the ever increasing costs of maintaining large estates, a lack of business acumen and a number of poor business deals, it became necessary for John to sell the Manor and estate. His daughter, Emily's unpublished letter outlines her family's concerns over his debts. He moved his family to Hawkhurst Court, Billingshurst, West Sussex and left Osmaston.

DECISION TO SELL THE OSMASTON ESTATE

1883-The Manor remained unoccupied though fully furnished until 1883 when the whole of the estate along with the Wright's other properties at Langar and Barnston were put up for sale. On 25th May 1883, the Derbyshire Advertiser announced that the estates had been advertised for sale in The Times. The advert showed that property in Nottinghamshire at Langar and Barnston comprised purely agricultural land of 3000 acres and "several fine sites for the erection of a mansion" and the Nottinghamshire estates were sold separately. An inn in the village of Langar named "The Feathers" was recorded as purchased by his grandfather in 1799. Its name had been changed to "The Unicorn" to reflect the existing family crest motif.

1883- OSMASTON ESTATE – ADVERTISED AGAIN
A comprehensive sale catalogue, held by Derbyshire Record Office, was produced to describe the Estate. It details all estate rental properties, 40 cottages, buildings and land in addition to the Manor and gardens. An initial offer was received from a Sir Samuel Wilson which was accepted and was then withdrawn.

A further offer was very promptly accepted from Mr. Andrew Barclay Walker, a wealthy brewer and coal mine owner, who is said to have paid £206,500 for the Manor and estate including all furniture and contents.

A NEW OWNER-In January, 1884, Mr. Andrew Barclay Walker took over Osmaston Manor and Estate. John Osmaston was in Dinan, Normandy at the time of the sale.

JOHN OSMASTON CONTINUED TO SELL OFF EVERYTHING HE COULD

1884-Sale of Lordship of Ashbourne and Osmaston

In 1884, John Osmaston sold the Lordship of Ashbourne to the Town of Ashbourne for the sum of £3000. After the death of Francis Wright in 1873, it could be assumed that his son would have held the title for Osmaston along with the estate. Kelly's Directory of 1876, however, lists a John Godber as Lord of the Manor. In the Directory for 1888, the title is shown as held by William Richard Smith J.P. of Clifton House, Clifton. By 1900 Sir Andrew Barclay Walker owned it.

1884-Sale of Remaining Paintings John Osmaston had retained ownership of the Manor paintings, bronzes, statuary and object d'art which he sold at the following auction:-

> "The purchaser of Osmaston Manor had not taken to the pictures, so had been thought best to sell them in Derby, in order that friends of the family might have the opportunity of securing some relics of the place with which they were intimately identified.
>
> The conditions of sale were then read, and from these it appeared that Messrs. Earp and Huggins did not hold themselves responsible for the correct description, genuiness, or authenticity of lots, and made no warranty whatever." Derby Advertiser and Journal 21 3 1884

PRELIMINARY ANNOUNCEMENT.
THE
OSMASTON MANOR GALLERY OF PAINTINGS,
To be Removed to the
LECTURE HALL, WARDWICK, DERBY,
For convenience of Sale.
EARP & HUGGINS
ARE honoured with instructions from JOHN OSMASTON, Esq., to SELL by AUCTION, early next month, at the LECTURE HALL, Derby, the whole of the HIGHLY VALUABLE and IMPORTANT COLLECTION of OLD and MODERN PAINTINGS, including the two well-known works, "Monna Lizza," by L. da Vinci, and "The Magdalen," by Murillo, purchased direct from the Queen of Spain; "The Annunciation," by P. P. Rubens; "The Fight for the Standard," the engraved work by R. Ansdell, R.A.; "A River Scene," by Constable, R.A.; three grand works by J. M. W. Turner, R.A., &c., &c.
Further particulars may be obtained of
EARP and HUGGINS,
Auctioneers and Valuers,
7, London-street, Derby.

The newspaper article listed sales including artists of great renown. Sales included "The Annunciation" by P P Rubens; "The Fight for the Standard", the engraved work by R Ansdell, R.A.; "A River Scene" by Constable, R.A.; and three grand works by J M W Turner. There were however, concerns regarding the authenticity of some of the works.

The Derbyshire Times and Chesterfield Herald gave a word of caution:
"Old Masters are dubious things to buy from an auctioneer unless he knows something about art. It is difficult, above all things, to estimate the real value of works by the old masters. Experienced picture-buyers sometimes fall into pit-falls ruinously expensive, victimised by false work which has the irresistible charm of plenty of brown varnish employed by scientific swindlers, who, by their clever counterfeits obtain rashly artificial prices."
"On the day of the auction, John Osmaston answered his critics by stating he had offered the pictures in Derby because he thought many of his friends in the country would be glad of an opportunity of purchasing some of them. Mr Huggins, the auctioneer, said that one of the conditions of the sale was that he could not guarantee the authenticity of any of the lots and that considerable doubt was cast upon their genuineness. In the end, the bidders were unconvinced. Proceeds from the entire auction raised a paltry £7,000. The "Magdalen" sold for 1900 guineas and the "Monna Lizza" scraped a mere 50 guineas".

Chapter 4. A CHANGE OF OWNERSHIP AT OSMASTON MANOR

SIR ANDREW BARCLAY WALKER

1884

Sir Andrew Barclay Walker, a wealthy brewer, had agreed to buy the Osmaston estate and Manor house from John Osmaston.

John Osmaston had inherited the estate from his father, Francis Wright.

He received the sum of £206,500 for the estate and the house which included the furniture and contents.

Photograph of Sir Andrew Barclay Walker
Courtesy of Sir Andrew Walker-Okeover Bt.

EARLY LIFE OF THE WALKER FAMILY

Andrew Walker was born on 15 December 1824 at Auchinflower, Ayrshire, the son of Mr Peter Walker, owner of the Fort Brewery, Ayr. His grandfather, Mr Andrew Walker of Bonnvid, Maryhill, near Glasgow, was a prosperous coal mine owner.

Andrew's father, Peter Walker, moved from Ayr to operate a brewery business at Bewley Hall, Warrington. In Warrington, Peter Walker ran the business together with his eldest sons, Peter and Andrew, who both became partners in the business. The sons would later establish separate breweries – Peter at Wrexham and Andrew at Burton on Trent.

Andrew was never poor although his father was not wealthy during his childhood.

"He received an ordinary lad's education and at an early age was set to work, learning every detail practically of the business, and avoiding no labour, however unpleasant, so that he became familiar with the feelings and habits of all engaged in the public house trade and in brewing." Liverpool Legions of Honour. B.G.Orchard 1893

While living in Warrington, Andrew married Eliza Reid, of Lime‹iln, Fifeshire, in a simple ceremony within the family home. Her father was a boat builder and this is where the family would spend many holidays and where the family developed their love of boats. Andrew then moved to Liverpool continuing as a partner in his father's business. He is said to have brought huge energy and commercial talent to the business.

"He was a consummate organiser, a shrewd judge of men and events, an indefatigable worker, gifted with manners and personal appearance which, in all circles, at all times produced a favourable impression; and ere long he became prominent as proprietor of numerous public houses, and the most fitted of all in the trade to disarm hostility to it and himself……… "
Extract Liverpool Legions of Honour – B G Orchard 1893

Together with his brewery and public house trade, Andrew also acquired colliery properties in Ayrshire and South Wales, which combined to provide a substantial income. He is remembered for the innovations he made to the public house trade by establishing numerous Walker public houses selling their Walker beers, and which were run by his own employees who were regularly inspected. Combined with the "long pull" which gave customers more beer, his business was very successful.

His main residence at this time was Gateacre Grange in south Liverpool which, as a large detached house, with 21 bedrooms, would remain his main residence following his purchase of Osmaston Manor.

Gateacre Grange, Photograph Courtesy of Liverpool (Liverpool City Group)

Andrew was a supporter of Conservative politics. It was said that there were benefits from his support by way of sympathy from Conservative magistrates regarding licensing and also an introduction to public life. With growing business expansion and growing wealth, he also looked to helping the poor.

> "His wealth was becoming great and he saw that it would become immense, whereupon, like other capable men to those nobler prizes in life which wealth, judiciously used, can buy to use his wealth to assist distressed acquaintances and benefit the poor".
> Extract Liverpool Legions of Honour. B G Orchard 1893

1867-With an increased interest in local politics, Andrew aged 43, joined the Town Council for South Toxteth Ward – a poor area just south of the city centre.

1872-HE BECAME AN ALDERMAN AND SUBSEQUENTLY, BECAME MAYOR OF LIVERPOOL

Once elected as Mayor, he announced his intention to present £20,000 to the city to build an Art Gallery for Autumn Exhibitions. He was neither a patron nor a collector of art. His funding of the gallery was welcomed by the council who elected him as mayor for a second year.

> "On assuming the duties of the Mayoral Chair, Mr Walker after thanking the Council for the honour conferred on him, said for some time, in anticipation of the honour, he had been considering in what way he could best mark his sense of the high dignity conferred on him in a manner which would be most conducive to the interests and wishes of the town. After consideration of the subject, he had come to the resolution to give £20,000 for the building of an Art Gallery to be presented to the town."   Glasgow Herald 6 9 1877

1874-On 28 September, Prince Alfred, Duke of Edinburgh laid the foundation stone of the Walker Art Gallery. The council set aside £1,200 for the purchase of works of art.

The Foundation of the Walker Art Gallery

Autumn exhibition select committee

1873 and 1876- He was appointed High Sheriff of Lancaster. In 1876 he also expanded his business by building a large new brewery at Shobnall Road, Burton upon Trent and also bought an Irish distillery. At this time, collieries he had bought as exhausted mines, also became profitable.

1877-THE 15TH EARL OF DERBY OFFICIALLY OPENED THE WALKER ART GALLERY on 6th September 1877 with 324,117 visitors in four months.

**The Walker Art Gallery
Liverpool**

Photograph Osmaston History Group

ANDREW BARCLAY WALKER WAS KNIGHTED AT WINDSOR CASTLE BY QUEEN VICTORIA on 2 December 1877 in recognition of his public services.

1879-On the death of his father, Sir Andrew gained control of the business. His business acumen continued. The Liverpool Post reported that at one time, Sir Andrew, recognising that foreign brandy might become scarce due to crop failure, bought up all stocks of brandy that he could find. His foresight proved accurate and he made a substantial fortune.

PRIVATE LIFE

1882-Sir Andrew was a great yachtsman. He owned a number of yachts including the 'Cuhona', a famous steam craft which he sailed at the North Shannon Yacht Club in Ireland. He entertained on board several members of the Royal Family, including the Prince of Wales. He had spent a number of years cruising with Lady Walker who had been suffering from a long illness from which she died in 1882.

Lady Walker died in 1882, leaving behind her six sons and two daughters, the eldest son being Peter Carlaw Walker (1854-1915). She was buried in Childwall church, Liverpool, in the presence of a very large concourse. A decorative and costly memorial was erected by her husband to her memory.

Lady Walker's Grave, Childwall

Sir Andrew's Yacht "Cuhona" Was Refitted In Grand Style-As indicated by the following extract from the "Encyclopaedia of Interior Design", edited by Joanne Banham, during the 1880s.

"In their design for the principal rooms of Sir Andrew Barclay Walker's yacht "Cuhona" 1882, George and Petro chose to ignore any maritime connotations, instead deliberately treating the yacht as just another domestic interior.

The salon 24' x 20' was richly carved in dark oak, the panels above the dado line, carved in wood and lacquered in dull gold, were separated by fluted and carved pilasters. The ceiling was painted by G E Malims.

A rich curtain enabled the limited space to be divided – an arrangement often favoured by George & Petro to convert the hall into more intimate areas – into a drawing room and dining room. The side of the curtain facing the drawing room was maize brocade, the reverse stamped velvet.

A mirror, surrounding the fireplace was another device to extend the limited space. The sideboard, piano, writing tables, chairs and even the wine glasses were all specially designed by George & Petro in accord with the scheme.

The sofas were covered with antique Persian rugs."

The "CUHONA" Courtesy of Sir Andrew Walker-Okeover Bt.

1884-SIR ANDREW PURCHASED OSMASTON MANOR By this time, Sir Andrew was the head of Peter Walker and Sons and a very wealthy man. He purchased the Osmaston Manor estate complete with furniture and contents, apart from the works of art. The local newspapers reported that there were great rejoicings when Sir Andrew came into possession of the estate and the garden party which he gave on that occasion would long be remembered.

The Derbyshire Advertiser of 20th July gave an account. It stated that "the house was delightfully situated on an elevation commanding a most extensive and lovely prospect over the adjacent country, more especially towards the South. From the last point of the mansion, which overlooked the terrace, the lake with its islands and flocks of wild fowl; beyond that, and rising so high as to shut out all further view to the east, is Shirley Wood. The estate consists of 3400 acres of land, a portion of which had been laid out with great taste and regardless of cost by the founder of the mansion, the late Francis Wright Esq. JP" It also stated that the cost of the house alone was £200,000. This account was repeated in his obituary written by the Derbyshire Advertiser on 3rd March 1893.

LIFE AT OSMASTON MANOR

1885-In January, 1885, Sir Andrew and some of his sons held two events to wish his Osmaston tenants and staff a Happy New Year.

OSMASTON-BY-ASHBOURNE at Osmaston Manor "On Monday and Tuesday evenings, the 12th and 13th instants, the Manor House, the seat of Sir Andrew Barclay Walker, was the scene of gaiety and pleasure. On Monday the tenant farmers, their wives, and friends were the invited guests of Sir Andrew, and right well were they entertained. Amateur theatricals were the first item of the programme, and two pieces were produced. The first play was entitled, "Little Mother." of which the following is the cast:

Mr. Doubleprong (a dentist), Mr. G. H. Cartland – *Christopher (his son)* Mr. A. K. Batchelor- *Frank Singleton,* Mr W. H. Walker - *Bobby Grimes,* Mr. P. C. Walker - *Adolphus (page to Doubleprong),* Mr. A. B. Walker- *Kitty Clark,* Miss M. Turner - *Fanny (her sister),* Miss A. Pearson. The second was Larkin's Love Letters, the characters being sustained as under:—

Littleton Lynx - Mr. P. C. Walker, *Mr. Benjamin Bobbins* - Mr. A. B Walker, *Col. Bobbington Boyleover,* Mr. H Walker, *Isabella* (Bobbin V.- wife), Forwood; Sally (servant), Miss Forwood.

Continued ...

Both pieces were admirably played, and were productive of much laughter. Great pain had evidently been taken in getting them up, and the masterly manner in which the performers took their respective parts was no doubt the result of frequent rehearsals. Of Mr. Peter Walker's acting one can only say that it was about the best amateur performance we ever had the pleasure of seeing."

"A most sumptuous repast had been provided, and after supper Sir Andrew said that he wished them each and all a very happy and prosperous New Year, and was very pleased to see them all, and to become intimately acquainted with his Derbyshire tenantry. Mr. Silcock, of Wyaston, on behalf of the tenants, thanked Sir Andrew for his good wishes, and for the kindness of himself and family in providing such an agreeable evening's entertainment for them.

Dancing was then entered into with spirit, to the strains of Mr. Wildsmith's quadrille band (of Alvaston), and kept up until some hours in the morning. On the following evening, about 150 of the cottagers on the estate were entertained to supper, and the amateur performances were repeated, much to the delight, of them never having witnessed anything of the kind before.

The proceedings were enlivened by the strains of Mr. Alfred Barton's quadrille band."
Derrby Advertiser & Journal 23 1 1885

1885-Sir Andrew's eldest daughter, Mary Carlaw and her husband, William Hubert Roylance Court bring a son into the world at Osmaston Manor. Sir Andrew's grandson is called William Hubert Roylance Court.

1886-Osmaston School In January a concert was given in the Osmaston Schoolroom "in aid of the funds of the reading room", and notwithstanding the inclemency of the weather, the room was filled to overflowing. Sir Andrew then presented the Reading Room Society with a magnificent library. The charge for using the Reading Rooms was 4 shillings p.a.

1886- SIR ANDREW BARCLAY WALKER CREATED BARONET WALKER OF GATEACRE

JANUARY- A celebration Ball was held at Osmaston Manor which was attended by a large number of guests, who were the elite of the County and to their amazement electric lighting had been installed at the Manor.

Sketches were made during the evening to record events. Here Sir Andrew and Lady Walker are pictured greeting guests in surroundings decorated with palms.

The sketches are annotated:
Ernest, George & Pete, Architects.

Rambling Sketches by T Raffles Davison No.380.

Courtesy of The British Architect Magazine 19 2 1886.

ELECTRIC LIGHTING AT CELEBRATORY BALL

The first mention of electric lighting comes from the Derby Mercury of January 1886. The following newspaper article describes the ball in detail. In 1886, electric lighting was something very new and it is likely that Osmaston Manor, at this time, would have been unique in this respect in this county.

Derby Mercury 3rd February 1886

"Sir Andrew Barclay Walker Bt. gave a ball at Osmaston Manor. A temporary ballroom was erected on the lawn facing the drawing and morning-room windows. It consisted of a pavilion 71 ft. long by 15 ft. wide, made of wood covered with double texture mackintosh sheeting, and notwithstanding the severe weather (rain and snow now falling heavily upon it), not a drop of water penetrated through. The floor was laid with inlaid parquet flooring and the sides were draped with Madras muslin. Mr Sherwin the head gardener carried out all the floral decorations throughout the house. A raised dais ran along the entire length of the side of the room, and was so arranged that the guests could see into the pavilion from the drawing and morning room.

The entire colonnade had been secured from the weather by waterproof sheetings, and was laid with crimson cloth. It also led to the conservatory, in which the supper was laid. The entire floor space was carpeted with crimson cloth and the room was illuminated with a large number of Japanese lanterns. The whole of the work was carried out by Mr Eastwood of Manchester. Supper was laid out in the conservatory, and in lieu of the usual long tables a new departure was made, and small tables were arranged amongst the orange trees and large fern trees to accommodate four persons each, presenting a very pretty appearance. A large decorative table was situated in the centre arranged round the fountain, which was kept playing. The supper was supplied by Messrs Gunter and Co of London.

The famous Vienna band, under the leadership of Herr T Ouer, performed the programme of music, which included twenty dances.

The whole of the room was lighted by electric light. The permanent plant to light the whole of the Manor was laid down in an extraordinary short space of time, Sir Andrew only having decided to adopt this mode of illumination some three weeks ago. The fittings throughout were entirely in character and had been designed to suit the requirements of the various rooms. The whole of the work had been carried out by the Liverpool Electric Supply Company, under the superintendence of their managing engineers Messrs Holmes and Vandrey, and the brickwork by Mr Edward Wood of Derby.

Temporary stabling had also been provided to accommodate 140 horses, at the cottage, farm and saw mills, and the telephone was fixed from the front door of the manor to the stables to call up the coachmen at leisure. The guests commenced to arrive about ten o'clock and numbered about 350, and the dancing was kept up until about 4. am.

The scenes presented in the ball-room where the dancing was at its height was of a most brilliant description; the scarlet coats of the hunting gentlemen, the beautiful dresses of the ladies, the subdued light of electric lamps, the foliage of the plants, and the various coloured tapestries on the walls, all combined to make a very animated tromp d'oile."

1886

The above picture shows the furniture used by the ladies in the sketch opposite on display in the Manor many years later.

Continued Links With Liverpool-During this period, Sir Andrew served as High Sheriff of Lancashire. In that year, he also made a further donation to benefit Liverpool.

"Sir Andrew gracefully announced that in honour of the Jubilee he would defray the cost up to £15,000, for the building of Engineering Laboratories in connection with the Liverpool University College and again more than carried out the promise, as he defrayed the entire cost up to £20,000."
extract Liverpool Legions of Honour. B G Orchard 1893

Local Involvement & Tradition-Sir Andrew continued local traditions established by the Wright family. In 1886, he contributed £1000 towards rebuilding the Derbyshire Royal Infirmary, where he served as President of the Board. He was also Vice President of Derbyshire County Cricket Club and Derbyshire Natural History & Archaeological Society.
He also became a Director at Trent College which was founded by Francis Wright.

1887-Ill Health In November, Sir Andrew visited Mr. Orchardson, a famous portrait painter in London, to sit for a portrait which was to be presented to him by a number of Liverpool friends.

Portrait of
Sir Andrew
Barclay
Walker Bt.

By W.Q.
Orchard.

Photo from
Illustrated
London News
4 3 1894

Up to that period, Sir Andrew had enjoyed excellent health, but while in the artist's studio, he was suddenly taken ill. He was found to be seriously ill with doubts for his recovery. He did however, recover and arranged a voyage on his yacht, the Cuhona, to recuperate.

"Lady Wilmot hosted a garden party for Sir Andrew for which the whole county was invited- a never to be forgotten event- the popularity of its owner ever increasing with all classes. Sir Andrew is known to be a munificent subscriber to all charitable and religious agencies for good, but with all he gave with discretion. He was a familiar presence at county gatherings and with the middle classes and poor, he made his name a household word."
Derby Mercury 22 06 1887

A reporter from the Liverpool Mercury visited Osmaston Manor in June 1887 and described the house and the popularity of its new owner.

"The entrance hall is a spacious and pleasant chamber, as are the principal rooms, but the smoke room is evidently much appreciated. Though its appointments are good, and its panelled ceiling of timber very fine, it has an essentially cosy appearance. Like the rest of the house, it is lit with the electric light. I found Mr Richard Keene, the well-known photographer of Derby, taking a variety of views of the mansion and its surroundings. For many years Sir Andrew Walker Bt. had known Sir Henry Wilmot, by whose advice, rumour has it, he bought Osmaston Manor. Be that it may, ever since that never to be forgotten garden party, to which the whole county was invited for Sir Andrew by Lady Wilmot, the popularity of its owner has gone on increasing with all classes. Only at the last county ball at Derby the guests were equally astonished and delighted at the sumptuousness of the supper and the excellence of the wines, and it only accidentally oozed out that the supper was the generous gift of Sir Andrew."

A new snooker room was built at Osmaston Manor.

Photograph Courtesy of Sir Andrew Walker-Okeover Bt.

1887
20TH JUNE-QUEEN VICTORIA'S GOLDEN JUBILEE CELEBRATIONS

This year saw the fiftieth anniversary of Queen Victoria's accession to the throne. The Golden Jubilee was celebrated in the village on 20 June 1887. A Mr A S. Hutchinson, who was a taxidermist, was given the heads of two bullocks to preserve. The two bullocks were then roasted whole in honour of Her Majesty's Jubilee at Macclesfield and at Osmaston. One was given by Sir Andrew and the other by Thomas Crew and Son of Macclesfield. The heads were mounted on massive oak shields, with a silver plate bearing an inscription to commemorate the Jubilee. It is said that one was displayed in the hallway of the Manor.

Changes to St Martin's Church

Sir Andrew made alterations to St. Martin's chancel.
To celebrate Queen Victoria's Jubilee new leaded
painted glass windows were installed. The floor was
re-laid with mosaic tiles, new stalls were added and
the walls and roof decorated.

11th OCTOBER-SIR ANDREW BARCLAY WALKER Bt. MARRIES AT OKEOVER HALL

Sir Andrew Barclay Walker Bt. married the Hon. Maude Okeover. Their marriage had been postponed on two occasions, firstly from 29 April 1887 and secondly from 14th of June, 1887, when Sir Andrew had become unwell a few days earlier. He had travelled to Germany for a "course of waters". The wedding was rearranged for the autumn.

"On 11th October, Sir Andrew married the Hon. Maude Okeover, the second daughter of Haughton Charles Okeover, a family of very old standing and who had held the lordship of Okeover for over 700 years. Maude had served Queen Victoria in the capacity of Maid of Honour and was rewarded with several wedding presents including a beautiful diamond, ruby and pearl brooch, with a piece of hair and a photograph of her majesty in a silver frame.

Amid great rejoicings, although the wedding itself was a ceremony in accordance with the desire of Sir Andrew. The guests at Okeover were Lady Waterpark, aunt of the bride, the Hon. Mrs. Clowes, the Hon. Susan Cavendish, Dowager Lady Vernon, the Hon. Alice Vernon, Mr and Mrs. Rowland Scott, Mr. Hamilton Pelly, Mr. Anson, Mr. Court. All Sir Andrew's sons were present."

Derbyshire Times & Chesterfield Herald 15 10 1887

1887

> "Demonstrations of welcome were frequent in both villages, and arches of evergreens were raised here and there by the tenantry of the respective estates to celebrate the joyful occasion. The arch of evergreens, interspersed with appropriate sentiments which was erected in the main avenue to Okeover Hall, was particularly striking. The town of Ashbourne was also en fete on the interesting occasion numerous and sincere being the wishes expressed for the future happiness of Sir Andrew and his bride who, as well as her family, are beloved both in this picturesque little town as well as the surrounding district. The ceremony was performed by the rector of Longport, Staffordshire and the reverend John Young vicar of Blore, Staffordshire. After the ceremony, the bridal pair drove to Bentley Priory, near London, for the honeymoon.
>
> Mr and Mrs Okeover entertained the guests to a garden party. Presents were, of course, both "numerous and costly". Derby Daily Telegraph 12 10 1887

The interest in the event was not limited to Derbyshire and Staffordshire, but attracted considerable attention in fashionable circles over the country based on the fact that the Hon. Maude Okeover was one of the maids of honour to Queen Victoria.

CHRISTMAS HOUSE PARTY FESTIVITIES AT OSMASTON MANOR

Sir Andrew and Lady Walker held a family Christmas Celebration at the Manor with Sir Andrew's daughters, son in law and children and four of his sons. Also in attendance were Lady Walker's family – Hon. Mrs Okeover, Master Okeover and Miss Edith Okeover.

> **Ventriloquism at the Manor** "Entertainment at Osmaston Manor on Friday last. About 120 of the tenants of Sir Andrew Barclay Walker Bt., were entertained in sumptuous style at Osmaston Manor. Sir Andrew was presently entertaining a number of gentlemen belonging to the Eyrie Society of Amateur Minstrels, and these gentlemen gave an entertainment in the racquet court which was thoroughly appreciated by all present. Captain William Hall Walker then gave the company considerable amusement by an exhibition of his ventriloquism skill and the wonderful performance by his terrier dog, which is understood to have been trained by the Captain himself.
>
> After the entertainment, supper, which had been laid out in the conservatory was partaken of and Mr F Jackson proposed the health of Sir Andrew Barclay Walker Bt., which was heartily drunk. Captain William Hall Walker thanked them all so kindly receiving the toast and apologised for the enforced absence of his Father." Derbyshire Advertiser & Journal 28 1 1887

1888-CHILDREN'S PARTY FESTIVITIES

> "The festivities at Osmaston Manor were continued on Saturday week, which was a red letter day in the lives of the children. The whole of the school children from Osmaston, Shirley, and Wyaston were, with their mothers, invited to the Manor in the afternoon. A conjuring and punch and judy entertainment was provided for the youngsters in the Racquet Court, causing intense amusement, not only to the younger members of the audience but also to the mothers, who laughed as heartily as the children at the well-known frolics of punch.
>
> On Tuesday evening a juvenile ball was given by Miss Walker. The children began to arrive about six o'clock and soon after that hour 150 young people from the surrounding neighbourhood were present. Mr. Dodd's band from Derby, was in attendance, and dancing was held in the large hall. Supper was served in the large dining- room about nine o'clock, and after supper the dance was kept up until nearly 12 o'clock." Derby Mercury 4 1 1888

63

1888-Foreign Travel On 23rd July, Sir Andrew's eldest son and heir, Peter Carlaw Walker at the age of 23 left Liverpool to continue his foreign travels. He left for New York via Queenstown on the SS Aurania as a first class passenger. His love of adventure and travel was evident from an early age and would continue when he eventually inherited Osmaston Manor.

MRS SELINA WRIGHT'S DEATH-(WIDOW OF FRANCIS WRIGHT)

Mrs Selina Wright, who had been living at Yeldersley Hall with her daughter Judith, died on 30th December 1888. In her will she left £5281 with probate granted to sons, Francis Beresford Wright of Wootton, Warwickshire and Fitzherbert Wright of Breadsall. She was laid to rest within the family vault under the chancel of St Martin's Church.

> "Eleven carriages formed the funeral procession to St Martin's Church in Osmaston. The first carried Reverend Nicholson who officiated, the second carrying Mrs Selina Wright. The remaining carriages transported family members.
> Sir Andrew Barclay Walker, who by 1888 owned Osmaston Manor, followed the family cortege. During the service, the bells of St. John's Church in Ashbourne together with muffled bells at St Martin's, rang out throughout the service. A hymn was sung as Mrs Wright was laid to rest in the family vault within the church. The vault was decorated with moss."
> Reported in Derby Mercury, 16 01 1889

1889-Donation to Liverpool University

In November 1889, the Walker Engineering Laboratory was formally opened by Lady Walker in the presence of distinguished guests. The Laboratory had been gifted by Sir Andrew Barclay Walker Bt. to Liverpool University College at a cost of £20,000 and was reported to be the most complete of its kind. Lord Derby presided over the opening and Sir John Cooke, Engineer, also gave an address. Sir Andrew was present although in very poor health.

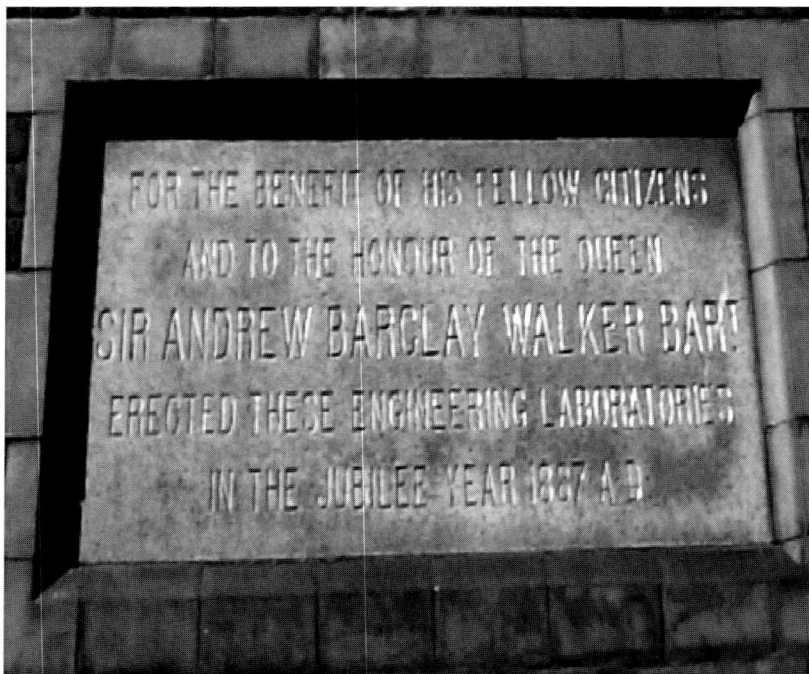

> "For the Benefit of his fellow citizens
>
> And to the Honour of the Queen
>
> Sir Andrew Barclay Walker Bart Erected these Engineering Laboratories
>
> In The Jubilee Year 1887 AD"

1890-A LIMITED COMPANY IS FORMED

During the year, Sir Andrew continued his extensive business activities by arranging his businesses under one limited company to raise the sum of £3,250,000, one million of which was paid to him in cash.

In April 1890, the businesses of Messrs Peter Walker and Son, Liverpool and Warrington; Messrs. A. B. Walker and Co., Liverpool and Burton-on-Trent; and Messrs. Monro Co, at Warrington and Liverpool, were registered as a limited company, under the name of "Peter Walker and Son, Warrington and Burton Limited."

Sir Andrew was chairman of the company and his sons had a large share in its management. The capital was £2,000,000 with £1,000,000 in debentures. The ordinary shares are held by the vendor, the preference shares and debenture being taken up by investors at a premium.

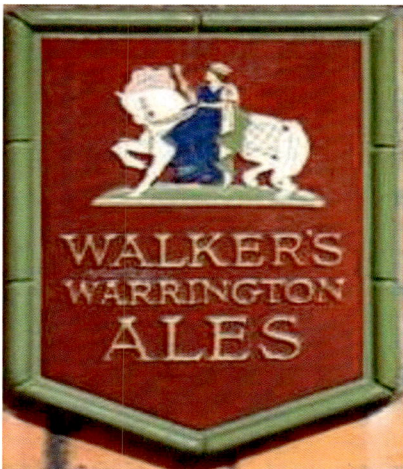

Around 150 public houses in Liverpool, and many in the north west of England, bore the name of Walker's Warrington Ales on doors, windows and lights. Many remain today.

1890-FREEMAN OF LIVERPOOL

Shortly after the formal opening of the Walker Engineering Laboratories, on November 2nd 1890, Sir Andrew was made the second honorary freeman of the City of Liverpool and presented with a Freedom of the City of Liverpool Plaque.

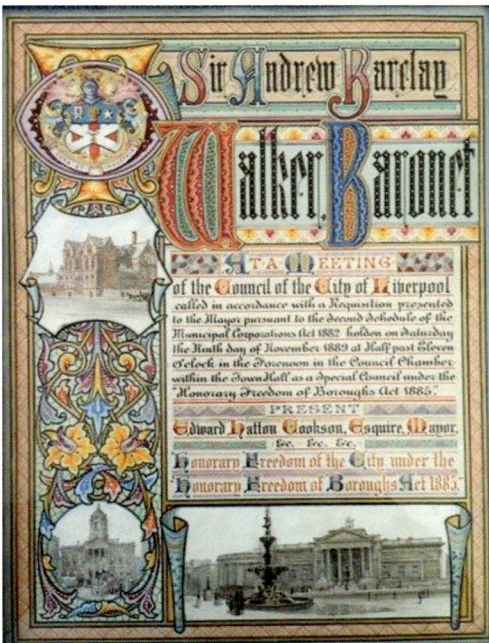

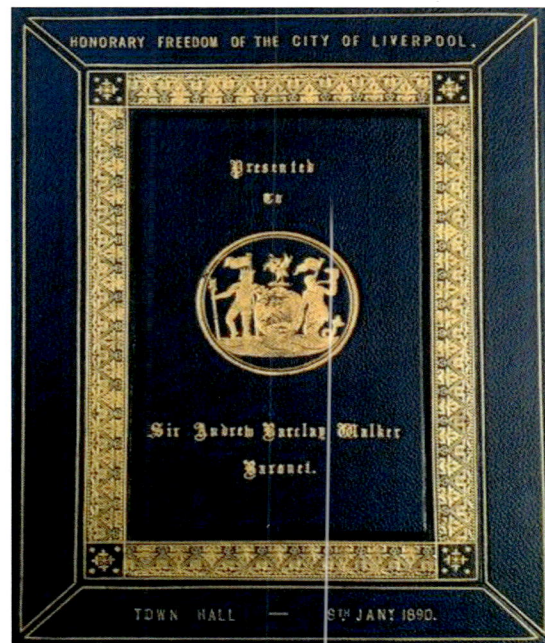

Freedom of the City of Liverpool Plaque – Courtesy of Sir Andrew Walker-Okeover Bt.

1881-1891 THE FIELDING FAMILY IN OSMASTON

1881- A John Fielding was living in Moor Lane, Osmaston, described as a 'farmer of 34 acres' at New House Farm. Before moving to Osmaston, he and his wife Sarah were living in Swinscoe where John had a grocers shop. Amongst their 5 children was their second son John Harvey Fielding.

1881-Grocer and farmer Martha, then aged 34,was described as a 'grocer and farmer of 6 acres'

1884-Postmistress Martha Wibberley still fulfilled the role. Her niece Anne Marie lived with her at this time.

1891-Postmaster, grocer and provision dealer The census shows a John Harvey Fielding, married to Anne Mary Wibberley, as the 'postmaster, grocer and provision dealer' in Osmaston. John Harvey had 5 children Margaret, Francis John, William Harvey, Kathleen Amy and Harold Arthur.

His father was still at the same address (Newhouse Farm) and then shown to be a 'farmer and drainage contractor'. Following the loss of his wife, Sarah in 1900, John (sen) then married Martha Wibberley at Osmaston in October 1901.

John Fielding, Senior, outside the shop (now known as Challow Cottage) with two grand-children, thought to be William Harvey and Harold Arthur. John Harvey Fielding is on the pony and trap. Photo courtesy of the Fielding Family.

The Fielding family at the Post Office. John Harvey Fielding is at the back on the left

Annie Marie Fielding (nee Wibberley) married to John Harvey Fielding

1897-1920s MEMORIES OF KATHLEEN AMY (KITTY) FIELDING AT OSMASTON POST OFFICE/SHOP

Written by one of her children

"Kitty was born in Osmaston in 1897 the daughter of John Harvey Fielding and Annie Mary Fielding. She lived with her parents, 3 brothers and 1 sister in the house attached to the shop. Her bedroom was at the front of the house overlooking the lane toward the Shoulder of Mutton. She, as all the children, attended the village school until she left to work in the shop. She delivered the post in the village and made the deliveries on horseback when the snow was too deep to walk through.

John Harvey, her dad, was a regular at the pub and even though it was a short walk he would take his horse and cart. At the end of a merry evening he would be bundled in to the cart by his drinking companions with the knowledge that his horse knew the way home!

When Lord and Lady Walker held events at the house, she and her family were called upon to help.
She met my dad (Edwin Harold Peplow) around 1919 when he came to Osmaston, from his home in Kilburn, London and was employed as a chauffeur by Lady Walker. His military service was cut short by illness and he was unable to continue active service. When he first came to the village he lived in Rose Cottage . He must have made an impression on the young Kitty as he persuaded her to go out for a spin in Lady Walker's Rolls Royce.

Unfortunately for him, he had an accident which damaged the car, resulting in him being dismissed. However, smitten by Kitty he stayed in Osmaston driving for anyone who would give him work - local farmers taking livestock to market etc. Apparently, she gave him his first taste of alcohol in the Shoulder of Mutton!

The pair of them ran away to London and lived in lodgings in Boniface Street at the back of Waterloo Station where they were involved with the Salvation Army. They married in June 1920; they were both 22 years old and my brother Ronnie was born in July of the same year-just 1 month later!

Kitty and Edwin moved to Kilburn, London and went on to raise me (b:1926), my two brothers and two sisters. We all lived on the top floor of a house in two rooms, which we also shared with my uncle and his wife."

A number of the Fielding family were involved in

WW1 – 1914-18

Details in the next Section on Sir Peter Carlaw Walker and WW1

1891

Osmaston Village Life-The Kelly's Directory for 1891 lists the following as living in Osmaston Village.

Names and occupations of people living in the village listed in the Directory	
Charlesworth John-	Farmer & carpenter
Collins Augustus -	Head gamekeeper to Sir A B Walker Bt. Copse House
Evans Jas. -	Farmer & registrar of births & deaths for Brailsford sub dist. Blake House
Fielding John-	Farmer – New house
Fielding John Harvey-	Shopkeeper Post Office
Francis Richard-	Farmer, wheelwright & carpenter, The Grange Farm
Jackson Fred-	Farmer, The Glebe farm
Kirkland Hannah Mrs-	Farmer
Millward Thomas-	Relieving officer, Ashbourne Union, Registrar of birth & deaths, Ashbourne
Millward Thomas-	Junior farmer
Shaw Ann Mrs-	Cow keeper
Taylor Charles-	Shoemaker
Warner Charlotte Mrs-	Farmer
Watkinson Emma Mrs-	Shoulder of Mutton PR & farmer
Wright John William-	Farmer, Deputy Registrar, births & deaths Brailsford, White Meadow Farm

Osmaston School – Sir Andrew is a board member

A School Board of 5 Members	Commercial
Bateman Mrs, The Cottage Brownson William Hall William Rose Cottage Nicholson Rev. Lancelot (Vicar) Walker Andrew Barclay Bt., Osmaston Manor	Bagshaw Thomas (excrs of) - farmers - The Pastures Bardney John -head Gardener to A B Walker Bt. Bestwick John- Farmer Brown William –farmer- Osmaston Fields Brownson Wm sec. to John Osmaston esq

Yeldersley Hall-Judith Wright, daughter of Francis Wright, now aged 48 was still living at Yeldersley Hall with two temporary wards, girls aged two and five. Her sister Frances and husband, the Rev. Frederic Wigram and their six children were also there at census time. They had seven female servants and a coachman. A gardener was living in the Lodge.

1891-6TH JANUARY GRAND BALL

"A magnificent Ball was given by Sir Andrew at Osmaston Manor on the occasion of the debut of Miss Walker. The arrangements for the ball were of the most elaborate nature, the whole of them being in the hands of Messrs. Grater & Co. of London.

There was a very large and brilliant gathering including representatives of all the leading families in the district, whose invitations numbered upwards of 700. In addition there was a huge house party of distinguished guests.
The ballroom was a temporary erection built on the lawn in front of the Manor by Messrs Eastwood of Manchester. The decorations and arrangements of the ballroom were excellent. The walls were draped with pink and white linen and muslin and the room was lit with electricity."

1893-27TH FEBRUARY DEATH OF SIR ANDREW BARCLAY WALKER Bt.

"While Sir Andrew Barclay Walker was a popular and kindly landlord, his stay at Osmaston Manor was relatively short lived. He had suffered ill-health and even his wedding to Maude Okeover in 1887 had to be delayed several months while he recuperated on his yacht and a visit to Scotland. Just 5 years after his marriage, early in 1892, he was confined to his room at Gateacre Grange for several weeks with a severe illness. On Sunday, there was a decided change for the worse and about seven o'clock on Monday morning, February 27th, 1893, Sir Andrew passed peacefully away, in the presence of Lady Walker and all the members of his family.

Directly the melancholy became known, Liverpool flags were hoisted half-mast at the Town Hall, St George's Hall, the Walker Art Gallery and other public buildings as well as the political clubs and elsewhere, Derbyshire people in all ranks of life also shared the deep and sincere regret with which they mourned the death of Sir Andrew Barclay Walker, Bart. J.P. of Osmaston."

Derby Daily Telegraph 27 2 1893

INHERITANCE OF SIR ANDREW BARCLAY WALKER'S ESTATE

"Probate was granted at the Liverpool District Registry, of the will and three codicils of the late Sir Andrew Barclay Walker, Bt. of Osmaston Manor, Derbyshire, and The Grange, Gateacre to the executors Sir Peter Carlaw Walker, Bt., John Reid Walker, William Walker, Andrew Barclay Walker, Joseph Gilstrap Branston and John Hughes, the gross value of the personal estate being sworn in £2,876,781 18s 10d.   The will dated the 14th July 1891, the first codicil 23 June 1892, the second codicil 13th July 1892 and the third codicil 11 August 1892. Testator confirms the settlement made upon his marriage, and bequeaths to his widow provision for a dower house and furniture. After leaving various legacies to members of his former staff and others, testator bequeaths to each grandchild living at his decease, £2000 and the following legacies free of duty:-

Liverpool Legions of Honour. B G Orchard 1893

CHARITABLE BEQUESTS

Royal Infirmary	Liverpool Newsboys' Home	Liverpool Blind Asy.
Liverpool Deaf & Dumb Institute	Liverpool Eye & Ear Infirmary	Seamans Orphan Inst.
Liverpool Consumption Hospital	Liverpool Magdalen Institute	Liverpool Boys Asy.
Stanley Hospital	North Hospital	Liverpool Inf. Asy.
Bluecoat Hospital	Royal Southern Hospital	Liverpool Female Asy.
Liverpool M.S Indefatigable	Ayr Infirmary for Children	
Liverpool Infirmary for Children	Liverpool Home for Incurables	

BEQUESTS : "Testator bequeaths his yacht, the Cuhona, to his eldest Son, Sir Peter C Walker, and his son, Mr J R Walker, the residential property, The Knoll at Barton Under Needwood, and to his Son, Major W H Walker, the residential property at Gateacre, called The Grange, with the land and properties adjoining, and the contents of the house.

The Osmaston Estate, together with all the contents of the mansion, the Belle Vale Estate, and the adjoining property at Little Woolton near Liverpool and a sum of £700,000 are settled by testator upon his eldest and other sons successively in tail male. Testator bequeaths £10,000 to his son in law, Mr W R Court, and settles upon Mrs Court and her children £150,000, and upon his daughter Ethel Lisette in like manner £120,000 and upon his son Arthur Carlaw Walker in like manner £100,000. The residue of the testator's estate is directed to be divided between testator's sons, J R Walker, W H Walker, A B Walker and J M Walker...."

Liverpool Legions of Honour. B G Orchard 1893

COMMEMORATION IN VILLAGE CHURCH

Sir Peter Carlaw Walker Bt. installed a new painted lead glass window in St. Martin's Church as a tribute to his father.

Photograph Osmaston History Group.

Surviving children of Sir Andrew and his first wife were:

Mr. Peter Carlaw Walker, succeeded to the baronetcy, and would eventually move to Osmaston Manor.

Mr. John Reid Walker, Managing Director of the Burton Breweries resided at The Knoll, Barton-Under-Needwood. His main interests were Horse Racing and Polo. He established the Ruckley Stud farm at his home, Ruckley Grange, in Shifnal, Staffordshire.

Mr. William Hall Walker, Managing Director of the Northern Breweries. He owned stables at Gateacre, which he inherited from his father, where he bred and raced horses. His main interests were Polo, racing and breeding horses. He also owned a stud in Ireland and he gave the nation his bloodstock of horses to form the national stud 2 miles from Newmarket. He was given the title of Lord Wavertree. The Wavertree Charitable Trust was formed in his memory.
In 1933, the Walker Art Gallery in Liverpool held an exhibition that included the works of Picasso and Gauguin. William Hall donated £20,000 and his painting collection to the gallery. For many years, he continued to help hang Exhibitions at the Walker Gallery.

Mr. Andrew Barclay Walker was born in 1865. He was a keen sailor and owned sailing boats, "Ailsa" and the "Esquimaux" which he bought and fitted out for a Whaling trip.

Other children were Mr Arthur Walker, born in 1859 and Mr Joe Monro Walker born 1866. His daughters were Miss Mary Carlaw Walker, who married Mr Roylance Court in 1883 and Miss Ethel Lisette Walker who married Henry Edwyn King-Tenison, 9th Earl of Kingston and became known as The Countess of Kingston.

From 1893, Osmaston village was part of the Estate of Sir Peter Carlaw Walker Bt.

Chapter 5. SIR PETER CARLAW WALKER - 2ND BARONET 1854-1915

1893-Sir Peter Carlaw Walker, at the age of 39, inherited the title of 2nd Baronet, on the death of his father, Andrew Barclay together with the Osmaston Estate and Manor. His father's main residence at Gateacre, south Liverpool, was left to Sir Peter's younger brother, William Hall Walker.

Unlike his brothers, he was educated at home. When the brewery business became a limited company in 1877, he was a director with his father. His brothers John Reid and William Hall were managing directors.

He was a keen sailor and a member of the Royal Yacht Squadron at Cowes and had spent 6 months in the South Seas sailing a 30 ton coasting schooner.

Courtesy of Sir Andrew Walker-Okeover Bt.

Articles in local Derbyshire newspapers provide an indication of life at the Manor and Sir Peter's involvement with the local community. It would appear that whilst his father was ill in 1892 he had taken some control of the Estate and became involved with the Derbyshire Yeomanry where he rose to the rank of Captain and would regularly visit the Manor.

> "At the Invitation of Captain Walker of the Derby Troop, about 120 members of the Derbyshire Yeomanry Cavalry journeyed to the Manor in brakes provided by Captain Walker and on arriving at the Manor after a short interval for refreshments." Derbyshire Advertiser & Journal – 21 10 1892

1893-TRAVEL IN USA He toured the USA visiting Colorado and Wyoming where he acquired a small herd of elk which he brought to the Manor and established a herd. The arrival of the Wyoming Elk at Osmaston.

> **IMPORTATION OF ELK-**"Sir Peter C Walker Bt., during a recent tour through the United States, entered into a contract with Col. W H Root, of Laramie, Wyoming, to furnish him with twenty head of Wyoming elk, one-third to be male the remainder to be female...... After a journey of 2600 miles across the continent, he landed them safely at New York. Here they were shpped for Liverpool in the "Runic of the White Star" line on October 9th and were trucked with the assistance of Mr Cross, a naturalist from Ashbourne arriving on 21st. Mr Brownson and others connected with the Osmaston Estate at once set about getting them to their final destination, which was expeditiously accomplished all being safely within the enclosure prepared for them near Copse Hill by noon the next day......The elk seem to be taking well to their new quarters, and no doubt under the careful treatment which they will receive, will thrive well. Sir Peter C Walker Bt. sailed for England from the United States, in the s.s. Teutonic, on Wednesday last". Derbyshire Advertiser (extract)

1893

The elk seemed to take well to their new quarters, and with careful treatment they thrived well.
Miss Jane Walker-Okeover recalled "iron railings surrounded the grounds and the park between the House and the lake were deer fenced as our Great Grandfather had imported some American Wapiti."

Photograph courtesy of Sir Andrew Walker-Okeover Bt.

To this date there is an area on the Estate still called the Elk Pen.

Sir Peter had enjoyed worldwide travel prior to his inheritance of the baronetcy.
He continued to travel extensively, enjoying sport, big game hunting and sailing.

Among the countries visited were Mexico, Ceylon, South Africa, British Columbia and the U.S.A.
Trophies from his game hunting were brought to the Manor and decorated the hallway.

A large grizzly bear or two greeted visitors to the Manor.
Photograph
courtesy of Sir Andrew Walker-Okeover Bt.

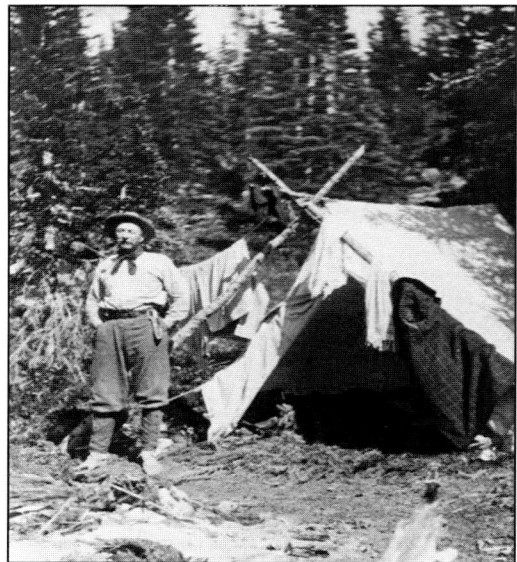

As a huntsman, he continued sporting pursuits when at home at the Manor. The following article shows the extent of an estate shoot.

"Sir Peter C Walker Bt., who has lately returned from the United States, gave his first shooting party at the Manor on Monday last." "On Thursday and Friday in last week the "Old Warren" and the coverts around the Manor were shot through by Sir Peter C Walker Bt., W R Court, Colonel Paget, W Jones Cross Esq. and H B Greenfield Esq. As game was plentiful, some good sport was enjoyed. During the two days shooting, 1304 head fell to the guns, including 548 pheasants, 686 rabbits and 4 woodcocks. Sir Peter afterwards gave large dinner parties at the Manor".
Derbyshire Advertiser & Journal 10 11 1893

1894–SIR PETER SETTLES INTO COUNTRY LIFE

Politics-The Derby Beaconsfield Club made a trip to Osmaston

> "It may be said without fear of contradiction that the seat of Sir Peter Walker Bt., ranks high amongst the stately homes of England. Like the ever popular Palace of the Peak, it has many attractions."   Derbyshire Advertiser and Journal 1 6 1894

Yeomanry-Sir Peter invited 120 men of the C & D Troop of the Derbyshire Yeomanry Cavalry to attend a church parade at Osmaston Manor.

Hunting

> "The last meet of the Season of the famous Dove Valley Harriers was held at Osmaston Manor, the seat of Sir Peter Walker Bt., the popular owner of the pack, although this was not a very large meet. They had 20 couples of 21 inch foxhounds and met three times a week. Their kennels and headquarters were in Mayfield."
> (Source H A Bryden, Hare Hunting & Harriers, 1903. Published Grant Richards, London)

New Stud Stables At Osmaston
Sir Peter undertook a new building project of Stud Stables for his Race Horses

A newspaper correspondent wrote – "I was favoured the other day with permission to view the new block of stud stabling, recently erected at Osmaston Manor for Sir Peter Walker Bt. and which has now been in the hands of the builders for some time. I must say that I was greatly impressed with the first glimpse I got of this most artistically-designed and picturesque building, with its beautifully tinted tile roofs and timbered gables and which covers an area of about 1,400 sq. yards................

On your right and left are the boxes 16 in all, the exterior work of which is brick with stone dressing, intermixed with oak timbers, cement, stucco and rich coloured ornamental hanging tiling. Turning to our right we were first shown the sick box , which is of course isolated and we then enter the main building, and are at once struck with its very carefully considered detail and complete finish. .... The boxes are wainscoted with teak, and tiled above with tinted glass tiles..... The centre block consists of saddle room, cleaning room, wash box, drying room, boiler house etc. and above these are the men's bedrooms, mess rooms and bathrooms which are reached by a teak staircase. The Architect was A Macpherson of Derby and the Builder was Ford & Co of Derby."
1893 – Derbyshire Advertiser (extract) 1893

GARDEN PARTY
"At Osmaston Manor on Saturday last at the invitation of Sir Peter Walker, Bt. a large and distinguished company attended the garden party at Osmaston Manor. The grounds, as it is well known, are very picturesque." Derbyshire Advertiser & Journal – 18 05 1894

1894-95 Osmaston School

> "The return Cricket match between Osmaston School and Cubley School played on the Osmaston Manor Ground on Saturday —Osmaston Score: Wright b Ford, Williamson b West, Green run out 7 Brown hit wicket." Derbyshire Advertiser & Journal 7 9 1894

> "A scholar of the National School by the name of Collins had obtained a scholarship at the Derby Organised Science School, granted by the Derbyshire County Council." Derbyshire Advertiser & Journal 9 08 1895

Lady Maude Walker Marries

Sir Peter's step mother, Lady Maude Walker, continued to live at the Manor following the death of Sir Andrew Barclay. Sir Peter had a good relationship with her and in 1895 when she married, Sir Peter gave her away. Lady Maude Walker married Lori Phillips, of Lawrenny Park, Pembrokeshire, Master of the Pembroke Hounds.

Duke And Duchess Of Teck Visit Osmaston Manor

"The Duke and Duchess of Teck had been invited to Open a Fund Raising Event at the Derbyshire Hospital and had been invited to stay at Calwich Abbey. A large number of people had gathered at Norbury Station which was gaily decorated with flags and streamers and evergreens. Mr A C Duncombe and Col. Barrington Foote assisted H.R.H. out of the carriage and drove through Ellastone which again was decorated and Mr F D Palmby of the Bromley Arms had constructed a splendid Welcome Arch. The Church bells rang and the school children were waiting on the lawn in front of Calwich Abbey. On the following day the Duke & Duchess of Teck arrived in Derby by train to open a Bazaar in aid of the Derby Infirmary at the Drill Hall and was met by the Mayor, Sir Henry Wilmot, and a guard of honour furnished by the Sherwood Foresters. Sir Peter had invited the Duke and Duchess on the following day to Osmaston Manor and as soon as it was known they were due to drive through Ashbourne action was taken to decorate the town and extend a cordial welcome."

Derbyshire Advertiser and Journal 26 04 1895 (extract)

1896

Derby Children's Hospital

Sir Peter had been President of the Board for the Derby Children's Hospital for 1895-96. This followed on from the support his parents gave this charity and although he had been unable to attend many meetings he wanted to assist in writing off a hospital debt and he donated £150.

Ladies' Cricket

A novel cricket match was played at Osmaston Manor. The team consisted entirely of ladies.

1897- QUEEN VICTORIA'S DIAMOND JUBILEE CELEBRATIONS

Throughout the country events took place to celebrate the Queen's Diamond Jubilee.

> "Osmaston Jubilee beacon fire was already in preparation on Shirley Common Hill, many loads of fuel already having been carted th ther at the expense of Sir Peter Walker Bt".
> Extract from the Ashbourne News Telegraph 13 08 1897

Ox Roast-Sir Peter had been away from the Manor travelling, and so celebrations had been suspended until his return. On the previous evening, an Ox had been roasted whole on the Cricket ground.

Photograph Osmaston History Group

> "Thursday, August 5th 1897 was a red letter day in the Parish of Osmaston, long looked forward to and still to be remembered. As the happy event drew near, the prospective enjoyment of which had been whetting the appetite, especially of the younger portion of the community for many weeks, suppressed excitement grew.
> Various sections of the village were busy adorning their horses, others making gay the streets and others busy on the cricket ground putting up tents and there was hardly a house in the village which was not decorated."
> Extracts from the Ashbourne News Telegraph 13 08 1897

> "The proceedings commenced as they should with a Jubilee Service in the fine church built by the late Francis Wright. Sir Andrew Walker had commemorated the Queens 50 year Jubilee in 1887 by installing the painted glass windows. After the service a procession was formed headed by the Osmaston Band and commenced its march to the Manor.
> Extracts from Ashbourne News Telegraph 13 08 1897

Diamond Jubilee Continued

A Procession from St. Martin's Church and Village Dinner for 600 at the Manor

Photograph Osmaston History Group

Sir Peter Meets His Tenants For The First Time

"On arriving at the grounds Sir Peter Walker planted a memorial tree near the Manor in commemoration of this great event.

They sat at tables and Sir Peter toasted the Queen and the tenants toasted Sir Peter. The Rev. L. Nicholson, vicar, said the pleasing duty devolved upon him of proposing the health of their worthy chairman, Sir Peter Walker.

They were all pleased to meet him that day and he believed that this was the first occasion on which Sir Peter had met his tenantry altogether. This meeting was all the more pleasurable as Sir Peter was an excellent Landlord, and had the interests of the tenantry at heart. It had been remarked in the village that it was a pity Sir Peter was not married and he himself thought that no man's education was complete until he married (laughter). He asked the company to drink the health of Sir Peter and to wish him health, prosperity and a good wife. (loud applause).

Sir Peter responding said it gave him the greatest of pleasure to meet his tenantry that day. For some time past he had wished for an opportunity to meet them and he did not think he could have chosen a more suitable occasion than the Jubilee Year of our beloved Queen"

Derbyshire Advertiser & Journal 18 06 1897

Jubilee Celebrations For Children

About 450 children sat down to tea and each was presented with a penny bearing the date of 1897 from Sir Peter Walker.

1898-CORPORATE ENTERTAINING BY PETER WALKER & SONS
100 plus servants travelled by train from Liverpool to cater for this event.

Peter Walker & Son Limited tries a new business promotion when the directors invited 484 of their customers and partners to visit Osmaston Manor, the home of the Chairman of the Board. "A train brought the Guests to Derby Station and a luncheon with music was provided at the Drill Hall with a choice of 17 courses.

At 1.30 the guests then proceeded to Osmaston Manor where a couple of hours were spent inspecting the gardens and interior of the Manor.   At 4.00pm dinner was served in a Marquee at the Manor.

Speeches: A Mr Turner addressed the guests after the meal and referred to the cordial relations that existed between the firm and their customers and to the commercial stability of the firm whose shares he said were as good securities as the best corporate bonds.

Col. William Hall Walker, who presided in the absence of his brother (Sir Peter Walker who was at present in America) thanked the company for their presence and how he wished he could have had the intimate personal connection with the customers that his father had. His father thought more almost of the customers than he did of his own, and they, his sons, had endeavoured to continue this work.

He hoped that whatever happened in the future they would all stand together and be able to defeat their enemies. The party eventually left Ashbourne Station on the North Staffs Railway embarking in the special train, they returned to Liverpool."

Derbyshire Advertiser & Journal 10 06 1898

1899-A FASHIONABLE WEDDING AT OKEOVER ON TUESDAY MAY 30TH 1899.
THE MARRIAGE OF SIR PETER CARLAW WALKER Bt. TO MISS ETHEL BLANCHE OKEOVER

"At the Hall gates was a well-designed arch of evergreens – and banners, flags fluttered amongst the fine old trees.   Then at Dove House Green, Ashbourne extended its first message of "God Bless the Happy Pair." The Market Place, St John Street, Church Street and the approaches to the Railway Station were abundantly decked with bunting, union jacks and ensigns flying side by side with flags of all nations.

The Ceremony -The fine band of the Derbyshire Yeomanry appeared on the lawn and under Bandmaster King played a choice selection of music.   Then came a dash of the military element, the B squadron of the Derbyshire Yeomanry lining up on the right with drawn sabres, and with their blue uniforms, glittering helmets and nodding plumes and the glint of the sunlight on their accoutrements, they made a brave display. Sir Peter Walker is a major in the Yeomanry, and this was his squadron – come to do honour to his wedding and to form an escort for him and his bride after the ceremony.

The bridegroom entered the church with his best man Mr Nugent Howard.

Shortly afterwards the bride appeared, wearing a lovely bridal gown of rich ivory duchesse satin, exquisitely embroidered with pearls and silver and draped with flounce of beautiful Brussels Lace. A scarf of the same lace was attached to the left shoulder with a cluster of orange blossom and draped the entire length of the train. A lace veil was also worn. The bride was given away by her father.

Extract Derbyshire Advertiser & Journal 10 06 1898

The Ashbourne townspeople had apparently turned out en masse, lining the route to the station, all eager to catch a glimpse of Lady Walker and the genial baronet.

The wedding party left by special saloon train for St Pancras en route to Paris where the honeymoon was to be spent.

Lady Walker (formerly Ethel Okeover) leaving for her Honeymoon at Ashbourne Railway Station. Her Husband, Sir Peter Walker Bt., appears in the centre in the light suit and bowler hat. Miss Ethel Blanche was the fifth daughter of Mr H C Okeover of Okeover Hall J.P. and D.L. and Hon. Mrs Okeover, daughter of the third Baron Waterpark of Doveridge Hall.

Photograph Osmaston History Group

The engine was gaily decked with flags and flowers. Twenty one shots, a regimental volley, were fired over the line at Ashbourne and at Rocester. Clifton, Norbury and Rocester stations were all decorated. As the train slowly steamed out the Yeomanry escort waved their helmets and gave three stentorian cheers and the good wishes of an enthusiastic crowd. The bells peeled merrily from the noble spire of the old parish church of St Oswalds and the town was en fete."
Ashbourne News Telegraph Friday 2 06 1899

1. Silver Cups were given by the Tenants of Osmaston with a list of contributors.

2. Silver Bowls and a Gold Bracelet gifted from the Townspeople of Ashbourne with a list of contributors.

Courtesy of Sir Andrew Walker-Okeover Bt.

1899-IT WAS NOW OSMASTON'S TURN TO CELEBRATE

Sir Peter and Lady Walker returned from honeymoon by train to Derby on July 6th and were met by a cavalcade escort to accompany them back to Osmaston. Celebratory flower arches decorated the roads in Brailsford and Shirley and every house in Osmaston was decorated, with the school children ready to sing their welcome song for Sir Peter to welcome his new wife to Osmaston.

The School children were waiting outside the decorated School to sing. Flowers were thrown into the carriage. At the school, Miss Bardney presented a bouquet as did Miss Madge Brownson.

Photograph Osmaston History Group

Traditional Procession- Once in Osmaston, the horses were removed from the carriage and ropes of blue and yellow attached. Accompanied by hearty cheers, local people took up the ropes and manually pulled the carriage with Sir Peter and Lady Walker on board towards the Manor. The band headed the procession with villagers and visitors following in line. Mr Brownson, estate agent greeted Sir Peter and his bride at the terrace gates followed by Mr Turner, the butler, and the servants at the Manor.

Sir Peter made a speech "Friends and Neighbours. Any few words I may say now to try to thank you for the very hearty welcome you have given myself and my wife today will very inadequately express what I really feel. To me it is only another instance of the many kindnesses you have shown me since I have come here to live, although I have been more or less an absentee landlord. As for my wife, I am sure she will long remember coming to her new home, and it is a day that she will look back to with pleasure all her life. I beg to thank you most heartily in the name of my wife and myself, for the very kind way in which you have given us a homecoming. I thank you most sincerely."

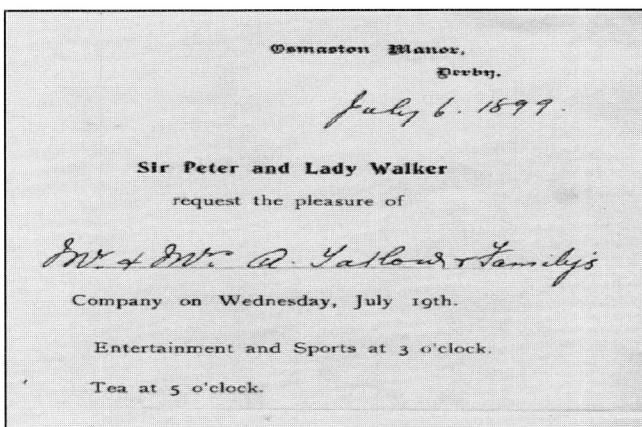

Osmaston Manor,
Derby.
July 6. 1899.

Sir Peter and Lady Walker
request the pleasure of

Mr & Mrs A. Tatlow & Family's

Company on Wednesday, July 19th.

Entertainment and Sports at 3 o'clock.

Tea at 5 o'clock.

Invitations were issued to all tenants to join Sir Peter and Lady Walker to celebrate on their return to Osmaston after their honeymoon.

This particular invitation was issued to Mr and Mrs Tatlow and family who lived in a thatched house in the woods near the Osmaston village duck pond known as the Tatlow Plantation.

THE TATLOW FAMILY LIVED IN THE HOUSE (NOW DEMOLISHED) AT THE EDGE OF THE POLO FIELD AND OPPOSITE THE DUCK POND

A water pump was situated by the village duck pond. Photograph shows Mr Tatlow collecting water.
Mr Arthur Tatlow (1860-1937) was employed as a Gardener at the Manor. Emily Tatlow his wife lived until 1960.
Photograph Osmaton History Group

The Tatlow Sisters - Eliza, Edith and Amy. Daughter Eliza also worked at the Manor as a seamstress.
Eliza 1898 - 1975
Edith 1893 - 1965
Amy 1890 - 1969
Photographs Osmaston History Group

1900-1902

OPEN GARDENS AT OSMASTON MANOR In 1900 Sir Peter opened the gardens at Osmaston Manor to the general public. An entry fee was charged which Sir Peter donated to charity. Garden openings would continue for many years with open days advertised in Derbyshire newspapers and coaches would bring in visitors. The open days would finish with dancing on the lawn to a brass band.

The couple dancing in the centre (man wearing the bowler hat) are Mr. & Mrs Getcliffe, great, great Grandparents of Dinah Archer of Yeldersley. Photograph courtesy of Dinah Archer

1900-Celebrations Sir Peter & Lady Walker's first child Enid Walker was born.

1901-Osmaston Census details
Staff working at the New Stables: Grooms: Joseph Babbington and Simeon Finney.
Garden Staff William Bardney as Head Gardener with wife and 3 children
Foreman Gardener in The Bothey was George R Mountford plus 6 men.
Coachman in the stables, William Warlow, and Wife and 4 children.
The Cottage, Osmaston, Lydia C Bateman as Cook and housemaid .
Osmaston School- Census details- Walter and Hannah Beeby were still running the School
Yeldersley Hall-Census details, Judith Wright, Francis Wright's daughter was living alone in the house along with six female servants and a coachman.

Delayed Coronation Celebrations for King Edward VII

"The Festivities which were arranged to take place in June last, and deferred in consequence of the serious illness of His Majesty, were held on the Manor Cricket Ground, where a large marquee had been erected." Derbyshire Advertiser & Journal 22 081902

LIFE IN OSMASTON VILLAGE 1902-04
HEIR OF OSMASTON MANOR ARRIVED- THE BELLS RING OUT

"Mr Brownson (Sir Peter Walker's steward) did all he possibly could to ensure a successful day and his efforts were much appreciated. During the afternoon there was a champagne luncheon. Sir Peter Walker presided with Lady Walker on his right. This day will long stay in the memories of the people of Osmaston who celebrated the birth of the Heir to Osmaston Manor, Ian Peter Andrew Monro Walker". Derbyshire Advertiser & Journal 7 08 1903

Lectures Held In Osmaston School

"The annual report from H M Inspector of Schools had recently come to hand. It was gratifying to learn that order and attainments were very satisfactory, and that the sewing was reported to be good. Excellent grades had been awarded."
Derbyshire Advertiser & Journal 9 05 1902

"Second of the series lectures – First Aid Injured, was kindly undertaken by Dr Boswell of Ashbourne, was given in the schoolroom on Tuesday evening last."

Derbyshire Advertiser & Journal 13 11 1903

In 1904 a series of lectures had been allocated to Osmaston by The Derbyshire Technical Education Committee.
One lecture on laundry work was given by a Miss Sinclair shown as having a first class diploma from the Edinburgh School of Cookery and Domestic Economy.

The Royal Liverpool Seamen's Orphanage Visit
Each year, Sir Peter invited the Liverpool's Seaman's Orphanage to Osmaston Manor, as his father had before him. Approximately 300 children would visit for the day.

Derby Royal Infirmary
Sir Peter contributed £1000 to the Derbyshire Royal Infirmary where he became President of the Board which again followed on from both his father and Francis Wright who had been a founder member involved in building the Hospital.

Sir Peter was also Vice President of the Derbyshire County Cricket Club and Derbyshire Natural History & Archaeological Soc. and Lady Walker became involved with the Derbyshire Children's Hospital and was also Vice President of the Derbyshire Red Cross Society.

Sporting & Social Events
Elvaston Handicap Steeplechase Plate race. Sir Peter and his son, John Reid Walker attended the Steeplechase race where Sir Peter's Horse "Flutterer" ran and also Mr Walker's horse "Monksilver".
(Sporting Life 17 03 1903)

1903 YELDERSLEY HALL-Death Of Judith Wright Daughter Of Francis Wright

Judith died, aged 61, on 23rd May 1903 and was buried at Osmaston on the 27th. She left £15,793. Her will was proved by Frederick Beresford Wright and Fitzherbert Wright.

She was very well thought of in the area and was a member of the Ashbourne Board of Guardians for the Union Workhouse, situated on Belle Vue Road, Ashbourne and was a regular visitor there. Each year she invited and paid transport costs for the female inmates to visit Yeldersley Hall for tea. Judith also held an annual treat at Yeldersley Hall for Osmaston school children and their parents, annual fetes in support of the Missionary Society and was a teacher in Osmaston Sunday School.

Yeldersley Hall was thought to have still been in the ownership of the John Osmaston (Wright) family and was passed to, or purchased by, Fitzherbert Wright of The Hayes, Swanwick. In 1903, it was leased to Ernest Beresford Fitzherbert Wright for 21 years at £180 per annum.

OSMASTON VILLAGE SPORTING CLUBS

1904-Osmaston Manor Cricket Club – The AGM was held in the reading room on the 13th December 1904 when a "goodly number" of members attended.
Derbyshire Advertiser 23 12 1904

1905-Osmaston Manor Football Club was formed in September. Those who joined were either from Osmaston Manor Estate or others living in the village and neighbourhood. Details appeared in the Derbyshire Advertiser & Journal

1905-Bowls Club
"The Osmaston Bowling Club, which only initiated this year, has been well supported and is due to the Hon. Secretary for the excellent arrangements made for the benefit of the members and good of the club." Derbyshire Advertiser & Journal 13 10 1905

1906-DANCE CARD FROM OSMASTON MANOR showing the dances of the day from 1906

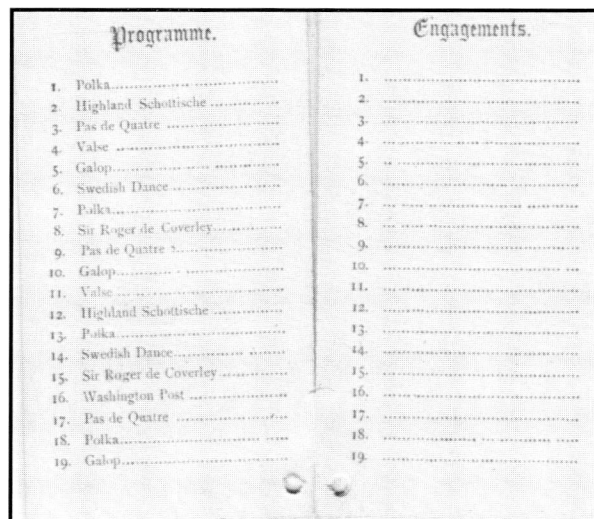

This Dance card had been saved by Enid Walker, Sir Ian Walker Okeover's sister, and eventually passed to her friend Phyllis Sadler. The dances on the Card are: 1.The Polka 2.Highland Schottische 3.Pas De Quatre 4.Valse 5.Galop 6.Swedish Dance 7.Polka 8.Sir Roger de Coverley 9.Pas De Quatre 10.Galop, 11.Valse 12.Highland Schottische 13. Polka 14. Swedish Dance 15. Sir Roger de Coverley 16. Washington Post etc.

1906 SIR PETER REACHED THE RANK OF COLONEL WITH THE DERBYSHIRE YEOMANRY

Derbyshire Yeomanry at the Manor with Sir Peter, centre, Lady Walker to his left, Reverend Titmuss, to his right and his son, Ian and daughter Enid stand to their mother's left.

SIR PETER WALKER Bart. OSMASTON MANOR - FIRE ENGINE

"If you can imagine something from Charlie Chaplin or a Laurel and Hardy film, it looked like a smallish version. Manned by men on the estate, probably grooms and gardeners, they were summoned by a bell from the kitchen tower. There were long rolls of canvas hoses on reels at strategic points in the house and these were tested yearly by, I think, a representative of Merry Weathers, and then stretched out to dry in the arcade. I remember a red fire bucket of sand on the nursery landing" (Extract from Memoirs of Miss Jane Walker-Okeover) (daughter of Sir Ian Walker)

1906-DEATH OF MR WILLIAM BROWNSON - LAND AGENT FOR THE ESTATE

"On the 8th June it was reported that Mr William Brownson, who was the Agent for the Osmaston Estate, had died of a heart condition at the Derbyshire Royal Infirmary.

Mr Brownson had lived at the Manor Farm in Osmaston and would be sadly missed." Derby Daily Telegraph 7 0 6 1906

Mr Brownson's funeral was at Osmaston Church and his burial was in Osmaston churchyard.
Photograph Osmaston History Group

Mr Brownson funeral cortege-Photograph Osmaston History Group

1906-"An Osmaston Manor Bowling Club competition was held for the set of bowls kindly donated by Sir Peter. The winner - the final best between Mr Latham and Mr C A Beeby - being the former, who thereby became entitled to the set of bowls." Derbyshire Advertiser & Journal 1906"

1906-"The Annual trip of the choir, Sunday School teachers took place numbering over 30. They were conveyed to and from Ashbourne in conveyances kindly provided from the Manor Farm." Derbyshire Advertiser and Journal 7 09 1906

1907
SIR PETER FULLY IMMERSED HIMSELF IN VILLAGE LIFE

"**AGM Osmaston Manor Cricket Club**, which Sir Peter Walker Bt., is the active president, was held at the Schoolroom, Osmaston, the Rev. H Titmus presiding. The secretary's accounts showed the finances be a sound condition. The officers mostly re-appointed, and Sir Peter Walker thanked for his services and generous support. Messrs. May and Bramson were chosen as Hon. Secretaries, Mr F Brown captain of the first team and Mr Barnard of the second team. It was decided to join the Ashbourne League, and also the Junior League, should the proposal to form the latter be carried out."

Sheffield Daily Telegraph 26 08 1907

Cricket matches from 1907 onwards are recorded as being played at Osmaston

TRAVEL TO THE USA In October 1907 Sir Peter travelled out again to New York on the SS Umbria. Records show that he travelled with his valet, John Harry Boston.

ESTATE GAME KEEPERS

1908-Deer Catching In Osmaston Park "Last week 14 head of the splendid herd deer belonging to Sir Peter Walker Bt., located in the Manor Park were deported to Killiechonate Forest, Spean Bridge." Men on horseback divided the herd using a ten foot net to catch them.
Derbyshire Advertiser & Journal 7 02 1908
1909
The Keepers Entertainment "Keepers employed by the Osmaston Estate, together with the beaters for Sir Peter Walker's shooting parties during the last season, were entertained to a hot supper served "old English fashion". Derbyshire Advertiser & Journal 19 07 1909

Shooting Party "Sir Peter and Lady Walker of Osmaston Manor entertained a distinguished shooting party on Monday last. Some excellent sport was provided and some excellent shooting was witnessed". Derbyshire Advertiser & Journal 10 12 1909

FISHING COMPETITION

Osmaston Estate at the Wyaston Lake

on Wednesday, 16th June, 1909.

Start time 1.00 p.m. Finish time 6.30 p.m.

Any kind of fishing tackle permitted.

Derbyshire Advertiser & Journal – 21 05 1909

CARS-A wide variety of cars were used, seen here housed in the Stable Courtyard at Osmaston Manor.

Photograph courtesy of Sir Andrew Walker-Okeover Bt. Date unknown

LOVE OF HORSE RACING-
EXTRACT AND PHOTOGRAPH FROM BAILY'S MAGAZINE OF SPORTS AND PASTIMES. JULY 1909 NO.593

"The sport of Steeplechasing has no more staunch supporter than Sir Peter. Although an ardent admirer of the English thoroughbred, Sir Peter loves best to see him performing steeplechasing.

For years he has been trying to breed a good class of horse to be raced in steeplechases only, and for quite two decades now has Sir Peter been associated with sport under National Hunt Rules.

Col. Hall Walker and John Reid Walker have long been supporters of flat racing even in the early days of Polo and Galloway Pony Racing, Sir Peter has stood loyal to the so-called illegitimate sport.

Lady Ethel Walker also owned a number of National Hunt horses of her own called Shirley Park and shared Sir Peter's love of flat racing.
There are a dozen steeple chasers housed at their home at Osmaston Manor with John Latham the little cross country jockey, a superb horseman."

87

1909-Donations to Derby Royal Infirmary "During the year the President of the Infirmary, Sir Peter Walker of Osmaston Manor, signalised his year of office by presenting the institution a room and apparatus for the treatment of lupus, by the Pinsen light system."
Derbyshire Advertiser & Journal – 26 11 1909

1910-Osmaston Manor V. Clifton Cricket Club "Wright, H Scrimshaw, Page & Machin did not bat. These old rivets in the cricket field met for the first time this year at the Osmaston Cricket Ground. The game resulted in a draw much in favour of the visitors."
Derbyshire Advertiser & Journal – 24 06 1910

1910-Osmaston Manor Bowling Club "A general meeting was held on Monday evening, the 20th inst. When a good number of members were present. M J Jackson ably presiding. The Hon Sec. Mr Tally, submitted a statement of the accounts for the past year. "
Derbyshire Advertiser & Journal 01 01 1910

1910-Family Wedding At St. Martin's Church
Miss Ethel Carlaw Walker, niece of Sir Peter Walker Bt., of Osmaston Manor and Mr J Balfour Caldwell were married at Osmaston Church. Miss Walker and her brother, PAC Walker, had been living at Osmaston Manor for quite a period of time since their parent's death.
The sacred edifice had been very tastefully decorated by the Osmaston Manor staff, (under Mr J Tully) and there was a large assembly of guests. Derbyshire Advertiser & Journal 21 10 1910

1910/1911-Osmaston Band Play At The Manor   Photograph Osmaston History Group

Back row: Ted Morley, Billy Stubbs, Arthur Stubbs, George Riley, Horace Stubbs, George Slater, Unknown **Front Row**: Arthur Gamble, Albert Bull, Unknown, Jack Housley

1911-Open Gardens "By kind permission of Sir Peter & Lady Walker the Gardens will be open to the Public on Whit Monday 10th and Wednesday July 12th ".   Derbyshire Advertiser & Journal 19 05 1911

1911 CENSUS

Osmaston Manor-The Census shows there being seven male and fourteen female staff at the Manor. The Garden staff consisted of Mr Tully, Mr Salt, Mr Jones and Mr Kent.

The School-Mr & Mrs Beeby have left and Amy Conyard, a Certified School Mistress, has taken over.

Yeldersley Hall-Ernest Beresford Wright was still living at the Hall with his wife Lucy Adeline (née Fox) and their three daughters. They employed a chauffeur, a stud/groom and seven female servants. The head gardener was living in the Hall Lodge.

NEW TECHNOLOGY AT OSMASTON-In 1911 the first steam lorry was purchased by the Estate.
Frank Bull & Jim Gilman, outside the Station Hotel, Ashbourne

Photograph Osmaston History Group

In the early 1900s a new Laundry Building was built next to what was the Gamekeeper's cottage.
Photographs courtesy Audrey Tomlinson

1911-SHOOT AT OSMASTON

"On Tuesday, at this shoot, the following large bag was the result – Wild duck 777, pheasants 562, Woodcock 1, various 1, total 1341. In attendance Sir Peter Walker, Lord Grosvenor, Sir Philip Guy Egerton, Prince Colloredo Mannsfeld, Col Sandeman, Mrs R Bruce, F Cooper, Miss D Roylance Court, Lady Aylesbury, Mrs Hall Walker, Miss Enid Walker, Lady Walker, Master Ian Walker, Capt. R Bruce, Miss E Roylance Court, Col. K Hall Walker, Col M Hall Walker MP, Princess Colleredo Mannsfeld and PAC Walker (Jack)." Derbyshire Advertiser & Journal 17th 11 1911

Photograph Osmaston History Group

1912-There was much unrest with the Coal Miners over their working conditions and a strike was called.   The miners' strike only lasted from January 1912 until April 6th 1912 but the impact in some mining areas was great. The Wright family and the Walkers had all been involved in the coal mining industry.

1912-New Agent For The Estate Major George Page who had been Quartermaster Sergeant to the Derbyshire Yeomanry for the past 6 years was appointed.

1912-Osmaston Manor Gardens were again thrown open to the public for the charge of sixpence on Bank Holiday Monday and around 700 visitors attended. Mr Tully, an estate employee and his colleagues ensured it was a successful afternoon, Osmaston Manor Brass Band was present and Mr Bates of Ashbourne catered for the teas.

1912 SHOOTING PARTY – LARGE NUMBERS OF BIRDS RECORDED

"A select and distinguished shooting party was entertained at Osmaston Manor, when the Copse Hill, Boathouse, Osier, and Scarsdale Plantations were drawn, resulting in some very excellent sport and a record bag of 2,613 head game being accounted for - Pheasants 2,431, wild duck 182. The arrangements under the able control of the head gamekeeper.

Birds being plentiful and flying well, and the guns being excellent 'marksmen', ensured an enjoyable and successful shoot was the result. It is worthy of notice that 738 head of game fell to the guns at one stand, which was made at the Boathouse Plantation. The following were the guns: Duke of Leeds, Earl Kerry, M.P., Mr. G. Farquhar, Mr. E. Crosfield, Col. Fitzherbert and Sir Peter Walker Bt."
Derbyshire Advertiser & Journal 15 11 1912

1912 Village Wedding–Miss E Watkinson

"The bells of Osmaston Church rang out merry peals on April 29th, the occasion being the nuptials of Miss E. Watkinson, daughter of Mr. A. A. Watkinson (parish chairman), and Mr. R. Salt, late of Osmaston Manor Gardens, and now head of the staff at The Gardens, Ipswich.
Great interest was taken in the occasion and there was a large assemblage in the church to witness the ceremony, which was performed by the vicar, the Rev. H. V. Titmuss.

Later in the afternoon the ringers were entertained by the bride's parents to a rich tea, and on the following Thursday evening the members of the Osmaston Manor Bowling Club with other friends to a sumptuous supper. The bridegroom was a very popular member of the Bowling Club, and was the winner for one year of the Wright's Challenge Cup."
Derbyshire Advertiser & Journal 27 7 1912

1912-Yeldersley Hall New Occupant

Ernest Beresford Wright moved to Dorset, to be close to his wife's family. His elder brother, Captain Henry Fitzherbert Wright, moved into Yeldersley Hall with his family.
Captain Henry Fitzherbert Wright was the eldest son of Fitzherbert Wright and grandson of Francis Wright. He was born in 1870 and was educated at Eton and Trinity College. He was called to the bar in 1905. He practised on the Midland Circuit until he joined the family business at Butterley. In 1908, he was commissioned into the newly formed Derbyshire Howitzer Battalion of the Territorial Force.

1912-1918 He was Unionist M.P. for Leominster. He served as a Magistrate and became a member of the local County Council. He was also a Governor of Repton School, President of Derby Children's Hospital and on the board of management of Derbyshire Royal Infirmary. A sportsman in his youth, he had played cricket for Derbyshire at times between 1891 and 1905.

1912-Cricket Osmaston Manor V Kirk Langley

"The opening match of the season for the Osmaston Manor Club took place on Saturday last when they were opposed to a good team from Langley. Owing to the fine bowling of B Brown and A V Haywood, both bowling all through the innings, the Langley Team were only able to put on 48 runs. Brown capturing 6 wickets and A V Haywood 4 for 18. Haywood also gave an excellent display with the bat". Derbyshire Advertiser & Journal 18 5 1912

SIR PETER & LADY WALKER CONTINUE WITH VILLAGE LIFE AND THEIR CHARITIES

1913-Royal Liverpool Seamen's Orphanage Treat Once again, through the generosity of Sir Peter and Lady Walker, the children of the **Seaman's Orphanage, Liverpool**, numbering about 330, together with 14 from the Deaf and Dumb Institution of Derby, spent a very happy day at Osmaston Manor.

Photograph Osmaston History Group

"Ample provision was made for the enjoyment of the young people in the way of roundabouts, swing boats, and donkeys, and it is needless almost to add that the last, although there were twenty; in the field, were hard and well ridden. The order and behaviour of the children were all that could be desired, showing that they were under most careful supervision, and reflected the greatest credit on those in charge of them, and their cheerful and happy faces showed that kindness in their training was not wanting in these institutions.

Before leaving for home at 6 p.m. each child received from Sir Peter and Lady Walker a valuable book, new penny, and packet of sweets. The Brass Band, numbering 25, composed of orphans resident in the institution, discoursed a selection of music in an admirable manner.

Amongst those present, in addition to Sir Peter and Lady Walker and family, were Mr. Okeover, Hon. Mrs. Allsop, Mr. and Mrs. Slatter, Mrs. Knowles and party. At the close Sir Peter, Lady Walker, and family were the recipients of very hearty and prolonged cheers for their very happy day they had given the children of these valuable institutions." Derbyshire Advertiser & Journal 9 08 13

1913-Racing Successes

"The Rangemore Handicap Steeple Chase Plate, the chief event of the afternoon brought out 9 runners, and led to plenty of speculation, which half a dozen were backed between 5:2 and 6:1. Mask Off was favourite from Savannah 11 and Legalite but Long Water made all the running and scored a popular win for Sir Peter Walker.

It was reported that Sir Peter had great success with his horse Ben a Beg (or the Baker) that out of Sure Haven, won the two miles flat race at Cheltenham on Wednesday March 12th and on the following Friday, he won a Steeplechase of 25 miles and on the 25th he won the Jubilee Hurdle Race at Manchester". Derbyshire Advertiser & Journal 9 08 1913

Shoot records for 1912/1913-the Osmaston Manor Estate show the numbers of birds and wildlife shot during the season– Wild Ducks 3,238, Snipe 3, Pheasants 7628 Partridges 61, Hares 2, Rabbits 624. Mr Affleck would have been the Head Gamekeeper at this time.
Derbyshire Advertiser & Journal – 28 03 1913

1913-"The following party of gentlemen took part in the shoot in the Osmaston Manor preserves, given by Sir Peter & Lady Walker on Friday – Lord Enniskillen, Sir Peter Walker Bt., Sir D Gooch, Mr G Farquhar & Mr Darcy, Mr Taylor, Mr W L Fletcher, Mr C Marcham, Mr J C Colobald.

Considering the auspicious weather the shoot was very successful with highly satisfactory management. Bad weather for guns up until lunchtime but a good number of pheasants bagged. Shooting at ducks in the park pond gave splendid sport, the ducks flying high in strong winds. Total bagged 1148."   Derbyshire Advertiser and Journal - 29 11 1913

1914-Osmaston Manor The Annual Servant's Ball - Photograph Osmaston History Group

"Through the kindness of Sir Peter and Lady Walker the Household, staff and other invited guests, the Annual Servant's ball, took place under the Head Butler and Mrs Thompson, the Housekeeper. Dancing commenced at 9pm until the early hours including supper. The singing of Auld Lang Syne in the good old British fashion and God Save the King brought this very happy evening at Osmaston Manor, which will long be remembered, to a close." Derbyshire Advertiser & Journal 31 1 1914

Osmaston Manor Open Gardens

Photograph Osmaston History Group

Sir Peter and Lady Walker again opened their Gardens at Osmaston Manor to the public on Whit Monday June 1st 1914 when the Osmaston Brass Band would be in attendance. Dancing on the lawn, weather permitting, from 4.30. Any funds raised on the day would be distributed to Lady Walker's chosen charities.

Sir Peter became involved with the Ashbourne Cottage Hospital, the Uttoxeter Agricultural Society, Ashbourne Rifle Club and the Ashbourne Cycling and Athletic Club of which he was President. He also was involved with other Institutions and a supporter of the Warrington Band who visited Ashbourne to play at the Garden Open Days.

1914-Osmaston Garden Society Flourishes And Prizes Are Awarded

"The following prizes have been awarded by Sir Peter Walker, Bt., for the best cultivated cottage gardens on the Osmaston Manor Estate, as follows:

Osmaston, —1, H. Allen, 21s., and 2s. 6d. special prize; 2, A. Tatlow, 18s., and 2s. 6d. special prize; 3, . Mould, 15s., and 2s. special prize; 4, C. Allen, 13s. 6d, and 2s. special prize; 5, J. Holloway, 10s. 0d.; 6, F. Brown, Bs.; 7, W. Brownson, 6s. 6d.; 8, M. Brown, 5s.; 9, A. Wright, 4s.; 10, A. Hawksley, 3s.; 11, W. Oakden, 2s. 6d.; 12, J. Housley, 2s.

Shirley—l, T. Hough, 12s., and special prize; 2, W. Sefton, 10s., and 4s. special prize; 3, J. Maskrey, 6s., and 3s. special prize; 4, W. Harper, 5s., and 2s. special prize; 5, W. Stubbs, 3s, and ls. 6d. special prize.

Wyaston. —1, H. Williamson, 10s.; 2, J. Woolley, 5s.

In future the villages of Osmaston, Shirley, and Wyaston would not compete separately, but altogether, the whole of the circumstances, such as difference of soil, etc., to be taken into consideration in awarding the prizes.

The following is a list of the vegetables for which the judges will award marks when inspecting the gardens:—Peas, broad beans, runner beans, beetroot, broccoli , Brussels sprouts, red cabbage, carrots, cauliflower, celery, herbs, leeks, salad, onions, parsley, parsnips, turnips, vegetable marrow, shallots, potatoes, fruit trees, flowers, neatness and order. Twenty prizes, ranging from one guinea to ls. 6d. will be awarded.

1914-THE FIRST WORLD WAR BEGINS AND OSMASTON PLAYS IT'S PART

APPEAL FOR VOLUNTEERS
Territorial Forces

At the time of the outbreak of war in August 1914, a number of men of the area were members of the Derbyshire Yeomanry or the Derbyshire Howitzer Brigade. These were part time territorial forces with weekly training sessions and an annual camp. These units were immediately mobilised at Siddals Road Barracks in Derby and were then moved by train from Derby Friargate station to Reading.

Lord Kitchener's Appeal for Men

With the obvious need for more troops, Lord Kitchener issued an appeal for volunteers. At the end of August, a parish meeting was attended by a number of young men and a committee was formed to "further the enrolment of men willing to serve".

This included Messrs. A.A. Watkinson, J.W. Brown, J.Francis, A.Botham, W.Weller, N.Jones and A.Coxon. Eight men signed to serve in the regular army and four in the Territorials.

Convalescent Home at Manor

Sir Peter and Lady Walker set up a convalescent home at Osmaston Manor. Rooms were changed at the Manor to be suitable for accommodating a hospital for wounded soldiers, Dr. H. H. Hollick, of Ashbourne was the commandant of the hospital, which had accommodation for ten patients.

Raising Funds for the War Effort

A week later on 4th September, another parish meeting was held in the schoolroom. The Chairman was again Mr Watkinson with the Rev. Titmuss and E.B.F. Wright as speakers. Sir Peter Walker was unable to attend but had wired his under-steward Mr Hall to "tell the men to attend the meeting".

 It was agreed that collections should be made to support the Prince of Wales Patriotic Relief Fund and that weekly collections should be made with a minimum of 1d per house.
Together with monies raised by a concert on the cricket field given by Osmaston Town Band, by the end of October about £23 had been raised.

Horses For The War

> "Ten horses from Canada have arrived at Osmaston Manor and these are being fed and trained at the expense of Sir Peter Walker Bt., soon to be ready to be transferred."
>
> Derbyshire Advertiser & Journal 21 11 1914

THE FIELDING FAMILY GOING TO WAR

John Harvey Fielding and his wife Annie Marie brought up 5 children at the Post Office/Grocery Store in Osmaston.   All pictures and information courtesy of the Fielding family.

Going to War 1914.

William H Fielding, back right, with family members. His younger brother Harold Arthur is on the right wearing his sword belt and carrying his carbine.

William Harvey Fielding. Born at Osmaston in 1895. Seen right (centre) as a member of the Derbyshire Yeomanry at Osmaston before 1914.

During WW1 he served with them in the Balkans from April 1915 until October 1917 and became a Lance Corporal in The Mounted Military Police. He married in 1924 and died at Cannock in 1950.

The eldest Son, Francis John Fielding, became a police officer and in WW1, although he enlisted in the forces in October 1916, he was placed on the reserve and not called up until 4th April 1918. He then served in the Coldstream Guards. He married twice and died in 1971.

1914- TRAGIC DEATH OF LIEUT P A C WALKER - SIR PETER'S NEPHEW

Peter Arthur Carlaw Walker, died September 13th 1914, aged 26 following a motorcycle accident at Maidenhead prior to mobilisation for active service.

"Lieutenant Walker, having, it might be said, been reared under Sir Peter and Lady Walker's loving care. The deceased, who was born in New Zealand, was only 26 years of age. Among the numerous letters of sympathy which have reached Osmaston Manor was one from Colonel Lord Henry Bentinck, who wrote to the effect that only a few days ago the Brigadier had complimented Lieut. Walker on his smartness and keenness, and considered him an excellent officer. He was a splendid fellow (Lord Bentinck added), and all were devoted to him, and death was a very great loss to the regiment. Lieut. G. Strutt also forwarded a feeling letter, in which he referred to the personal qualities and military abilities of the deceased gentleman, and said his troop were broken-hearted."
Derbyshire Advertiser and Journal 19 09 1914

"The coffin was covered with the Union Jack, on which were placed Lieut. Walker's helmet and sword. The Service was conducted by the Rev. H. V. Titmuss (vicar of Osmaston). The Family Vault was lined with ivy and white flowers. At the close of the service the firing party discharged and trumpeter A. Imeson sounded the 'Last Post.' The floral tributes were very numerous and beautiful."
Derbyshire Advertiser and Journal 19 09 1914

Sir Peter had a plaque placed in St Martin's Church commemorating the life of his nephew Lt. Walker and his name was also placed on the War Memorial. He was interred in the family vault within St Martin's graveyard.

1914-Osmaston Manor Cricket Club-Village Life Continues after loss of fellow member

"A committee meeting of the above club was held at the Village Inn, Osmaston, on Friday evening, when there was a good attendance of members. Mr. May ably presided, and in opening the proceedings said he was voicing the wishes of all the members of the club when he expressed the very deepest regret at the heavy loss the club had sustained by the death of their late highly esteemed and fellow member, Lieut. P. A. C. Walker, who gave such great support to the club financially, and also by his fine display in the matches. A sincere vote of condolence with the family and all so sadly bereaved was passed unanimously and silently.

Mr. Bloor—his colleague in the secretaryship, Mr. B. Brown, having joined the colours submitted the accounts for the past year to the meeting, and these were found quite satisfactory, and the club financially sound the outstanding subscriptions had been collected. The season's play was then scrutinised, and the following results were forthcoming:— **BATTING AVERAGES** of the first six. A. V. Haywood. 14 runs per innings. H. Tunstall 12.2, P. A. C. Walker 11.1, E. Wright 9.3, E. Bloor 7.3, G. Jones 5.3, The above have played in six matches or over. **BOWLING AVERAGES**. A. V. Haywood 4.06 runs per wicket. E. Bloor 5.0, B. Brown 5.5, H. Tunstall 8.7, Matches played, 14; won 9, lost 4, drawn 1. After fixing the date of the general meeting for about the middle of next month, and passing hearty vote of thanks to the chairman, a very pleasant meeting was brought to close".
Derbyshire Advertiser and Journal 23 10 1914

1914-Area's Roll Of Honour. Many men of the district signed up to serve their country by joining either the regular or territorial forces :-   The Derbyshire Advertiser & Journal 20 11 1914

OSMASTON		WYASTON
William Rust	Frederick Moffatt	Leonard Gamble
Charles Eldridge	William Weller	John Woolley
Arthur Gamble	Harry Sanderson	**YELDERSLEY**
Charles Bell	Walter Sanderson	Harry Williamson
William Black	Charles Buckland	Albert Taylor
Bertram Brown	Albert Allen	William Brownson
Joseph Bestwick	George Wright	Alb. Taylor
Henry Whylde		**SHIRLEY**
Thomas Ollerenshaw	**EDNASTON**	Thomas Titterton
Charles Taylor	William Slater	Herbert Moorhouse

1915-Wounded Soldiers At Osmaston Manor   On 2nd April, the Derbyshire Advertiser reported that nine men had been brought to the Manor from Derby Infirmary. Later in the year they also reported that there were ten beds for other ranks and six beds for officers, mainly Colonial men.

"On Monday last a number of wounded soldiers arrived at the hospital which Sir Peter Walker Bt., has generously provided at Osmaston Manor, where they will remain as his guests and will have every care bestowed upon them, in addition the many luxuries and comforts which Sir Peter's solicitude has furnished.

The men are indeed fortunate to have such an excellent host, and to be able to recuperate amid such beautiful surroundings as those in which the stately mansion is situated. It is understood that a further six beds for sick and wounded officers has been provided, and these are expected to be mainly occupied by representatives of the Colonial or Indian forces.

The names of the nine soldiers who have already arrived are as follows: Private H. C. Hammond, Army Service Rifleman, J. Heath, 2nd King's Royal Rifles, Lance-corporal J. Harper, Ist Sherwood Foresters, Private M. Seymour, 3rd Suffolk Regiment, Sergt. A. Bradshaw, Ist Duke Cornwall's McAdams, 2nd Buff*. -V K'Callum, 7th Argyle."

Derbyshire Advertiser & Journal 3 4 1915

LOSS OF SIR ANDREW'S GRANDSON/ SIR PETER'S NEPHEW

"Captain Court was Sir Andrew Barclay Walker's grandson who was born and christened at St Martin's Church, Osmaston. He was second in command of B squadron 9th (Queens Royal) Lancers and was shot through the head and killed instantly whilst near Hooge, Belgium aged 29 years of age."   (Information from the Canterbury 9th Lancers Roll of Honour).

"The ruthless hand of war does not discriminate between persons, and high and low, rich and poor, throughout the land have suffered, and are suffering bereavement." Sir Peter Walker had lost a nephew, Captain Court of the 9th Lancers, the second relative the family had lost to the war".
Derbyshire Advertiser & Journal 3 4 1915

1915

RED CROSS HOSPITAL REPORTS OSMASTON MANOR
ASHBOURNE NEWSPAPER REPORT -1915

Gunner, F A Dakin of Osmaston and formerly a gardener in the Manor gardens had enlisted in March and was now on active service with the Royal Field Artillery.

Private W Tully Mr & Mrs Tully of Osmaston Manor had received news that their son had been wounded near La Basse in France. He had suffered a head wound from shrapnel.

Ashbourne News Telegraph 25 2 1915

Home Guard-In January, the Derbyshire Volunteer Home Guard was formed.

"60 members of the Osmaston, Yeldersley, Shirley and Wyaston Home Guard under the Quartermaster A.V.May and Sergeant Instructor Salt carried out a route march headed by Osmaston Town Band under Bandmaster Stubbs."   Derbyshire Advertiser 28 5 1915

The Home Guard Met Regularly The drills, held Tuesday and Friday evenings at the Garage, Osmaston Manor, were well attended and were enthusiastically entered into with an average attendance of over 60 out of about 70 members.

At the April Meeting, Col. Sir Peter Walker Bt. presided over a parade of 60 members. Sir Peter had gifted fifty Martini rifles with bayonets and also uniforms. A rifle range was also made on the Osmaston Manor Estate for men to qualify for the "marksmen badges" and for general rifle practice.   War Office recognition badges, the "Brassards" were handed to every member.

Col. Sir Peter Walker Bt., Chairman, Rev H V Titmuss, Hon Sec., Mr A Tully, who was the Head Gardener, were appointed officers.

Firing Range In The Woods At Osmaston Manor

Firing Range Results- Osmaston Manor Detachment of West Derbyshire. Results up to date of mass firing – **Marksmen- Deliberate** Leslie Titmuss 97, W Normanshaw 97, T Affleck 96, J Chadfield 96, C Eldridge 96. **Rapid** C Eldridge 96, John Chadfield 94, T. Affleck 93, W Normanshaw 93 and L Titmuss 92.
First Class Deliberate Joseph Chadfield 94, **Rapid** Chadfield 88.
Mr Affleck was the Head Gamekeeper for the Estate and lived at Copsehill Cottage.
Derbyshire Advertiser & Journal 31 7 1915

---

*"**Memorable gathering** -* Inhabitants of the town and many visitors from the neighbouring villages thronged the streets a little later when the Ashbourne & Osmaston and Shirley Home Guards, numbering about 140, under the direction of Adjutant R Holland and Commandant J R Mellor, paraded through the streets". Derbyshire Advertiser & Journal 14th August 1915

1915-LIFE IN OSMASTON VILLAGE CONTINUES

Patriotic Support-Anniversary of the Declaration of War Friday August 6th

Festivities in Osmaston continued on July 19th when Sir Peter Walker entertained his tenantry and employees, together with the tradesmen of Ashbourne and the children attending the schools of Osmaston, Shirley & Wyaston.

August Gardens Opening The gardens and grounds at the Manor were again opened to the public on the August Bank Holiday Monday. A charge of 6d. for admission and 9d. for tea was made with the proceeds, as with previous garden openings, going to charities. There was a record number of visitors for the last opening of the year. Mr. Tully, Head Gardener, had ensured the gardens were at their best. The conservatory, rock and rose gardens, and greenhouses were very admired by visitors.

Mr Tully would also help in the decoration of the church for harvest festivals, weddings etc. and the Manor gardens would be used for the supply of flowers, fruits etc.

> **Harvest Festival-**" Report on the Harvest Thanksgiving at Osmaston. These services were held in the parish church on Thursday evening the 14th inst., and the following Sunday. The church was tastefully decorated under the surveillance of Mr Tully the head gardener at Osmaston Manor."
> Derbyshire Advertiser & Journal – 22 10 1915

> **Dove Vale Harriers-**"The last meet of the season of these famous harriers was held at Osmaston Manor, the seat of Sir Peter C. Walker. Bart., the popular owner of the pack, on Saturday last. There was not a very big meet owing to the market day at Ashbourne, and to the entire home parade also at Ashbourne on that day. Some good sport was found for those who followed the harriers during the afternoon." Derbyshire Advertiser & Journal 3 4 1915

1915 DEATH OF SIR PETER WALKER, Bt. – 18th OCTOBER

Dominating the newspaper columns this week in 1915 was a death, not of a serviceman killed in action, but a prominent member of the North Derbyshire community. The local paper, Ashbourne Telegraph, reported his passing on October 18th.

A summary of the article: "Sir Peter Walker, "a typical English gentleman", died at Osmaston Manor on October 18, aged 61. The paper described him as a "popular and philanthropic benefactor". The baronet's passing received the full obituary treatment, detailing his life and family, noting his military career, his involvement in horse racing, his sporting achievements (which included shooting a 7ft 2in bear in Canada and landing a 195lb fish), his role as a landlord and agriculturist and his "unostentatious generosity".

He was a supporter of the National Hunt and a generous land owner and follower of the hounds and an Officer for 35 years in the Lancashire & Derbyshire Yeomanry. It was noted that Sir Peter had supported the Osmaston Home Guard, supplying men with rifles and uniforms.

The paper's Notes and Comments column stated: "By the death of Sir Peter Carlaw Walker Bart, of Osmaston Manor, there is removed from our midst one of the most prominent and esteemed gentlemen of the county, and in this critical period of our history, his loss is irreparable." "Such was his popularity that the paper announced only ticket-holders would be admitted to the funeral service at Osmaston Church. "

Photograph Osmaston History Group

FUNERAL PROCESSION-The procession started from the Manor soon after 1.30, the band of the Nottingham and Derby Regiment from Normanton Barracks (under Bandmaster Moull) playing the "Death March" Saul, and Chopin's and Beethoven's Funeral Marches as the cortege wended its way through the Park to the Church. The coffin was conveyed by motor and was covered by the Union Jack, on the top of which were the deceased colonel's helmet and sword. Preceding the coffin was Major Harding, the deceased Baronet's Estate Agent.

SIR PETER WAS LAID IN THE FAMILY VAULT AT ST MARTIN'S CHURCH, OSMASTON

The entrance to the Walker's family vault was adorned with white chrysanthemums, spires and evergreens under the supervision of Mr J Tully, the head gardener at Osmaston Manor. The hymn "Now the Labourer's task is o'er" was sung to the band accompaniment and the rifle squad discharged three volleys after which a trumpeter sounded the Last Post.

Photograph Osmaston History Group

A MEMORIAL SERVICE

The service was held in Osmaston Church the following week attended by staff, tenants and Home Guards etc.

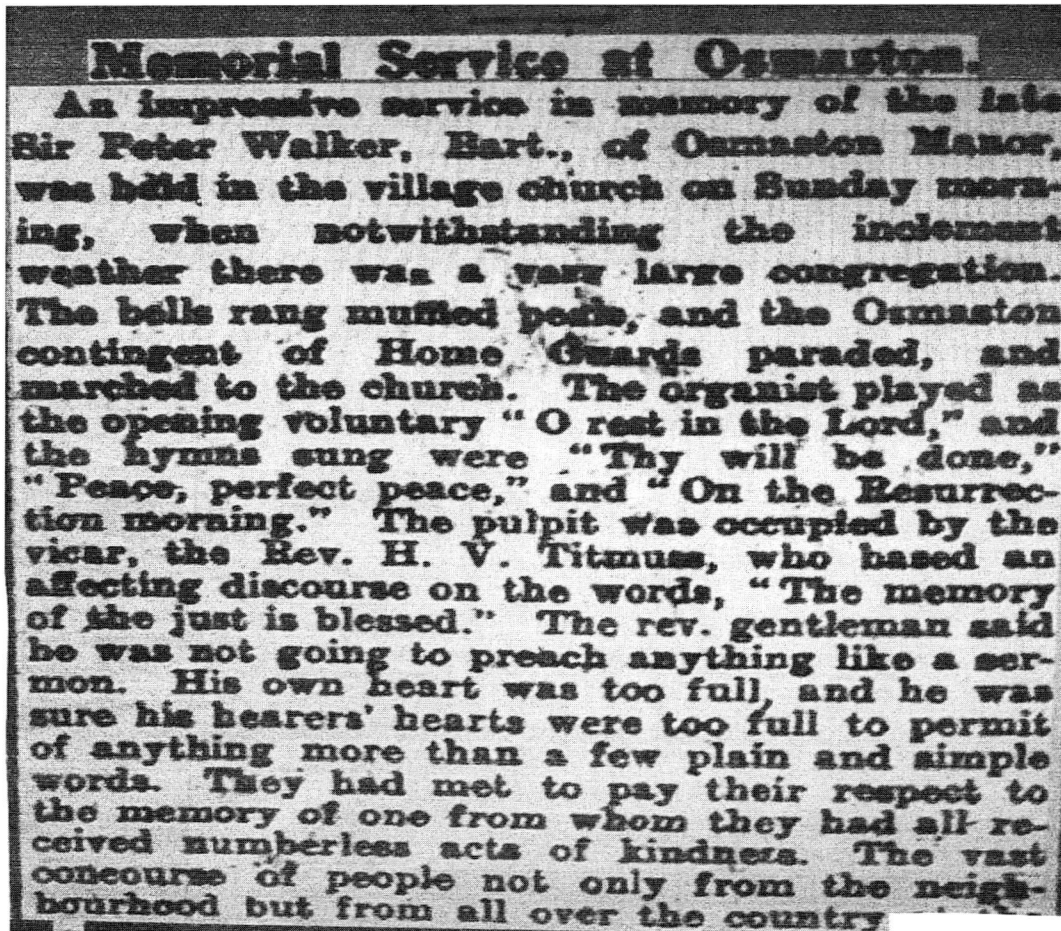

> **Memorial Service at Osmaston.**
>
> An impressive service in memory of the late Sir Peter Walker, Bart., of Osmaston Manor, was held in the village church on Sunday morning, when notwithstanding the inclement weather there was a very large congregation. The bells rang muffled peals, and the Osmaston contingent of Home Guards paraded, and marched to the church. The organist played as the opening voluntary " O rest in the Lord," and the hymns sung were "Thy will be done," "Peace, perfect peace," and "On the Resurrection morning." The pulpit was occupied by the vicar, the Rev. H. V. Titmuss, who based an affecting discourse on the words, "The memory of the just is blessed." The rev. gentleman said he was not going to preach anything like a sermon. His own heart was too full, and he was sure his hearers' hearts were too full to permit of anything more than a few plain and simple words. They had met to pay their respect to the memory of one from whom they had all received numberless acts of kindness. The vast concourse of people not only from the neighbourhood but from all over the country

The Rev. Titmuss conducted the service and reflected on Sir Peter's connection with the village where he had made his home.

He commented that the Church, the School, the Reading Room, every club and institution owed much to his liberality, and that men of the Home Guards, who formed a large part of the congregation, knew the deep interest with which Sir Peter took in the welfare of their Osmaston unit and they would not forget that it was entirely through him that they were one of the best trained and equipped units in the County....It was Sir Peter's desire that every available man in the Osmaston District would play his part.......

INHERITANCE

His son, Ian Peter Andrew Monro Walker would become the 3rd Baronet at the age of 13 and would inherit the Manor Estate, together with the death duties.

Chapter 6. SIR IAN PETER ANDREW MONRO WALKER, 3RD BARONET (1902–1982)

1915-Sir Ian Walker, at the age of 13, inherited the title of 3rd Baronet, together with the Osmaston Estate & Manor, on the death of his father Sir Peter Carlaw Walker .

Sir Peter Carlaw Walker Bt. photographed with his son, Ian Peter Andrew Monro Walker at an early age.

Sir Peter Carlaw Walker had died as WW1 had started. With the guidance of his mother, Ethel, Sir Ian took on his responsibilities.

He was educated at Eton and Oxford and had a great love for the outdoors.

Photograph Osmaston History Group

WWI CONTINUES

Many men of the area enlisted under the Lord Derby Scheme or, from March 1916, were conscripted into the forces.

Osmaston Manor continued to be used as a WW1 Red Cross Hospital as part of Lady Walker's involvement with the Red Cross.

1915-1916 Lady Ethel Walker continued to live at Osmaston Manor and ensured that on Christmas Eve 1915, the residents and employees on the Osmaston Manor Estate received large and prime cuts of venison.

Sir Ian Walker Bt.
Photograph courtesy of Sir Andrew Walker-Okeover Bt.

103

Advertisement 24 6 1916
Osmaston Shoulder of Mutton Hotel,
Osmaston near Ashbourne & Dovedale.
Families and Tourists, with or without
board.

Motorists and Cyclists catered for (by
notice)

Excellent accommodation.

September 1916
Shoulder of Mutton Inn Osmaston
Up for Let
Possession in October
Peter Walker & Son Ltd
Shobnall Brewery
Burton on Trent

1917-School Photograph is taken with the group in front of the village church gateway.

Photograph Osmaston History Group

1918-Alcohol Sale

"Lady Walker instructed John Wilkinson & Son to sell 900 bottles of wine & brandy by auction at 12 o'clock at Osmaston Manor on Thursday July 18th 1918:- The lots comprised of Taylors Port 1873 & 1896, Rogers Port 1878, Sherry 1844, Sauterne, Walkers Brandy 90 years old and others. Catalogues were still in the course of preparation." Derbyshire Advertiser & Journal 28 6 18

1918- Appeals against Conscription Appeals for exemption from conscription, from 1916, were considered at local Military Tribunals. As the number of volunteers from 1914 had fallen, the Lord Derby Scheme in 1915 appealed for volunteers, permitting volunteers to choose the service in which they would serve. By 1916, as the number of volunteers was much lower than needed, conscription was brought in with men serving wherever they were needed. Appeals were permitted.

No records of these appeal tribunals remain and newspaper reports rarely name the appellants. An exception to this is the case of an Osmaston man in 1918, a period of great manpower shortage in the forces.

104

WW1 Continues This article reflects the impact of WW1 on a small village.

Thomas Affleck, Estate Gamekeeper, then aged 47, appealed on the grounds that he was the head gamekeeper on the Osmaston Estate and that of the 12 gamekeepers under him, 11 including his son, had joined the forces and it was now no longer a question of managing the game but controlling the vermin.

He also stated that between 60 and 70 estate workers had joined up and that the estate staff had reduced by 75%.

He was also in charge of the Volunteer Home Guard.

He was granted an exemption of six months.

He remained in Osmaston until his death in 1938.

Derbyshire Advertiser, July 1918.

> allowed.
>
> Mr. R. Williams (Messrs. Holland, Rigby and Williams) appeared to support an application in respect of T. Afflick (47), grade 2, gamekeeper for the trustees of the Osmaston estate, and stated that this was the first application made for any employee on the estate, from which between 60 and 70 men had joined the army, and of the staff of 12 under Mr. Afflick 11 had joined the colours. As the Tribunal were aware, the preservation of game was a thing of the past, and Mr. Afflick's duties were principally those of keeping down vermin and rabbits, which were liable to do a great deal of damage, and as the staff of workmen had been reduced by 75 per cent, Mr. Afflick lent a hand in an emergency. His son had served in France for two years, and he himself was in charge of the Osmaston detachment of the Volunteers. — Six months' exemption was granted.
>
> George Brown (45), grade 1 gardener for Gen

WW1 FINALLY ENDS – Flags fly and Bells Ring

There is no record of celebrations on the occasion of the Armistice but on 12th July 1919, following the signing of the Treaty of Versailles the Derbyshire Advertiser carried the following report :-

Osmaston by Ashbourne

"On the news that the Peace Treaty had been signed reaching here about four o`clock on the 28th ult., the relief and gratification felt by the villagers was soon in evidence. Flags were soon flying from many of the cottages , the church bells were rung and in the evening startling explosions were much in evidence. On the Sunday following, the historic event was referred to by the Vicar, who advised his hearers not to feel too assured until the Peace Terms had been fully ratified. On Sunday, in accordance with the command of the King, special thanksgiving services were held in the Parish Church"............

Early 1920s Osmaston School-Mr W Talley, headmaster and Miss D Shenter, schoolmistress

Photograph Osmaston History Group

OSMASTON SCHOOL

Mid 1920-1930 There were 2 classrooms and 2 Teachers, Miss Grindey and Miss Jones.
The **Infants Class for 5-9 years**

Tables used in classroom   -   Photograph Osmaston History Group

The Senior Class for 10-14 years

Desks now used in classroom   -   Photograph Osmaston History Group
Miss Grindey remained at the School until 1992

OSMASTON VILLAGE.

Late1920s (Exact dates unknown) The Post Office-Mr & Mrs Austin are living and running the Post Office in a thatched cottage near the Shoulder of Mutton with Mrs Austin delivering the post. Mr Bill Austin worked for the Estate and then Rolls-Royce in Derby. Unfortunately the thatch roof caught fire (see cottage roof on the right) and the cottage was pulled down and the post office was moved.
Photograph Osmaston History Group

Yeldersley New Houses

In 1920, a row of four cottages were built on Painters Lane to accommodate Yeldersley estate workers. The photograph shows the new Yeldersley Jazz Band!!!!!!

Photograph Osmaston History Group

1921-The War Memorial

Now a Grade II Listed War Memorial, Osmaston Memorial was erected in 1921, designed by Walter Knight Shirley, the 11th Earl Ferrers to commemorate those lost in the First World War.
Photograph Osmaston History Group

Dedication of Osmaston War Memorial

It was unveiled on 29th July 1921 by General Ponsonby of the North Midland Brigade and dedicated by the Bishop of Derby. The sandstone memorial bears the names of thirteen men of Osmaston and Yeldersley who died during the conflict. While some of these were local men, others, who were not born locally, were employees of the Osmaston or Yeldersley estates.
On Friday, 11th November 1921, a group of former servicemen, together with children from the school, were present at the first service of remembrance to be held at the memorial. At 7pm that evening a service was held in the Church. The day was the feast day of St Martin.

The men who lost their lives in the First World War appear on the memorial as follows:

Peter Arthur Carlaw Walker- 2nd Lieutenant : Derbyshire Yeomanry. Died in a motorcycle accident at Maidenhead Berks on 13th September 1914, age 26. Buried at St Martin's Church Osmaston.

Frank Allen- Rifleman : 2nd Batt. Kings Royal Rifle Corps Killed in Action on 26th June 1916, aged 23. No known grave.
His name is engraved on the Faubourg d'Amiens Memorial at Arras.

Peter Clossick- (named as P Classic on the memorial) Lance Corporal : 9th Batt. Kings Royal Rifle Corps Died of Wounds on 13th April 1917, aged 36.
Buried at St Sever Cemetery Extension, Rouen.

Arthur Hammersley- Lance Bombardier : 17th Battery Royal Field Artillery. Died of Wounds on 5th May 1919, aged 22.
Buried at Doullens Communal Cemetery Extension, Somme.

John Hellaby- Signaller : 1st Batt. Sherwood Foresters. Killed in Action on 7th July 1917 aged 36.
Buried at Vlamertinghe New Military Cemetery, Belgium.

Albert Housley- Private : 6th Batt. Sherwood Foresters. Killed in Action on 3rd April 1916 aged 20.
Buried at Ecoivres Military Cemetery, St Eloi, France

Percy Mellor- Private: 1/6th Batt. South Staffordshire Regiment. Killed in Action on 1st July 1916 aged 29. No known grave.
His name is engraved on the Thiepval Memorial to the Missing, Somme.

Joseph Naylor- Private : 1/7th Batt. Royal Warwickshire Regiment. Killed in Action on 25th July 1916 aged 27. No known grave.
His name is engraved on the Thiepval Memorial to the Missing, Somme.

Walter Sanderson- Gunner : B Battery 76 Brigade Royal Field Artillery. Died of Wounds on 26th August 1918 aged 23.
Buried at St. Hilaire Cemetery Extension, Frévent, France

Harry Thomas- Lance Corporal : 9 Batt Sherwood Foresters. Killed in Action on 21st August 1915 in Gallipoli aged 20. No known grave.
His name is engraved on the Helles Point Memorial, Gallipoli.

H.Willis- No details known. Probably Herbert Willis who in 1913 was employed as 'assistant Chauffeur' to Sir Henry Fitzherbert Wright at Yeldersley Hall. A number of men of this name died in WW1.

George Wright- Private : 14th Batt. Durham Light Infantry. Killed in Action on 17th February 1919 aged 19. Buried at Cambrin Churchyard Extension, France.

William Bardney- Gunner : B Battery 235 Bde Royal Field Artillery. Killed in Action on 20th July 1917 aged 24. Buried at La Clytte Military Cemetery, Belgium.

1921

Sir Ian used the clay and brick works he had inherited on his land on the Yeldersley side of Painters Lane.   The bricks all bore his initials IPAMW.

There was a fine bed of excellent pure clay capable of manufacturing sound hard bricks, pipes and earthenware goods and substantial kilns.

9 September 1921
Bricks and Pipes – all handmade and well burnt. Can be delivered if desired – Prices on application to the Estate Office, Osmaston

1923-Sir Ian purchased Glen Avon Deer Forest in Banffshire which consisted of 40,000 acres of stags, grouse shooting and fishing.

1924-CELEBRATION OF SIR IAN'S 21ST BIRTHDAY (celebrated one year late) July

What a swell party this is

THIS fine body of people, the tenants of the Osmaston Estate, are rightly dressed up in their Sunday best, for they are seen at a celebration to mark the coming of age of Sir Ian Walker (later Sir Ian Walker-Okeover).

Sir Ian's 21st birthday had been on November 30 1923, but the general celebrations had — sensibly it would seem — been held over until the following summer.

Then on Wednesday afternoon July 23 (1924) a "sumptuous luncheon" was held "in a large marquee on the cricket ground," when Mr Ramsden of Derby served "in his best style" salmon mazonnaise, roast chicken, roast duckling, York ham, ox tongue, Derby round of beef, salad, trifle, compote of fruit, strawberries and cream and cheese and biscuits.

A report of the occasion in the *Ashbourne Telegraph* of Friday July 25 1924 records the names of the special guests, with a toast to Sir Ian proposed by Mr T Kent whose speech

indicates he had been a tenant for 60 years.

Speeches by Sir Ian, Major Harding, Mr A A Watkinson, Lady Walker (mother of Sir Ian) and Capt H E Okeover were also reported.

It must have been some celebration, for later in the afternoon about 500 people were entertained to tea — though it is not clear if those same people were also at the luncheon.

Osmaston Band, under Mr C Stubbs, played selections during the afternoon and, according to the report, "the various diversions provided included steam roundabouts, juvenile roundabouts, Punch and Judy, bowling match for a prize given by Sir Ian, and concluding with a grand display of fireworks supplied and discharged by R Ward, St John Street, Ashbourne. Sports were also arranged and these included: boys' race (handicap); girls' race; boys' sack race; skipping competition (girls 10 to 15); musical chairs; egg and spoon race; three-legged race; band race; married women's race; sinbgle

women's race and tenant farmer's race."

This photograph comes to me through Babette and Tom Lawton of Holly Meadow Farm, Bradley, to whom I'm most grateful.

Seated at the front and second from the right is Mr Lawton's grandfather and namesake, Tom Lawton, with his wife Anne, who is seen fourth from the right on the first standing row, identified by a white blouse beneath her coat and with dark brimmed hat with light coloured ruched crown.

Kneeling at the left shoulder (as you look at the picture) of Mr Lawton, in a striped dress, is Mrs Fred Atkin of Shirley Common Farm (with her husband next to her.

Seated on the ground two along from Mr Lawton is an easily identified man, Roger Wright.

The clergyman behind Mr Lawton is believed to be the Rector, the Rev Coates whose wife is in black, seen between Mr and Mrs Atkin.

Older readers will doubtless recognise many other faces.

The small child on the above photograph is Audrey Normanshaw.

Memoirs of Audrey Tomlinson (nee Normanshaw)

photographs courtesy of Audrey Tomlinson & Osmaston History Group

Audrey went with her parents to Sir Ian's 21st Birthday Celebration in a marquee on the Polo Field. Audrey was born at Park Lane Farm, Shirley, an Estate property in 1921 and remembers a wonderful childhood as she and her friends walked and played in the woods all day long and she remembers the summer house and the lake. Her father kept chickens and Audrey used to pluck and dress them, for which her father gave her sixpence and she would walk through the woods from Shirley to Osmaston to deliver the chickens at Christmas, very often in the dark.

Her father died when she was 17 and her mother managed to keep the farm going for a couple of years until the estate found them a thatched cottage in Osmaston, in an area known locally as Sludge Alley near the village duck pond.

Some years later Muriel, Audrey's sister, had come home from school at lunch time one day to check the fires and found the house on fire. All the children came out of school and formed a bucket chain between the duck pond and the house whilst waiting for the fire engine to arrive from the Manor, which was manned by estate staff. Luckily no-one was hurt and everyone came to help including the remount soldiers, who worked tirelessly and they managed to save the contents. After the fire the cottage was found to be badly damaged and was eventually pulled down. They then moved to another house within the village.

When her husband went to war, she didn't see him for two years and she went to live in Ashbourne with her mother and her stepfather.

Audrey met Walter Tomlinson who was a local boy and they married at St Martins, Osmaston on November 21st 1942 (Ashbourne News Telegraph of November 27th 1942)

A postcard to Walter when he was stationed in Dewsbury, Yorkshire from Audrey's sister, Muriel.

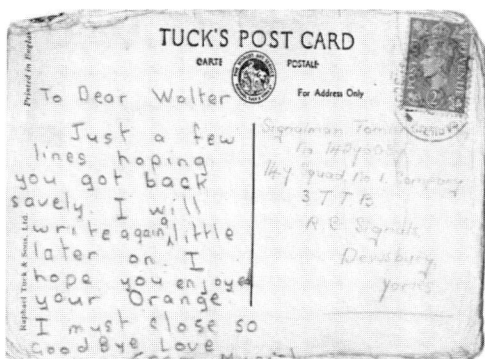

After Sir Ian had left Oxford he was fortunate enough to gain experience of the world outside Britain by being posted as Hon. Attaché to the British Embassy in Brussels.   In the 1920s he toured Germany, later South America, playing polo.

1926

General Strike-This is the year a General Strike was called – the TUC hoped the threat of a general strike would force the government to guarantee miners a living wage, but this did not work and the strike went ahead.   From 1910-1914 Britain was racked by a series of strikes that were noted for their militancy and for their refusal to follow the dictates of union leaders. This militancy shook the British capitalist state to its core. 2 million workers went on strike and lasted 10 days. This combination of who will control the labour process: employer or employee, with the added pressure of the declining standard of living ensured that class tensions were slowly building up throughout British society.

Osmaston Bowls Club-A Bowls Club was formed in Osmaston Village in 1926. The bowling green and small pavilion were near the village pond and a Silver Challenge Cup was donated by Captain H. Fitzherbert Wright and presented each year.

Winners of the Challenge Cup	
1927	F Titterton
1928	T Brown
1929	H Booth
1930	N T Brown
1931	W J Mould
1932	G Mellor
1933	G Mellor
1934	W Ruscoe
1935	Frank Titterton
1936	T Gadsby
1937	N T Brown
1938	T Gadsby
1939	T Gadsby
1948	R Hankey
1949	W Walker

1928-OSMASTON. R.S.P.C.A. Effort On Friday last, a whist drive and dance was held in the Victory Hut, Osmaston, in aid of the R.S.P.C.A. Fifteen tables were occupied for whist, and a good number of visitors took part in the dance. The prizes were given by Miss Enid Walker, of Osmaston Manor. Mrs. Beardsmore kindly presented them - the winners as follows: —
Ladies: 1 Mrs. Hudson, 2 Miss E. Naylor, 3 Mrs. Grime, booby Miss A. Sutton. Gentlemen: 1 E. Hughes, 2 Proctor, 3 A. Swindell, booby F. Titterton. A cake was drawn for which had been given by Mr. Bates, the winner being Mr. W. Morley. Mr. J. Hunt efficiently carried out the duties of M.C., and Mrs. Tatlow had charge of the refreshments. The music for dancing was supplied by the Ashbourne Five.
Derbyshire Advertiser & Journal 13 1 1928

1929-Wall Street Crash many of the Aristocracy and business people were involved in financial losses.

1928/1930s CHANGES AT YELDERSLEY HALL

1928-Henry Fitzherbert Wright bought a 3000 acre Estate at Alderwasley Hall and stated that he intended to spend more time in Ripley.

1929-The Yeldersley Estate was subsequently offered for sale 13 lots, to include the Hall, Lady Hole House, Lady Hole Farm, Home Farm, War Farm, Old Hall Farm, Bradley Wood and other properties. His herd of shorthorn cattle was sold at War Farm in October.

In December, his wife, on opening a sale of work in Wirksworth was described as Mrs Fitzherbert Wright of Alderwasley Hall.

1930s

A change of mind. The Derby Telegraph showed the Wright family had made the decision to stay at Yeldersley Hall.

Some parts of the Alderwasley estate were sold in August.

Sale of Yeldersley

The Hall and rest of the estate was advertised for sale in the Derbyshire Advertiser in February 1931.

CAPT. WRIGHT AND YELDERSLEY

Alderwasley Hall, recently purchased by Captain FitzHerbert Wright, of Yeldersley, is being offered for sale. Captain Wright told a "Derby Telegraph" representative to-day that he had decided to stay at Yeldersley.

The sale of the property is now in the hands of a London firm of estate agents.

By Order of Captain H. Fitzherbert Wright.
DERBYSHIRE.
FOR SALE BY PRIVATE TREATY.
SEVEN VALUABLE FREEHOLD FARMS (2 with Vacant Possession) as under :—

The Remaining Portions of the YELDERSLEY HALL ESTATE situate within 2 miles of Ashbourne and within 10 miles of the County Town of Derby.

1. "THE HOME FARM." 164 acres. Good house. Modern Farm Buildings. PRICE,—£5,250.
2. "THE WAR FARM." 158 acres. Modern House. New Model Farm Buildings. With Vacant Possession. PRICE,—£5,250.
3. "THE LADYHOLE FARM." 204 acres. Good House and Splendid Buildings. PRICE.—£4,250.
4. "THE OLD HALL FARM." 120 acres. Good House and Buildings. PRICE,—£2,450.

The above Four Farms are well situated on good roads, close to Town and Station, with splendid bus services. They are well fenced and watered, in perfect repair, and the Land is in good heart and condition.

At this time, a new company, the Shirley Park Estate Company, was formed with Sir Ian Walker of Osmaston Manor as the permanent governing director. This private unlimited company had an initial capital of £140,000 and its stated objectives were to "acquire estates in Derbyshire and purchase chief rents; to construct and improve roads railways and watercourses etc."

Although this company acquired both Yeldersley Hall and Lady Hole House, Captain Henry Fitzherbert Wright continued to live in the Hall for the rest of his life.

Open Garden During the 1930s, the gardens at Yeldersley were opened to the public on regular occasions to raise money for various charities.

Derby Daily Telegraph February 1934

"Yeldersley Hall Gardens opened to the public to view the massed crocuses. All of the proceeds of this event were given in aid of the Derbyshire Children`s Hospital."

YELDERSLEY HALL GROUNDS OPEN TO THE PUBLIC

Yeldersley Hall grounds should be a popular resort over the holiday. Captain and Mrs. H. FitzHerbert Wright opened them yesterday to the public in aid of the Derbyshire Children's Hospital, and visitors will be allowed to inspect them to-morrow and on Saturday, Sunday, and Monday.

Visitors will be admitted at any time of the day. The massed crocuses in full bloom make a wonderful display, and if the weather remains good the flowers should be at the height of their glory at the week-end.

1926-1930-POLO PLANS FOR OSMASTON Sir Ian started building stud stables under the management of Major Vere Foster and a Riding School for schooling and housing the Polo Ponies. Great care was taken in the selection of a suitable stallion and eventually the four year old Belgian bred Tabarin was purchased. Tabarin went on to win five consecutive championships at Islington and two at the Royal. Sir Ian bred Polo Ponies at his newly built stud and was very successful. The family colours were Peacock Blue and Old Gold.

Polo Stables and Stud-Photograph Osmaston History Group

THE MAIN STABLES: Going out for exercise at Sir Ian Walker's Stud.

The Riding School

In 1928 Sir Ian made a considerable contribution to the future of Polo by bringing back valuable ponies from the Argentine.

Polo week became one of Derbyshire's main attractions and polo matches were held between 1930 and 1936.

Riding School photograph Osmaston History Group

1930-POLO BROUGHT BACK AT OSMASTON "Careful preparation had been lavished on the ground at the Manor, and the beautiful level expanse of green, which was considerably larger than a football pitch, looked in perfect condition. Polo teams consisted of four mounted players, and the intelligence of their fleet ponies played a large part in the game. The Polo Week in Osmaston got off to a good start with over 1000 people watching. Captain C T J Roark, who played for England in America, scored three goals for Osmaston in their match against Foxhunters which resulted in a draw 7 – 7 and was one of the most evenly matched and hotly contested games in the week's programme."
Derbyshire Advertiser and Journal 5 7 1930

1930s-POLO

A POLO TOURNAMENT WILL TAKE PLACE AT Osmaston Manor Polo Ground NEAR ASHBOURNE, On MONDAY, WEDNESDAY, and SATURDAY, August 4th, 6th, and 9th, Commencing 3 p.m. (Weather permitting). The following Teams are expected to take part

THE ROYAL HORSE GUARDS (Blues) A* THE ROYAL HORSE GUARDS B * WINDSOR DATCHET MANCHESTER P.C. OSMASTON P.C. THE RED DIAMONDS YELDERSLEY ADMISSION each day 1/6 (including tax). Motors parked 2/6. Proceeds in aid of Local Charities. On Saturday, August 9th, The Famous RIPLEY SILVER BAND will be in attendance in the afternoon, and will give a CONCERT IN THE RIDING SCHOOL, from 8 to 10.30. ADMISSION 1/3 (including tax). DANCING 8-10.30 on the POLO GROUND. REFRESHMENTS Walton & Peart, Derby. For Bus Services apply Local Bus companies. Notices will be posted in the Bus Stations.

Derbyshire Advertiser & Journal   01 08 1930

The ground was unfit for play on Monday owing to rain, but a large crowd saw yesterday's matches. The Windsor team included the Duke of Norfolk. The results were: Osmaston 7 goals, Datchet 5; Manchester 104, Red Diamonds 10; Windsor 11, Yeldersley 4. Manchester foiled the opposition again and again.

Photograph Osmaston History Group

THE OSMASTON POLO WEEK

LADY WALKER'S HOUSE-PARTY AT OSMASTON MANOR

Lady Walker, who is the widow of the late Sir Peter Walker, Bart., had this house-party for the polo week at Osmaston, Derbyshire, organized most successfully by her son, Sir Ian Walker. Included in this group are : Miss Langley, Miss Schreiber, Lady Bridget King-Tenison, Miss O'Brien, Lady Walker, Sir Ian Walker, Mr. Head, Mr. A. Dugdale, the Duke of Norfolk, Lord Erne, Captain and Mrs. G. Reid-Walker, Colonel and Mrs. D. C. Boles, Colonel T. P. Melvill, Colonel and Mrs. Vernon Keighley, Mr. Merry, Captain Herbert, Mr. Smith-Bingham, and Mr. R. B. B. B. Cooke.

Photograph Osmaston History Group

GOOD SPORT BOXING STAGED AT OSMASTON MANOR

1930s-EVENING BOXING MATCHES WERE HELD AFTER THE POLO MATCHES

A **Boxing Tournament** was held for the guests and assistants at the Riding School at Osmaston Manor on Thursday evening last week after the Polo Matches. The arrangements were made by Major J V Foster and a committee consisting of Messrs R Wibberley and G French. There were six bouts of three rounds each and prior to the commencement Major Foster introduced R.S.M. Warwick, the Imperial Army boxing champion to the audience.

Mee v. F Gilman – The first round was even, both men putting life into their floor work and getting home with lefts to the face and body. By a narrow margin - Mee was declared the winner. Mr Gilman worked as a Groom at the Polo stables and it is believed that he came from Shirley.

C Reddington v. Etherington – This was another rousing contest, both landing well to the face and body in the opening round. Reddington was bleeding freely from the nose and "saw red" hitting out fiercely. Reddington was the winner. Charlie Reddington was married and lived in Laundry Cottage in Osmaston and was a Groom at the Polo stables.

French v. Wigley – French won in the second round – both men were set in for a quick finish.

Lee v Gregory – Lee started as though the ring was a circus until he received a word from the referee and he was then guilty of head butting. Gregory won on points.

Botham v Fawcett –The best bout of the evening and the verdict of a draw was a popular one.

Webster v Lewis – Webster who was the most experienced won on points.

Derbyshire Advertiser & Journal 15 8 1930

Mr Gethin selling tickets at the Polo Match for the evening boxing matches.

Photograph Osmaston History Group

POLO THRILLING MATCHES The polo tournament held at Osmaston Manor, concluded on Saturday, when a large crowd watched the finals for the Osmaston Cup and the Junior Cup. Fortunately bright sunshine at the event enabled some excellent sport to be witnessed.

Derbyshire Advertiser & Journal 15 8 1930

> Capt. Prior-Palmer arrived by aeroplane on Saturday mornings and, he "took off" from the polo ground, giving the crowd an added thrill by performing "loops" overhead before turning Southward.

The proceeds from the Osmaston Manor Polo Tournaments were distributed by Lady Walker to the Derbyshire Royal Infirmary, Derbyshire Children's Hospital and the Mayor of Derby's appeal. There were reports in the local newspaper that Sir Ian Walker was to take his Polo Team to America in January following the success of the recent polo tournament at Osmaston.

1930-DOVE VALLEY BEAGLES

"The meet on Wednesday was by invitation at Osmaston Manor and expecting a good day's sport, there was a large field present, including several of the regular foot followers of the Meynell who had come from a considerable distance to see this little pack at work. They were soon, however, disappointed for instead of being put on to hare at once, as generally is the case, the hounds spent the day drawing in vain without even hitting upon the line of a hare, let alone finding one. Considering that Mr. Vaughan Thomas had, during the latter part of the summer, turned down about a score of hares on the Osmaston estate, it was naturally a great disappointment to have a blank day. Up-to-date these hounds have enjoyed very good sport."
Derbyshire Advertiser & Journal 14 2 1930

Ashbourne Shrovetide Football-Sir Ian was given the Honour of turning up Ashbourne Shrovetide Ball in 1931 and was accompanied by Miss Clowes of Norbury and Miss Wright of Yeldersley.

Shirley Park Estates-Sir Ian's Company in 1932, purchased Beresford Dale.

1932-OSMASTON MANOR POLO WEEK, PONY PARADE & BOXING MATCH
"Some of the finest polo in this country took place at Osmaston Manor, near Ashbourne, in aid of local charities. Sir Ian Walker, had a team on the field, while considerable interest was centred around the Gaddesby Hall team, formerly the famous Red Diamonds, of South Africa. The other teams were Tidworth, a team of officers of the Second Cavalry Brigade, the Royal Scots Greys and Sir Harold Wernher's Someries House Team. There were polo matches every day and on Monday Wednesday and Saturday there was the popular Parade of Ponies when some of the most celebrated ponies in England took part.

There was band music every day with Ripley Silver Prize band playing on Wednesday when there was also a boxing tournament staged in the evening. The principal bouts being a ten round contest between Ernie Plant of Hangley and "Battling" Charlie Parkin. The second contest was a ten round fight between Eric Grainer and Ron Adams. Admission including teas was 2s.6d."

1932-33 Polo Week

Photograph Osmaston History Group

Sir Ian also sponsored the Osmaston Team who were Winners of the Hurlingham Champion Cup and the Coronation Cups. He also won the Social Clubs and the Colts Challenge Cups and was President of the National Polo Pony Soc. in 1933.

Photograph of Sir Ian on Dusky Dancer his favourite horse.

1933 FORMATION OF OSMASTON & DISTRICT WOMEN'S INSTITUTE

After a preliminary meeting, Osmaston decided in 1933 to form a Women's Institute, meeting on the 3rd Tuesday of each month at the Victory Hut. Lady Walker proposed and Mrs Foster seconded that the WI would be called Osmaston & District Women's Institute. Also present at the meeting was Mrs Wright of Yeldersley Hall.

The Victory Hut in Osmaston Village used by the WI etc.

21st March 1933-Mrs Stanning 1st WI President The first meeting was held in the Victory Hut. Mrs Stanning was elected President and over the next few months they had demonstrations on Rug Making, Folk Dancing, tailoring and upholstery. Members were also asked to give help to motorists on the road by "judicious signalling at Cross roads, pointing out the usefulness of such service to the community and the importance of it". A decision was also made to purchase a piano.

Information courtesy Osmaston and District WI.

MRS MARY STANNING OF LADYHOLE HOUSE YELDERSLEY

From the early 1930s, Mr Joseph Edward Stanning and his wife Mary Gladys (née Haworth) lived at Ladyhole House. Ladyhole House was built along with the original Yeldersley old hall in the 1600s.

Joseph Stanning was born in 1880 in Chorley, Lancs. and later worked for the family firm of John Stanning & Sons, bleachers of textiles and leather at Leyland, Preston, a firm employing 220 workers.

Brief family background

Mary Gladys was born in Didsbury, Manchester in February 1883, the fourth of five children, and the only daughter of wealthy cotton manufacturer and merchant, George Chester Haworth and his wife Elizabeth. In 1901, the family was living at Bowdon, Altrincham and had six female servants. Mary was educated at Roedean, one of the top schools for girls, where she particularly enjoyed sports. She played hockey and was the wicket keeper in the school's cricket team, but the greatest love of her life was horse riding. She went on to finishing school in Paris and although she was able to ride horses in the parks, she was home-sick and returned to England. After her marriage to Joseph in 1909 they lived near Preston, Lancashire. During the First World War, during which one of Mary's brothers was killed, Joseph served as a corporal with the 23rd (First Sportsman's) Battalion Royal Fusiliers, arriving in France in November 1915.

On his demobilisation in 1919, the couple lived in Cheshire with Joseph, being by then, the owner of the Leyland Bleach Works. They made their first visit to Derbyshire in July 1926 and visited regularly until they moved to Ladyhole House in the early 1930s when Joseph retired from the business. He died in February 1939.

Mrs Stanning (centre) riding her horse "Rally Wood" with the Meynell Hunt.

Mrs Stanning joined the Meynell Hunt and cut an elegant figure,"immaculately dressed in long black skirt, black riding jacket and black top hat; her presence could never be overlooked as she rode side-saddle on her grey horse, Rally Wood, who commanded as much respect and admiration as his mistress. Rally Wood died out hunting on March 7 1959 which prompted scores of friends to write letters of condolence to Mrs Stanning". Information Courtesy of Betty Hardie

1933-Polo Week at Osmaston Manor was favoured with good weather when about 2000 people witnessed two well contested matches. The first was between Someries House and Wykham. The second match was between Borders and Norten Bavant. A Boxing tournament was organised for the evening entertainment. The following day a Polo match between Osmaston and Wykham -with an attendance of about 1000 people took place. Osmaston's team was Sir Ian Walker, Captain A C L Vincent, Captain R.B.B. Cooke and Captain W R Hinde. Colonel Sir Harold Wernher had Lord Louis Mountbatten playing back for him when Someries House won their tie against Wykham in Sir Ian Walker's American Invitation Tournament at Osmaston Manor. Lord Louis evidently found it warm work. Count de Pret-Roose was Wykham's No. 2.

1934-Conservative Rally Stanley Baldwin attended with 15,000 people at Osmaston Park.

OSMASTON VILLAGE LIFE

Osmaston Band
Back Row: Ted Mellor, Len Allen, Bill Morley, Harry Stubbs, Les Allen, Mr Oakden

Front Row: Billy Stubbs, Les Bull, Bert Brown, Harry Allen, Jack Housley
Photograph Osmaston History Group

MID 1930s-OSMASTON MANOR BICYCLE POLO TEAM
Left to Right – Joe Hogston, Not Known, Bill Leng, Fred Morley, Frank Warren
Each member of the 1936 Polo Team were presented with a Medal.

Photograph Osmaston History Group

1934-High Sheriff Sir Ian like his father was High Sheriff of Derbyshire.

1935-Death of Lady Ethel Blanche Walker It was sadly reported that Sir Ian's mother had died at Osmaston Manor and she was interred in the Walker family vault. There is a plaque commemorating her life in St Martin's Church, Osmaston.

1935-Osmaston Shoot In November after the Meynell Hunt Ball, it was reported that "eligible bachelor and well known polo player", Sir Ian Walker, had his first big shoot of the Season at Osmaston Manor. Eight guns accounted for over 500 high flying pheasants before lunch and the afternoon was spent duck shooting on the lake. One of the guests is reported as Miss Betty Heber-Percy, a popular young Warwickshire lady who lived at lovely and historic Guys Cliffe. This is the lady he would eventually marry. The Tatler 17 11 1935

1936-The last Polo Match at Osmaston   Sir Ian made the difficult decision that this would be the last Polo match and to sell off his Polo Ponies.

The Ladies had also taken delight in watching the Polo

POLO WEEK AT OSMASTON 1936

Photograph Osmaston History Group

1936-The Duke and Duchess of Gloucester "were due to visit Osmaston Manor on November 20th to spend a day pheasant shooting". It was reported that the Osmaston Estate was particularly well stocked and good sport was assured for the Royal Visitors. There were four pheasant drives in the morning, and the afternoon was devoted to duck-shooting over the lake. The weather was quite out of the top drawer brilliant sunshine and warmth, quite unusual for this period. The names, left to right, are, back row: Mr. Harry Brown, the famous trainer and ex-G. R. Brig. -Gen. Reginald Hoare, H.R.H. the Duke of Gloucester, Sir Ian Walker, Sir William Bass, M.F.H. (Meynell), Mr. E. T. Baring, and the Hon. H. Douglas-Home. Front row Mrs. Bagot, Lady Bridget King-Tenison, Lady Margaret Douglas-Home, Lady Noreen Bass, H.R.H. the Duchess of Gloucester, the Countess de Bosdari, Mrs. Hoare, and Miss Schreiber". The Tatler 2 12 1936

Photograph Osmaston History Group

120

1936-Boys' Club Sir Andrew and Sir Peter had both supported the Royal Liverpool Orphanage and arranged Summer camps at The Manor. Following this tradition, Sir Ian arranged for a boys' club to use Osmaston Manor grounds. Sixty boys employed by Leys Malleable Castings of Derby visited the estate.

1936-OSMASTON & DISTRICT WI As the Victory hut was to be removed, WI Meetings were temporarily held at Yeldersley Hall by Invitation of Mrs Wright. The old tin hut was lifted whole and transported to Marston Montgomery.

1937-CORONATION OF KING GEORGE VI Sir Ian continued to be a popular landlord and built four thatched Coronation cottages and a new thatched Coronation Hall for the village to celebrate the Coronation of George VI.

Photograph of Coronation Cottages Osmaston History Group

The New Thatched Coronation Hall

Photograph Osmaston History Group

The new Coronation Hall was to be formally opened on Coronation Day, the builder was Geo.Walker & Slater of Derby, the Architect, Arthur Eaton & Son.
A great deal of consideration had been given to the design to ensure it fitted in with the village. The main room was 50' x 26' and could be divided by a partition and had a permanent stage for concerts and theatricals.
At the rear was a committee room, kitchen and games room and central heating. The WI recommended their meetings in the new Coronation Hall.

121

Coronation Celebrations Continued Osmaston Coronation festivities had been postponed due to an outbreak of measles and was eventually held in July when 250 people were present for a children's sports day and Punch & Judy Show. Coronation Mugs were presented to the children by Mrs G E Raven after they had tea in the Hall.

Tom Brown remembers moving to Osmaston just in time to see the celebrations for the Coronation of King George and the bonfire at Shirley Common. Tom went on to work for the Estate for 44 years.

EARLY 1930s-THE POST OFFICE AND SHOP were being run by a Miss Hilda A V May who was born in Hendon. In 1931 she married Lancelot Warren and continued running the Post Office/shop until 1945 when she had a problem with some Milk Coupons. Mrs Warren's income was £1-5- 0d as sub-postmistress and £1-5s-0d from the shop. Mr Warren worked for the Estate and then Rolls-Royce in Derby.

1937 EXTRACT FROM JERRY SHENTON'S MEMOIRS OF OSMASTON

1937-"Jerry Shenton had previously lived in the Buxton area but in 1934 the family moved to Ashbourne.
Jerry attended the Church of England School.

In 1937, he applied for a job as an Apprentice Gardener on the Osmaston Estate.

Mr Peffers, a large Scottish gentleman, interviewed him stating that he was "awful wee" but he started him on a trial basis. Jerry Shenton would eventually become Head Gardener."

Mr Peffers Head Gardener, with his Wife

Photograph Osmaston History Group

"Mr Peffers turned out to be a fiery but knowledgeable taskmaster. He'd worked his way up through major gardens including the royal estate at Sandringham, and knew exactly how to achieve the results he wanted. Over 30 varieties of apples and pears were grown in the extensive orchards and earlier in the season there were abundant cherries and plums. The walled garden bursting with vegetables covered 3 acres. Two great boilers heated the glasshouses used for growing fine grapes, peaches, nectarines, figs, melons, cucumbers and out of season Strawberries.

Flowers for the Manor were grown in abundance, some – such as Orchids, and how the flowers brought the House alive for events such as the Annual Polo Week and Sir Ian and Lady Walker's homecoming after their wedding.

In 1941 Jerry joined the Royal Army Service Corps."

1937-Sir Ian made the huge decision to sell his horses and close his very successful stud. Over the next few years his horses were sold off and the Stud buildings were eventually left empty.

1930/1940s-THE GILMAN FAMILY-THE LOCAL MILKMAN (Memoirs of Gerald Parker)

Herbert and John Gilman were brothers and lived at Pond Farm, Osmaston together with their sister Annie. Herbert looked after the dairy farm and John had a milk round and delivered milk between Osmaston /Derby and Derby centre.

Cans would be left on gates in the village and filled when John did his rounds. John married Phylis and initially lived in Ashbourne, eventually moving to New House Farm, Osmaston. They had 2 children, Ann and Phillip, who commenced their education at Osmaston School.

When John died, Phylis eventually moved to No.2 East side and Herbert continued living at Pond Farmhouse.

1938 JULY-SIR IAN WALKER MARRIES DOROTHY ELIZABETH HEBER-PERCY

Photograph Osmaston History Group

A large Warwickshire and Meynell contingent were at St Mary's Church, Warwick, to see Miss Dorothy Heber-Percy daughter of Captain and Mrs Joseline Heber-Percy, and granddaughter of the late Lord Algernon Percy, married to the Joint Master of the Meynell. The reception was held at Guy's Cliffe, Captain Joseline Heber-Percy's house near Warwick.

The tenants gave the bride a hunting crop and the Duke and Duchess of Gloucester sent her a watch barometer.

Osmaston would have its own celebrations when Sir Ian brought his bride back to Osmaston.

1938-WEDDING CELEBRATIONS AT OSMASTON

There were great celebrations at Osmaston when Sir Ian returned with Lady Elizabeth as his bride from their honeymoon abroad. They were met by tenants, estate workers and Ashbourne tradesmen who had all been invited to attend a garden party arranged to celebrate their homecoming.

Flags & Garlands across the Manor drive and the carriage pulled by tenants and staff

Photograph Osmaston History Group

A Schoolboy's Memory of Event - Gerald Parker and his family moved to Coronation Cottages in Osmaston in 1937 and he had just started at Osmaston School. He remembers the whole of the school going to the Manor Site to welcome the Bride and Groom home. Everyone stood on the bridge and waved their Union Jacks before going into a marquee for a tea and cakes party. The adults celebrated with an evening celebration.

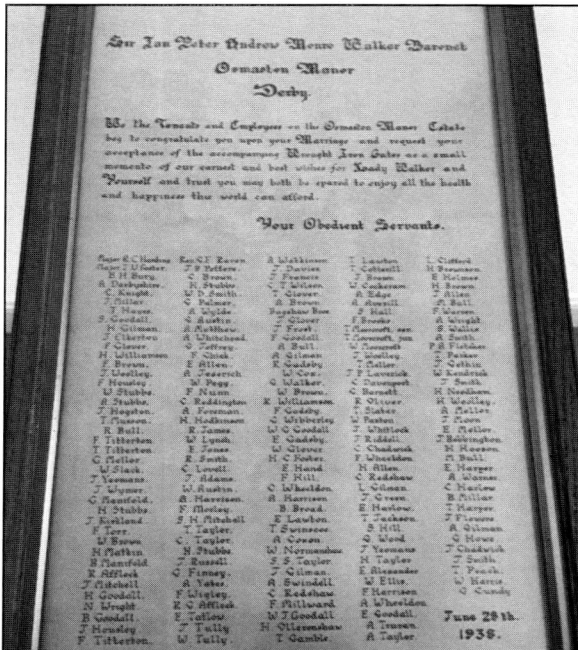

Photograph courtesy of Sir Andrew Walker-Okeover Bt.

New Gates. One of the features of the celebration was the unlocking of a pair of wrought iron gates which were given by many tenants and employees as a wedding present. (Listed).
The gates were made by Mr H Roberts, the Melbourne blacksmith, under the supervision of the Derbyshire Rural Community Council's Guild of Craftsmen and to designs supplied by them.

They were eventually placed in the Manor's walled garden.
The gates are still in position today.
Derby Daily Telegraph 29 7 1938

1939-WW2 BEGINS
BRITAIN AND FRANCE DECLARE WAR ON GERMANY
The country is on high alert of impending invasion and Osmaston plays its part.

Memoirs of Osmaston & District WI.

The WI continued to meet and at one of the meetings they practised "Gas Mask drill". The WI began preparations for fruit preservation and sugar was distributed to relevant members. In 1939 the Coronation Hall was temporarily used by the Armed Forces and Lady Walker invited the WI to meet at Osmaston Manor until use of the Hall could be resumed.

1940s-Rationing started in the UK
The WI ordered 20 dozen bottling jars & 6 cwt sugar for jam making. Requests for help were now moving rapidly. £50 was set aside for wool and material for making soldiers comforts. 3 Stirrup pumps were ordered at 25 shillings each. The Dig for Victory campaign was supported and a preserving centre was set up in the Hall for canning fruit and tomatoes. Members were asked to collect mint, parsley, dandelions and nettles for drying together with rose hips for rose hip syrup.

As this book is being written, we understand that the canning machine is still safely stored in the WI cupboard at Wyaston Village Hall – just in case!

Lady Walker remained at Osmaston but visited Sir Ian, who was in the Royal Naval Volunteer Reserve stationed at Grimsby, every fortnight. In 1940 Sir Ian & Lady Walker's first daughter, Elizabeth Anne Walker is born.

Open Gardens continue for charity "More than 200 people paid for admission to the gardens of Osmaston Manor, the home of Sir Ian and Lady Walker, which was thrown open to the public in aid of the Derbyshire Children's Hospital. Both Sir Ian's parents were presidents of the Children's Hospital during their lifetime, and Lady Walker herself the vice-president".

Photograph courtesy of Sir Andrew Walker-Okeover Bt.

1940-41 FOR THE SECOND TIME PREPARATIONS BEGIN FOR OSMASTON MANOR TO BE USED AS A RED CROSS HOSPITAL

Lady Walker was the Commandant and her mother, Mrs J Heber-Percy, Quartermaster. Additional family members moved into Osmaston Manor. The Walker children were moved out of the Manor into an estate cottage and in May 1941 the Red Cross Hospital opened at Osmaston Manor.

Memoirs of Miss Jane Walker-Okeover-The swimming pool was emptied and numerous baths were installed. The museum cabinets that used to be in the corridors were removed and the big hall partitioned off so that a sitting room could be made for Mr & Mrs Heber-Percy, the other end being used by everyone for meals. The drawing room stored the furniture from elsewhere as well as prams, bicycles and eggs in isinglass in large containers as they also had chickens on the lawns.

"Blue boys" at the Manor. The injured troops were all issued with blue suits and red ties and the children were not concerned with the injuries or missing limbs and she remembers the men playing bowls on the back lawn at the back of the summer house.

Local Memory:

Memoirs of Gerald Parker that two of the hospital patients came up to a dance at the Coronation Village hall. "When Matron did her rounds at the Manor Hospital, she found two patients missing. She got on her bike and came down to the Hall – but they were too quick and escaped out of the toilet window."

Bed patients passed the time doing carpentry, making soft toys, whist drives and other card games, bowls & fishing in the lakes.
Special buses were run by the Trent Motor Co. to take the men into Ashbourne every Tuesday & Thursday and were given free seats at the cinema by Mr F Bromwich.

Sister Riley together with Nurses and VADs
Photograph courtesy of Dinah Archer

In addition to the Sister-in-charge, there were 6 VADs (Voluntary Aid Detachment staff) in the wards and 6 for general duties. There were also 2 cooks, a secretary and a Sergeant- in-Charge. After the war had ended Sister Riley was presented with a cut glass perfume bottle for her services engraved "Osmaston BRCS Hospital 1941-1945". Sister Riley was the grandmother of Dinah Archer of Yeldersley.

1940s-MEMOIRS OF WARTIME OSMASTON BY BERKELEY COLE

Berkeley Cole was with the Cavalry Regiment at Colchester Cavalry Barracks and was posted to the No.2 Remounts Depot at Osmaston Manor. In 1940, they arrived at Ashbourne train station with 40 horses which they marched up to Osmaston on short reigns. The horse lines were behind the pavilion which became the NAFFI.

The hard standing near the pavilion was put down by the army and horses were kept near the pavilion under sheeting. Entrance to the Polo Ground was by a small gate where there was a sentry on duty. There was a cook house at Stud Farm where Major & Mrs Foster lived.

Berkeley Cole - The horses were exercised at what they called the sweating fields at full gallop past Stud Farm. There was a mounting block at Stud Farm and the area was used as the parade ground. Always at 10.00 pm, there was a Stand-Too when all the troops stood to attention.

Berkeley remembers going up the Manor drive and then bearing right which was a gated road. There was a large metal plate inset into the road and once you had stopped your car over it the gate opened automatically.

Berkeley Cole on his horse
Photograph Osmaston History Group

1940-Local Defence Volunteers

In May 1940, following the evacuation of British and French forces from Dunkirk, the fall of France and the threat of invasion here by German forces, a call was made by Winston Churchill for volunteers to assist the military in the defence of the country.

This force was initially called the Local Defence Volunteers (LDV) but in July was officially named the Home Guard. This force was organised into local units.

1940-1941 OSMASTON AND YELDERSLEY HOME GUARD

The following names of the Osmaston and Yeldersley section in 1940/41 were provided by Les Allen of Hulland Ward.

Bert Allen	Jack Jones	O.D. Dixon
Les Allen	H.Lowe	D.S. Harding
Keith Allen	Ted Mellor	E. Ahne
Bert Brown	Fred Nunn	J. Hulland
Baxter Eyre	Roy Oakden	Bert Hindle
H.Bull	Charlie Redshaw	Alec Wheeldon
Bill Cox	Arthur Thorp	J.H.Jones
Reg. Duffield	Edward Watkinson	Len Millward
James Elkerton	G.Wayne	Norman Brown
Tom Elkerton	Frank Warren	J.W.Durose
Bill Elkerton	D.Williamson	S.Bandy
John Foster	Alf. Wright	C.Botham
John Gilman	Eric Hankey	B.H.Bury
J. Gethin	Ron Hankey	Platoon Officers
Tom Glover	Tom Hankey	
Jim Glover	Gerald Torr	Capt. Heber-Percy
Bernard Goodall	W.Morley	Major P.W.Bell
Harry Goodall	W.Twigge	Major Clifford
Len Harrison	Bill Walker	C,Smith
Joe Hogston	Fred Walker	S.Smith
		E.Lee

ARMY HORSE TRAINING - REMOUNT HORSES OUT FOR EXERCISE

Photograph Osmaston History Group

In early 1940, No 5 Field Remount Squadron of the Royal Army Veterinary Corps moved to Osmaston Manor and were based at the Stud. Initially, 16 men rode 32 horses over from their previous base at Nottingham racecourse. Eventually, around 1000 horses and mules were accommodated in the fields and paddocks. They were to be trained for pack work, mainly in Burma, and exercises were carried out around all the villages in the vicinity. Map reading was a particularly important part of the training since during the war all road signs were removed. The Remount unit consisted of around 60 men.

128

THE INDIAN ARMY AT OSMASTON/SHIRLEY

In 1941, Berkeley Cole remembers they were given the job of preparing a tented camp and mule lines off Rough Lane, Shirley, for the arrival of the troops for the 32nd Mule Company of the Royal Indian Army Service Corps. Mules were most important to the RIASC, as was any form of transport animal, and in fact at one time, when an Indian joined up he had to take his own horse, sword and equipment. They had finished up in Dunkirk but now had to be moved. The tents were tucked amongst the trees in Shirley Hollow.

1941-ROYAL VISIT In Spring 1941, shortly after their arrival, and in great secrecy, King George VI and Queen Elizabeth came to inspect the troops. Berkeley was detailed to join the Guard of Honour as they walked from the Camp to Rough Lane, Shirley to join their waiting car.

Photographs courtesy of Berkeley Cole

● Playing their part ... Indian troops are seen (above) at the Royal Indian Army Service Corps Camp at Shirley, Derbyshire, in 1940, while (inset) they demonstrate throwing Molotov cocktails.

129

The Queen was interested as to what the men did with their turbans when they put their tin hats on. The reply was that the headgear helped the men to fill their time when not on duty, for a favourite occupation was rolling turbans, or puggarees. Each turban contained about 8 yards of cloth and took two men an hour and a half to roll.

1940-Asghar Ali who was a member of the Royal Indian Army Service Corp. was kicked by a mule and sadly died aged 37 on 13th September, 1940. He was buried in Ashbourne Cemetery and his grave is looked after by The Commonwealth War Graves Commission.

Picture Osmaston History Group

Gerald Parker remembers seeing two Indian soldiers in turbans walking down Osmaston Village with arms full of flowers – they were going into people's gardens and picking the flowers and no one dare say a word. No one had seen an Indian in a turban before.

Occasionally horses would escape and be found trotting down the village. Indian customs also caused some surprises – for the Indian soldiers, it was quite natural to walk into a stranger's house and quietly sit down, but for the households concerned, particularly the elderly of Shirley, it was quite unnerving.

Mr Peffers, the Head Gardener at Osmaston, said he never thought to see the day with Indian soldiers praying under his apple trees. Memoirs of Miss Jane Walker-Okeover

Memoirs of Pat Holland and Royal Visit- The Indian Soldiers came (1940) to Osmaston Park. The tents could be seen under the cedar trees on the right hand side of Shirley Hollow. There was great excitement when the King & Queen came to thank the Indian soldiers for their efforts during this time and Pat and her family went on the bus to Shirley Lane End to see them. This was quite an occasion, the Queen looking marvellous in her wonderful clothes. Pat also remembers the Indian Army walking from Shirley down the hill into Ashbourne with their turbans on and again they seem to have gathered flowers from somewhere which they would offer to her if she was at the house gate. They were not allowed to step out of line - she therefore would take them from the Soldiers.

Berkeley Cole remembers the telephone box in Osmaston Village being an important part of their lives as it was their only means of communication with family. He also remembered farmers with large fields were asked to erect tall posts in the middle of the fields to deter enemy aircraft from trying to land.

Berkeley was transferred from Osmaston in 1943 but the Army and war horses continued to arrive in Osmaston until there were around 700-1000 horses.

1939–1943 WW2 GERALD PARKER'S CHILDHOOD MEMOIRS OF OSMASTON AT WAR

Evacuees at Osmaston School

"The first evacuees came to the village from Manchester and attended Osmaston Shool. They came with their own teacher, a Miss Rabey but they didn't stay too long as the bombings in Manchester were not as bad as anticipated.

The second group of evacuees came from Leigh-on-Sea. They came by rail from Southend to Ashbourne and then by Trent bus from Ashbourne to Osmaston. Gerald Parker remembers he and some of his classmates sat on the wall outside the school watching as they all got off the bus with their labels attached to their clothing and carrying their belongings.

They all went to the village hall to be allocated lodgings. The council had previously visited homes in the village and if anyone had a spare room, they were allocated a child (or more if they had the space) – there was no discussion and they were expected to take them. They did try to keep brothers and sisters together but this was not always possible as in the case of Edna Westrop and Billy Westrop. Edna was placed with Mr and Mrs Brown at 1 East Side and Billy was placed at Whitemeadow Farm.

To help with the cost of looking after the new arrivals, the children brought ration books with them. School dinners were half a crown per week for which they received a wholesome hot dinner."

Evacuees at home

Mr & Mrs T Parker had two evacuee children at their house, a Brenda Gilchrist and a Joy Turner, but didn't keep in touch after they had returned home, although Gerald does remember that Edna Westrop came back to visit occasionally.

Parents of the evacuees were not really able to come and visit their children easily as few people had cars at that time and petrol was rationed.

A Ride on a Cow

Gerald also remembers coming out of school and Mr Bull would be moving his cows from a field near the school to a field near the duck pond. On numerous occasions Mr Bull would give 3 or 4 of the children a ride on his black cow down the village.

School holidays

were what every child remembered at Osmaston. They had the freedom to wander over the Estate and swim in the lakes. Many of the children remember even playing in the water wheel and going round and round.

Jack Wright remembers rushing home at 5.00pm to listen to Dick Barton & Snowy on the Radio.

OSMASTON C OF E SCHOOL-WAR DAYS

MEMOIRS OF GERALD PARKER

Gas Masks at School Gerald remembers that when at school, they had to wear a gas mask for half an hour at a time and complete lessons wearing it a few times a week. Unfortunately, the gas mask used to steam up and it was only by hooking a finger inside to allow air in could they then see what they were doing. They had to keep their gas mask with them at all times.

Dancing to Keep Warm at School-The school was heated by open fires and there were times when supplies of coal were low and the classrooms were cold. The answer was to push the desks back against the walls and they all had a dancing class with lots of movement to keep warm.

Pupils of Osmaston School from the 1940s-There is limited information as access to school and pupil information is limited by a confidentiality rule of 100 years.

Left to Right-
Irene Woolley
Muriel Richmond
Jim Chapman
Vera Slack
Ivy Kendrick

Left to Right-
Gladys Greenwood
M Hughes
Doreen Jeffreys
June Lindsay
Renee Brown

Left to Right-
Brenda Parker
Betty Hogston
Barbara Stockley
Betty Murray
Betty Wright

Left to Right-
Phillip Thorpe
John Chapman
Maurice Yeomans
Gerald Parker
Eric Slack.

RAF ACCOMMODATION BLOCKS AT OSMASTON

1941-Land was commissioned from Sir Ian Walker by the Government for building RAF accommodation blocks. A survey was carried out regarding Ashbourne Airfield and work began in the summer by the main contractors - Lee, McKenzie and Shand. Numerous Irish labourers arrived and the local children were fascinated watching the construction of the RAF accommodation blocks and runways.

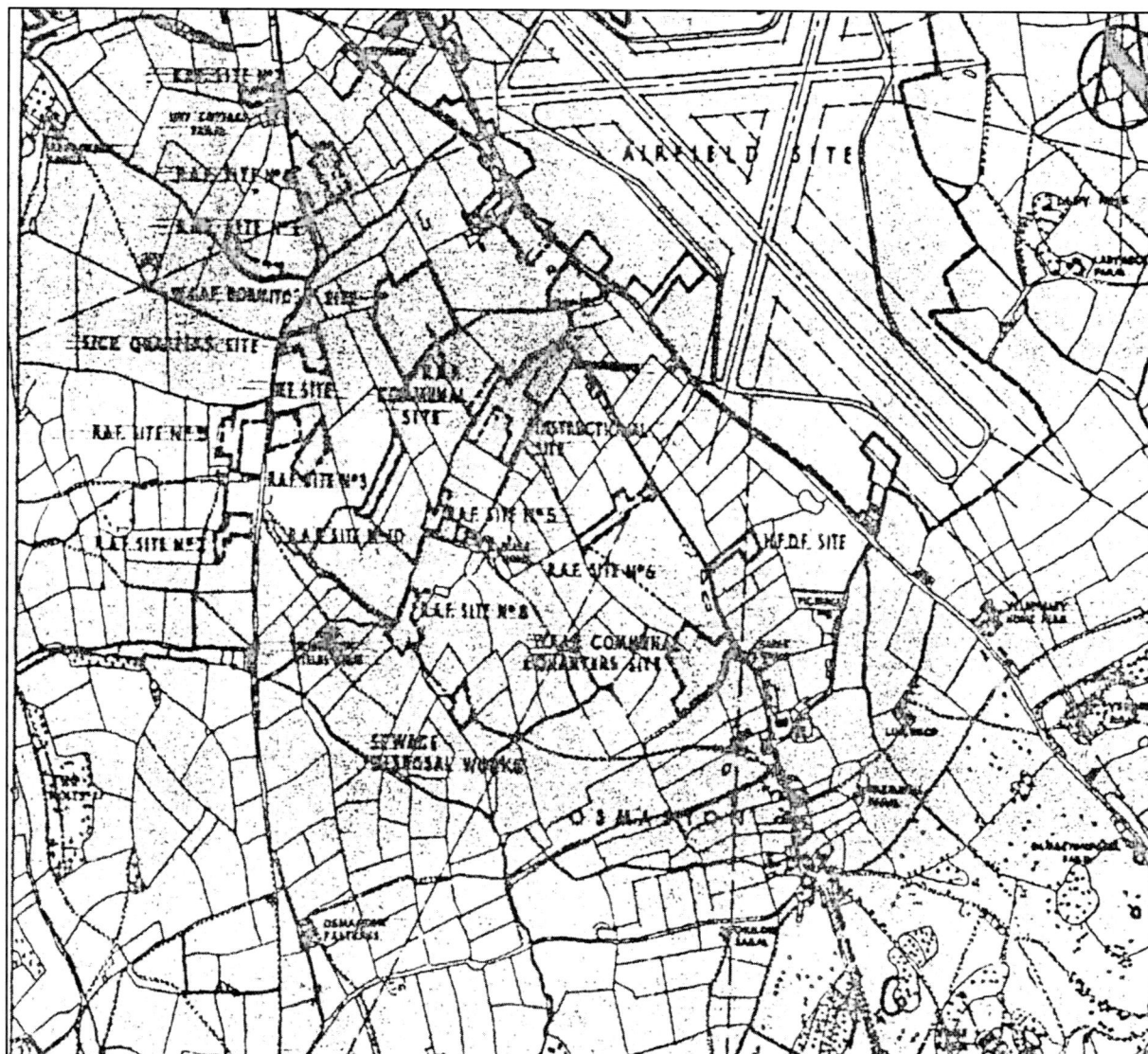

The airfield was not suitable for bombers and became an Operational Training Unit, 42 OTU, and remained until hostilities in Europe ceased in 1945.

The male and female accommodation blocks and hospitals were built and spread over a large area in Osmaston and Wyaston villages in case of an attack on the airfield. A female accommodation block was opposite Glebe and Newhouse Farm. The airfield was on the opposite side of the A52 (see the cross shape of the runways).

1942-RAF ACCOMODATION AT OSMASTON

The initial complement of around 80 men grew to about 700 by November of 1942. In December 1944, there were 2097 RAF Officers, and Other Ranks and 455 WAAF Officers, and Other Ranks. One of the lakes at the Manor was used for the aircraft evacuation and dinghy drill which formed a necessary part of the flying course. The impact on Osmaston village was extensive.

RAF Communal Site: Officers Mess, Bath/Shower/Latrines. Squash/Racquet courts. Sergeants Mess, Airmen Dining Room, Ration, Grocery & Cook Store, Gymnasium, Airmen's Showers & Latrines. Fuel Compound & Commanding Officers quarters, Water Tower & picket post.
Located in the middle of the Camp where the Caravan Site is now located.
Sick Quarters site: Sick Quarters & Annexe, Ambulance Garage & Mortuary & Latrines. **Situated off Wyaston Road**.
WAAF Communal Quarters **(Almost opposite Glebe House)** WAAF Officers Mess, Barrack Blocks, Decontamination, Bath House, Dining Room, Laundry & Drying Rooms, WAAF sick quarters
WAAF Dormitory Site – **Located in the middle of the Camp where the Caravan site is now located**

RAF Site 1 **off Wyaston Road** Officers/Sergeants Quarters, Airmen barracks & Latrines	RAF Site 8 **(near Osmaston Fields Farm)** Officers Quarters, Sergeants Quarters Latrines & Airmen Barracks.
RAF Site 2 o**ff Wyaston Rd. near Moor Farm** Officers/Sergeants Quarters , Latrines & Airmen Barracks	RAF Site 9 Latrines & Fuel compound RAF Site 10 Latrines & Barrack huts.
RAF Site 3 Officers Latrines, Sergeant Quarters & Airmen Barracks	Sewerage Disposal Works **Between Osmaston Fields Farm and Osmaston Pastures Farm.**
RAF Site 4 **Near Tutbury Hollow** Officers/Sergeant Quarters, Latrines & Airmen Barracks	--- HFDF Site-Enclosure & Rest Room **Land behind the Vicarage off Church Lane.** WT Site -Wireless Transmitting block
RAF Site 5 **Near Blake House** Officers/Sergeant Quarters & Airmen Barracks .Servants Latrines	In addition to the NAAFI associated with the Airfield, off duty activities and recreation opportunities for all of these service men and women were needed.
RAF Site 6 **Near Whitemeadow Farm** Officers/Sergeant Quarters, & Airmen Barracks	The RAF had football teams and other facilities such as a gymnasium but the increase in numbers of personnel must have put pressure on, and also created opportunities for local enterprises.
RAF Site 7 Officers Quarters, Sergeants Quarters & Latrines & Airmen Barracks.	

The cinema in Ashbourne changed the programme twice a week. Dances took place every week and pubs would have been full. In Osmaston, in addition to the weekly dances at the Village Hall and the hospitality of the Shoulder of Mutton, the Polo Field came into its own for concerts and other sporting events.

MEMOIRS OF BETTY HARDIE (NEE STEPHENS)

Betty Hardie (nee Stephens) lives at Ladyhole Lane, Yeldersley. The thatched cottages on Ladyhole Lane were built for the workers of Ladyhole House; her father, George Stephens, being the butler for Mrs Stanning and her mother, Ruth Stephens, helped in the house. Other cottages on the lane were occupied by the head gardener; Mr Jones the groom and the chauffeur.

Betty and her brother, Ellis, with a family friend with a Whittley Bomber parked on the runway behind their house
Photograph courtesy of Betty Hardie

Betty remembers that when aeroplanes were taking off from the airfield behind their house, as soon as her Mum heard the engines starting, she would run outside and get the washing in and gather the children, in case washing and children were blown away. During the war, Betty's Mum took in lodgers (whilst her husband was away at war) and these were people that worked on the airfield.

As a young child, when the war started, Betty remembers there being an indoor air raid shelter with a tin roof and netted sides in the living room, provided by Mrs Stanning – Betty and her brother enjoyed many hours playing in it. (This would be a Morrison shelter and over 500,000 were made. Although it was not designed to survive a direct hit from a bomb, it was really effective at protecting people from the effects of a bomb blast).

Betty's father was in the Derbyshire Yeomanry with Sir Ian Walker-Okeover and Sir Ian would often give him a lift home if they were coming home at the same time, otherwise Betty's father would have to walk from Derby. Betty also has fond memories of Mrs Stanning who would pick her up on her way to Osmaston Church in her Rolls Royce. It was a joy for Betty to arrive at Church in such style.

At Christmas, Betty, the Vicar and the village choir would go carol singing at The Manor. They would sing in the hallway and Betty remembers the "very imposing staircase."

Mrs Stephens from Yeldersley with her daughter Betty and son Ellis and friend, watching one of the RAF Sports Days on the Osmaston Polo Field.

Photograph courtesy of Betty Hardie

Plane Crash Memories

Memoirs of Gerald Parker- Gerald, aged about 12, was at school and 2 or 3 of the boys during lunchtime heard and saw an aircraft circling low, trailing smoke. They then heard it crash somewhere in a field near Blake House. The boys left school and went across the fields to see what had happened. The RAF were there and stopped the boys going any further but they could see the crashed aeroplane in flames. When the boys got back to school they were late, lessons had begun and they were in trouble.

Unfortunately, all three airmen were killed and the court of enquiry ruled that the plane had entered low cloud, and the pilot flying on instruments, had lost control and crashed — but Gerald still feels it was engine failure as they saw smoke — but no one asked them.

1942

New Scottish Estate. Sir Ian Walker purchased the estates of Slains, including the picturesque village of Collieston and the historic Old Slains Castle. The estate, bordering on the rugged Aberdeenshire coast, extended to 8,000 acres, and included 54 farms and crofts.

New Daughter. The second daughter of Sir Ian and Lady Walker was born in 1942 - Miss Jane Katharine Walker - all the staff were given a day's holiday to celebrate.

Memoirs of Osmaston Manor Gardener-"Jerry Shenton had joined the Royal Army Corps not knowing that he would be away from Osmaston for six years. He worked on ambulances, rescuing men with terrible injuries from battlefields in Iraq, Egypt, Sicily and Italy. He was at the appalling battle of Monte Casino, where a quarter of a million men died and were wounded. In a single week his ambulance group evacuated ten thousand injured men".

1940s YELDERSLEY HALL-WARTIME ASSOCIATIONS
Captain Henry Fitzherbert's Daughter and Son

Muriel Joyce Wright, daughter of Captain Henry Fitzherbert was born in 1909 . She was well known as a skier, a polo player and for her reputed good looks. When at Yeldersley, she was a keen follower of the Meynell hunt. During the war, she had an affair with a certain Ian Fleming, famous for his "James Bond" novels influenced by his wartime role in naval intelligence. He is said to have visited Yeldersley on several occasions.

During WW2, she joined the WRENS and was a despatch rider for the Admiralty in London until she was invalided out in late 1943. She was then involved in war work in a London factory. On 15th March 1944, Muriel was killed by a piece of masonry which came through the window of her Belgravia flat from a nearby bomb explosion during an air raid. A memorial plaque was placed in Osmaston Church.

Stephen Camplyon Wright, the youngest son of Sir Henry Fitzherbert Wright was born in 1907. Before the war he was employed at Butterley, the family firm.

TO THE DEAR MEMORY OF
MURIEL JOYCE
SEVENTH CHILD OF
HENRY FITZHERBERT
AND MURIEL WRIGHT
OF YELDERSLEY HALL

BORN 9th DECEMBER 1909
KILLED BY ENEMY ACTION
14th MARCH 1944 IN THE
CITY OF WESTMINSTER

THREE YEARS A DESPATCH
RIDER IN THE W.R.N.S.

FEARLESS AND FREE

In July 1940, while serving with the 9th Royal Lancers, was reported as missing in action. He was held as a prisoner of war. In 1945, some remarkable detail of his war experiences appeared in local newspapers. He had made five escape attempts from POW camps. One attempt was made from an asylum at Dortmund after he feigned mental instability. On recapture, he spent five months in solitary confinement, after which he was in an emaciated state. After a further attempt among 65 men who escaped via a tunnel, he was recaptured and finally sent to Oflag IVc – Colditz Castle. Here he described life as monotonous.

On the 14th February 1947, the London Gazette reported that he had been accorded a "Mention in Despatches" for "Gallant and Distinguished Services in the Field". He died in March 1977.

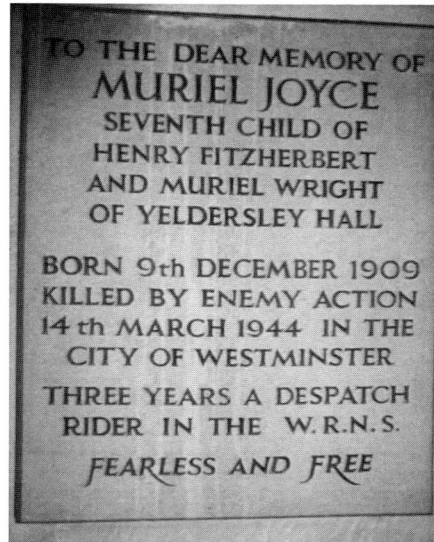

LIEUT. STEPHEN WRIGHT

YELDERSLEY HALL FOR SALE

1940s-Sir Ian's Shirley Park Company who owned
Yeldersley Hall, put the property and estate up for sale.

A charming garden and grounds, kitchen gardens, several plantations and two crofts of Old Turf were included.

A second local newspaper advertisement for sale stated that a Mr Fell bought it privately before an auction in 1947.

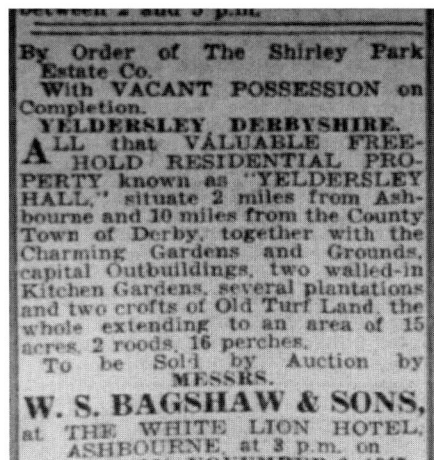

By Order of The Shirley Park Estate Co.
With VACANT POSSESSION on Completion.
YELDERSLEY DERBYSHIRE.
ALL that VALUABLE FREE-HOLD RESIDENTIAL PRO-PERTY known as "YELDERSLEY HALL," situate 2 miles from Ashbourne and 10 miles from the County Town of Derby, together with the Charming Gardens and Grounds, capital Outbuildings, two walled-in Kitchen Gardens, several plantations and two crofts of Old Turf Land, the whole extending to an area of 15 acres, 2 roods, 16 perches.
To be Sold by Auction by MESSRS.
W. S. BAGSHAW & SONS,
at THE WHITE LION HOTEL, ASHBOURNE, at 3 p.m. on

OSMASTON – EXTRACT OF MEMOIRS OF NORAH MOODY ATS

My family- My Life. Derbyshire Records Office. From 1942 to 1945

"In 1942, Norah arrived on a bus from Markeaton Camp and was greeted by Capt. Foster who took her by car to Copse Hill Cottage - a grey cottage where she was billeted with the Duffields. Mr Duffield was a groom/handyman to Lt Col Carver who lived in Copse Hill. Mr Reg Duffield was in the Home Guard and Mr Foster lived in the house opposite. They had a housekeeper, Mrs Knott, wife of a soldier with the Royal Artillary Vet Corp. She worked in Copse Hill House which was HQ RAV Remount Division.

Before the war, Capt. Foster had been the stud manager at the Manor for Sir Ian Walker but was now the Army Agriculture Officer for D, L,R & Nott. He supervised gardeners at the Manor and throughout all the counties. Norah's role was to contact the gardeners by telephone, taking orders, solve problems, order seeds, type letters and keep account books and was paid wages of 14 shillings per wk.

There were weekly hops on Fridays at the thatched Village Hall which had a good-sized dance floor with chairs around the edge, stage and kitchen. There was often a pianist, accordion, violin, drums and soldiers came from the Royal Artillery based on the Polo field and men & women from the RAF camp base and the Osmaston Airfield.   Music was also provided by the army band stationed at Osmaston Camp. Tea and sandwiches were available but no alcohol and the popular dances were the Excuse Me dance, Quickstep, Waltz, Gay Gordon's, Valetta, Lambeth Walk, & Hokey Cokey.

The Village Hall continued to play its part in organised village dances and the girls came up from Ashbourne and Derby and many friendships were formed with the airmen and soldiers. In March 1945 Norah's billet at Mr Duffield's house ended. "

Memoirs of Miss Anne Walker-Okeover-Derby didn't suffer too badly from bombing because it was difficult to locate but the string of three lakes at Osmaston on a clear night were thought to be a pathfinder. A string of incendiaries were ditched between Home Farm and the top lake and there are still holes where some stray bombs fell below Shirley Common Farm. The really serious experience was towards the end of the war when an off course VI chased by fighters went over the tower of the Manor at 100 ft., a miss of 10ft. It was shot down in open country and some of the village ladies went out with scissors to see if they could find the parachute to rescue the material.

Miss Anne went to the PNEU School in Ashbourne, then she had a governess at home, then at the age of 12 went away to boarding school in Hertfordshire.

Memoirs of Molly Silcock –

Post War we were never short of food.   There was plenty of game, rabbits, pigeons etc. and we had Pond Farm opposite which used to kill a pig occasionally and the village shared it. Food was simple and wholesome but we did not go hungry. Cooking was done on the range in the living room.

1944 - Allied Invasion Of France, Paris Is Liberated In August

Sir Ian was president of the Derbyshire Boys Clubs and Joint Master of the Meynell Hunt. He was acknowledged to be one of the best shots in Britain and took over command of the Derbyshire Yeomanry in May 1944. He was with them when they entered Austria in 1945.

**Memoirs of Gerald Parker who had previously lived in Coronation Cottages.
1946-Osmaston Post Office And Shop**

Mr & Mrs Parker and family, including Gerald, moved to the Post Office/Shop in Osmaston when Mr & Mrs Warren moved away. The family ran the shop, Gerald staying at Osmaston School until he was 14 then went to work on Mr Thorpe's farm at Yeldersley (Home Farm) and eventually owned a bike. Gerald remembers taking a mare and her foal to the Foal Sale on the Shaw Croft in Ashbourne and selling the foal and trying to bring the mare back home. The mare did not want to leave her foal and on numerous occasions turned back down the hill but eventually Gerald got her home –Gerald was aged 14, no saddle and hanging on for dear life. He earned 10 shillings and sixpence per week. He stayed at the farm for 18 months and at the age of 16 he moved to Miki Johns Electrical Engineers in Ashbourne staying until 1947 when the big snow arrived and everywhere was cut off.

Gerald then went back to farming at Quilow Farm, Osmaston and in 1952, joined the RAF based at Grove in Berkshire and eventually moved to Bicester from where he was demobbed.   By this time, Gerald had met Wendy and they married in 1956 at Challow Village Church. Eventually they moved back to the family home and Post Office/Shop at Osmaston, where their first son Stephen was born. They then moved to 2 East Side where Roy, Barbara, Alan & Trevor were born.

In 1963, Wendy took over the running of the Post office/Shop and they moved back to the Post office which they renamed Challow Cottage. Gerald worked for the Water Board for 29 years and Wendy continued running the Post Office/Shop until 1983. Gerald and Wendy were very involved with St. Martin's Church. Sadly, Wendy died in 2015 and Gerald still lives at Challow Cottage.

Gerald started collecting photographs relating to Osmaston at quite an early age and his interest grew as he acquired more photographs.

He has always been happy to share his interest with people and he is very proud of his collection.

WW2 ENDS

1945-July 6th The Manor Red Cross Hospital Closed   During the four years it was open, there were 1176 patients. Men from the three services, the Merchant Navy, Civil Defence workers and servicemen of different nationalities, all used the hospital. Even today 2018, families re-visit the village where family members had recuperated and had such wonderful memories of the Manor.

Sir Ian came home to Osmaston in July 1945. He had gained a Distinguished Service Order (DSO) and bar.

1940s- School Performances Resume

Mid 1940s "Ali Baba" School play. Edna Westrop, an evacuee, in centre with beard.
Photograph Osmaston History Group

Mid 1940s "Babes in the Wood", School Play – Photograph Osmaston History Group

1945-RAF ACCOMODATION CHANGES & RETURN OF SERVING OFFICERS

The Airfield and accommodation blocks at Osmaston started to be wound down from May 1945 until 1950 apart from routine care and maintenance. 28 Maintenance Unit from Buxton began to use the old runways and old bomb dumps for the storage and care of high explosives. During the Korean War, a specially assigned train would arrive at Ashbourne from Harpur Hill amongst tight security and would be laden with heavy explosives for delivery and storage at Ashbourne and Darley Moor. This involved the devices moving by road from Ashbourne Yard to the RAF station. The bombs would be stored and maintained at the airfield and when needed, they were moved by train from Ashbourne. This continued until 1954 when the site was disposed of. (RAF Ashbourne & Darley Moor by N Ryan & D Percy 2002).

Many local people who had served with Sir Ian, and also had a Derbyshire Yeomanry connection, found work on the Estate. George Mawbey started as a First Class Joiner and also as a barman at the Shoulder of Mutton. The Landlord then was a Charles A Robinson (Robbo). It was not long before Mr Brown (Reggie) joined Sir Ian as his private secretary. Eventually Col. E A "Nobby " Clarke, who took over the Yeomanry command from Sir Ian, joined the Estate as Agent.

Reg Bull can claim to be at least the third generation of his family in Osmaston. He was the Band Master and his father played the trombone. He was also head bell ringer just a bell rope distance from Church, in Church cottage where he lived with his son.

1945-Memoirs of Jerry Shenton Gardener at Osmaston Manor. After the War ended, the gardens at Osmaston Manor were revived and Jerry returned as Foreman Gardener but the itinerant workers never reappeared and were replaced with local men.

Some apprentices were recruited, including for the first time women. Working hours after the war were initially as long as before but in 1948 the Agricultural Wages Act set a maximum working week of 47 hours and a minimum wage. Jerry met his future wife in 1949 and they married and moved into a thatched cottage by Osmaston duck pond.

1946-George Teasdale became Clerk of Works for the Estate and lived at Stud House until 1961. He had previously been on the Strutt Estate in Belper but when the war ended he was looking for work. Sir Ian and Col. Clark offered him a job in Osmaston as they knew him from the Derbyshire Yeomanry.
Photograph & Information supplied by John Teasdale

Photograph of George Teasdale

One of the men employed by Sir Ian before the war was Sergeant Wallis Brown. He drives a tractor and is employed on the forestry staff. Driving a tractor in peaceful woods is a very different job from driving a Sherman tank, but both are all in the day's work to Wallis Brown, who won the Military Medal for his part in knocking out a German anti-tank gun while painfully wounded in the neck.

Sergeant Wallis Brown was employed on the Estate before the war and returned to became a tractor driver and a member of the forestry staff.
Derby Evening Telegraph August 1952

141

Memoirs Of Mr Winstanley- Under-Butler At The Manor

1947-Mr Winstanley had previously served four years in the Royal Navy and was working in Derby when he applied for a position of Under Butler/Handyman at Osmaston Manor. He was interviewed by Reg Brown and Sir Ian Walker and was offered the job. His wife was also given a job as back stairs maid and he and his family moved into a flat in the Manor. The Butler was Leonard Ancliffe, the Cook was Mrs Morley, with her assistant Margaret.

His day started at 6.30 am – open curtains, top up decanters, clean out all fireplaces and lay up for lighting, lay tables for breakfast and keeping the hot water boiler stoked etc. Duties also included rat catching for which he was paid 2 old pence each by the War Agency for each rat tail. Mr Buick was Sir Ian's valet. He had trained as a priest at Fort George on the Caledonian Canal, Scotland and was a "very dapper, smart and reserved man".

At the time, Sir Ian was one of the top twelve shotgun experts and in competitions used three Purdy guns, the valet acting as loader.

CONSIDERING THE FUTURE OF THE MANOR

The Walker family were now finding Osmaston Manor more and more difficult and uncomfortable to live in.

1947-Sir Peter Ralph Leopold Walker was born who would eventually become the 4th baronet. The Church bells were rung to announce his arrival.

SIR IAN WALKER'S SON

King Leopold of the Belgians is one of the godparents to Sir Ian Walker and Lady Walker's son, christened Peter Ralph Leopold. Sir Ian represented King Leopold at the ceremony.

Other godparents were Rt. Hon. M.S. McCorquodale and Major J.G.Morrison for whom Major L.A. Clowes stood proxy.

Derby Daily Telegraph 28th August 1947

Sir Ian and Lady Walker after the Christening with their two daughters Anne and Jane.

Photograph Osmaston History Group

1948-A New Company Sir Ian formed a new company, the Walker Scottish Estate Company at Glenmuick and eventually purchased "The House of Glenmuick" near Ballater, Scotland. This Estate backed onto the Queen's Balmoral Estate.

Memoirs of Sue and Molly Silcock-Molly came to the village with her parents when she was 2 years old and they moved in with family already living at Holly Cottage. Her father was Asst. Game Keeper for the Estate and her mother, Agnes, then had twins, Roger & Susan. The twins were brought up in the village and attended Osmaston School and then Ashbourne Queen Elizabeth Grammar School.

Mrs Silcock lived at Holly Cottage for about 40 years.

Christmas in the village
Susan & Molly Silcock & John Teasdale have all remembered being put into their Sunday best and going to the village hall to be presented with a Christmas present from Lady Walker and daughters, Miss Anne & Miss Jane.

The boys would bow neatly and the girls curtsied and afterwards enjoy the Christmas Party.

Talking to Miss Jane Walker-Okeover, many years later, she too remembered sitting with her mother and wrapping the Christmas presents which had been bought individually for each child on the Estate.

Hunt Ball-Memoirs of Miss Anne Walker-Okeover who lived at the Manor, remembers looking through the stair banisters at the Hunt Balls and watching the guests arrive. The Derbyshire Yeomanry also had their annual gathering at the Manor and how splendid the young men looked in their uniforms. There was a very good dance floor which had a water reservoir underneath it. Miss Anne Walker also recalls having a lovely childhood at Osmaston Manor and they were able to roam where they wanted and the Manor was so big there were rooms on the top floor which they never visited.

Memoirs of Molly Silcock-The Beaters Ball was held every year at The Green Man in Ashbourne. She also remembers that Harry Goodall, the Head Keeper, and her father, Douglas Silcock, used to go up to Glenmuick to help with the fishing and shooting. They took the gun dogs up on the train and always bought a new pair of plus fours for the occasion which were ordered by post from an outfitters in Hebden Bridge in Yorkshire.

Sad Loss-Harry Goodall, the Head Keeper, was doing the rounds with his dogs when he sadly collapsed and died. Mr Morley, the village Policeman, found him but they were unable to get close to him as Harry's dogs were protecting him. Harry Goodall used to live at Keepers Cottage.

1948 BRITISH JUNIOR RED CROSS- On 6th Dec. 1948, Betty Hardie (nee Stephens) enrolled.

Back: John Titterton, Ellis Stephens, Sheila Duffield, Barry Biffin, Barry Spruce, Peter Jones
Front: Norma Spruce, Maureen Cove, Betty Stephens, Pam Hill, Pat Jones

Photograph courtesy of Betty Hardie

1949-LONG SERVICE FARMWORKERS AWARDS

Thomas Titterton who had been employed by Sir Ian Walker at Osmaston Manor, for 44 years, has been awarded a long-service medal and certificate at the Council meeting of the Royal Agricultural Society of England. Two other farmworkers in Sir Ian's employ, **James Kirkland** and **Frederick Brown** were also to receive awards. Derby Daily Telegraph 07 04 1949

SIR IAN'S ASSOCIATION WITH THE BOYS CLUBS AND Toc H 1940s and 50s

1946-Sir Ian Walker was chairman of the Derbyshire Association Of Boys Clubs and in this role provided rooms in the disused Osmaston Manor Polo stables and stud which became known as the Derbyshire Boys' Country Club. He also promoted fund raising activities.

Derbyshire Boys' Country Club.

The Derbyshire Association of Boys' Clubs started its programme for 1946 with an experiment to try to ease the difficulties in bringing young people together in healthy country surroundings from various parts of the county, by forming a Boys' Country Club, where boys can intermingle for week-ends and holiday periods, and discuss problems relative to their clubs and localities, and join together for various sports and games. Through the generosity of Lt.-Col. Sir Ian P. A. M. Walker, Bart., D.S.O., chairman of the Association, the accommodation over the New Stud at Osmaston Manor has been loaned for experimental purposes, a delightful half-timbered building with adequate room to accommodate sixty boys, with club-rooms and games rooms for evening entertainment. Through the efforts of members of the Association, a unique club, being the first of its type in England, has been produced. Owing to its initial success, the Derbyshire Boys' Country Club will re-commence its activities on May 25th-26th, with a week-end Club Boy Training Course.

Derbyshire Times & Chesterfield Herald 21 7 1950

Derby Daily Telegraph 27 5 1946

Derbyshire Association of "Boys' Clubs.
GRAND FETE
Osmaston Manor Gardens,
(By kind permission of Sir Ian Walker,
Saturday, July 22, 1950,
Commencing at 2 p.m.
RIPLEY UNITED PRIZE BAND
FENCING DISPLAY.
ARCHERY COMPETITION.
MODEL AIRCRAFT
FLYING DISPLAY.
MODEL CAR RACING.
ALSATIAN DOG-DISPLAY.
GREAT BRITAIN'S
GYMNASTIC TEAM
(from the 1949 Swedish Lingiad).
Presentation of County Badges by
the Marquess of Hartington
Sideshows including Bowling for Pig
Punch and Judy
Children's Sports.
Teas and Refreshments, etc.,
Admission programme, obtainable at
gate,
1/6: Children 6d.
From 8 p.m. until Midnight:
DANCING in the CORONATION HALL to
THE BLUE QUAVERS BAND
Admission to Dance: 2/6.

Toc H is named after Talbot House, a refuge for WW1 servicemen, regardless of rank, in Belgium and founded by Army chaplains, Neville Talbot and Philip "Tubby" Clayton. Following WW1, the Toc H Movement was formed to continue the fellowship of Talbot House and, in the 1950s, local branches promoted projects such as play schemes, support for the disabled, elderly and activities for disadvantaged children. Girls were included in 1989.

Today, the tradition is continued with an Annual Summer Camp held on Osmaston Polo Ground, organised by Derby Toc.H, a charity which provides activity filled breaks for children from Derby schools who might not otherwise enjoy a holiday. It is thought the first camp was held in Osmaston around the 1960s and each year, around mid-July, the volunteers begin erecting the tents and marquees ready for camp. Over the years, thousands of children have benefitted from the summer camps.

Rain floods Toc H camp

A party of boys due to join a Toc H camp at Osmaston, near Derby, had to wait for 48 hours because of the rain, and will report to the camp today.

After 12 hours of rain, water seeped into some of the tents and boys had to be evacuated. After drying-out operations yesterday everything was declared shipshape again.

OSMASTON BEGINS TO RETURN BACK TO NORMAL AFTER THE WAR YEARS
1947-Ashbourne Shire Horse Show Moved to the Polo Ground in Osmaston The Ashbourne Shire Horse Society, which held annual shows from 1881, officially moved to Osmaston polo field in 1947. The first show at Osmaston was the Society's 58th show and had expanded to include a wide range of categories. Shows continued annually at Osmaston and developed into the popular agricultural shows now held each August. Sir Ian Walker was Show President in 1933 and 1958. He was delighted when his horse, Rangoon, won the Hunter Class and won a silver cup and rosette. Miss Jane Walker-Okeover later followed her father as President.

ASHBOURNE SHOW

WEDNESDAY, SEPT. 3rd,
on the
OSMASTON POLO GROUND,
Osmaston Manor, ASHBOURNE
CHILDREN'S GYMKHANA &
JUMPING COMPETITIONS,
Poultry, Rabbits and Bantams,
ROBBIE HAYHURST,
World-Famous Motor-cyclist.
Ring-side Car Park,
Luncheons and Refreshments,
Special 'Bus Service.

Photograph Osmaston History Group

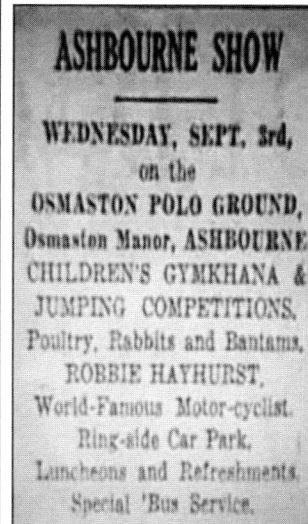

Memories of Jack Wright & Susan and Molly Silcock All attended Osmaston School during the 1950s. They all remembered Ashbourne Show being an exciting time in the village. At least a week before the show, lorries would start to arrive on the Polo Field and they would watch the erection of animal pens and marquees and last of all, the animals would arrive.

Photograph Derbyshire Life & Countryside Oct-Nov 1964

MID 1940s - MOTHERS UNION OUTING TO TRENTHAM GARDENS

Photograph Osmaston History Group

Memoirs of Mr. Winstanley – Under Butler to Sir Ian Walker

"One of my tasks was to help the Butler decant Sir Ian's own whisky brand, Glen Mist, from the barrel into the decanters for the library, study and the dining room. Soda water was also produced by placing a small bottle into a special holder, to which was attached an oxygen cylinder – two turns of the handle shot oxygen into the water and hey presto – soda water. Working at a big Manor House was a completely new style of living. Everything revolved around keeping things ship-shape for Sir Ian and her Ladyship. The hours were long and I found everything worked quite smoothly, almost like a well-run ship. Every morning, after breakfast, Lady Walker would come down to the kitchen to discuss the menu for the day and have a chat with everyone. She was the most charming and natural woman I have ever met. We already had a daughter, but when Stephen was born, Lady Walker gave us a christening robe from the nursery which was used at his christening in Osmaston Church."

Childhood Memoirs of Jack Wright – 3 East Side Jack's face lit up when he talked about Osmaston and the most idyllic childhood anyone could have. Memories came back to him of the Vicar tying the boy's sledges to the back of his car and towing them through the village. The best sledging run was the lane down to Lintwood Farm. There was no youth club or anything in the village but there was a cinema in Ashbourne but most of the time the children made their own entertainment.

1948-New Cottages Sir Ian built 4 new cottages in Osmaston to accommodate Estate workers.

146

1950-RETURN OF AIRFIELD LAND The Ministry returned the Airfield land back to Sir Ian Walker's Osmaston Estate and discussions were held as to what to do with it.

There were many RAF buildings remaining and local children used the air raid shelters as a playground. Many of these remain today, together with former wireless stations, and are now used as farm buildings.
Photograph Osmaston History Group

1940-50s Ballroom Dancing Classes Mr Tom Parker and Dorothy Fletcher started Ballroom Dancing classes on a Saturday night in the Village Hall which proved an instant success. Molly Silcock and Betty Hardie remembered the classes quite vividly and how these lessons stayed with them for the rest of their lives. Betty especially remembers learning to dance the waltz and quick step.

Payday-John Holmes remembers that in the early 1950s, Saturdays were payday for Estate Workers. After collecting their wages, the 26 gardeners under the Head Gardener, would assemble at the top of the drive with brushes and sweep the whole drive ready for Sunday Church and Manor visitors.

1950s-Decision on the Future of the Manor The Walker family considered options for reducing it in size. House rooms were far too big and ceilings too high with cast iron radiators which struggled to produce adequate heat. An architect looked at the problems and reported that a reduction was not possible. It was decided with regret to leave Osmaston.

1950s-Square Dance Classes
Dorothy Fletcher who lived in Coronation Cottages, organised Square Dancing Classes in the village hall and these proved to be a lot of fun. The Group, when requested, would provide demonstrations.

Left to Right-Square Dancing Demonstration Team.
G Parker/Barbara Hill,
Vera Fletcher/Percy Fletcher,
Tom Parker/DorothyFletcher,
Nancy Mellor/Ted Mellor.

Photograph Osmaston History Group

147

**DERBYSHIRE BOY SCOUTS ASSOCIATION – COUNTY CAMP AND RALLY
26-30TH MAY 1950 AT OSMASTON PARK**

1950- His Grace, The Duke of Devonshire KG (President), Lt. Col Sir Ian Walker Bt., DSO, (The Host) and AP Coote Esq (County Commissioner) welcomed boy scouts to Osmaston.

> **Message from Our Host: Lt Col Sir Ian Walker Bt., D.S.O. from Osmaston Manor**
> "I was very pleased when I heard that the County Rally for 1950 was to be held at Osmaston, and I extend to you all a most hearty welcome.
> I am firmly convinced that the Boy Scout movement brings out all that is best in the youth of the nation, and therefore anything that I can do to further the interests of the Movement, I do only too gladly.
> I hope you will enjoy yourselves during this camp, and when you leave you will take away with you happy memories of Osmaston and the 1950 camp."

The programme for the Boy Scouts included church on Sunday and rehearsals of "The Pageant" which they were presenting to the public and parents on Monday afternoon.

THE PAGEANT ENTITLED "BOY THROUGH THE AGES"

This was a production which enacted the development of boys through the ages. The opening sequence "Dawn" depicted when life and the universe met. Following scenes depicted various stages of development - a boy created, prehistoric life in caves, the age of tools, happy groups of simple people building homes settling to quiet domestic life only to be invaded by people from other lands, destroying and plundering. Later scenes depicted boys with finer ideas, tending the sick and dying and peace returned. A final fanfare of trumpets introduced the "aims and genius" of Lord Baden Powell represented by the books "Scouting for Boys" and "Boys Wolf Cub Handbook" which gave a boy a fuller life. It ended with the boy now a Scout and all Scouts rushed into the arena.
Extracts from the Programme

1951- Sir Ian is made Lord Lieutenant of Derbyshire. This was a post that was to last for 26 years from 1951 to 1977. Sir Ian was very well respected and "few men have brought more quiet distinction to public life in Derbyshire. In this difficult transition age when so many old standards are disappearing and new sets of values are taking their place, men like Sir Ian, with an understanding of the best in both old and new, are very rare."

1940s-50s ARMY CADETS AT OSMASTON.

The combined Cadet Force from Derby visited the grounds at the Manor during this time for training purposes and to practice manoeuvres.

Memoirs of a cadet in 1950s

A member of the Derby School Army Cadet Force recalls a visit to the Manor. Two buses of cadets arrived at the Park for a day's practical training. The quiet of the Park was disturbed as they practiced field-craft, landscape appraisal, signalling and mock section attacks. They were equipped with Mk1 and Mk2 short magazine Lea Enfield 303 rifles and a Bren gun. Although blanks were fired in place of live ammunition, they were warned not to fire their rifles close to anyone as they could cause burns. Thunder flashes were also let off. This mainly took place in the Elk park.

At the end of the day, they gathered for the bus at the Lodge in Shirley Hollow. Only one bus arrived so that half of the group had to wait for it to go into Derby and come back out again. Eight of them, instead of waiting, thumbed a lift on a passing army lorry which dropped them at the outskirts of Derby. They then decided to march into Derby down Friargate, in formation, with shouldered rifles and the Bren gun, back to the school at St.Helen's House. These events happened annually.

EARLY 1950s GRASS TRACK RACING ON OSMASTON POLO FIELD

Photograph courtesy of Mark Weston

1952-W.I. ANNUAL GARDEN PARTY Sir Ian greeted thousands of Women's Institute members who were meeting at Osmaston Park for their annual garden party of the year. "So nice of him to join us"– said one of the members, catching sight of his tall figure on the lawns. "So much easier for a man to hide from this monstrous regiment of women".

WASHING DAY MEMORIES-Memories of Molly Silcock at Holly Cottage. "Washing was done in the wash house outbuilding (which most cottages had), which had a copper boiler under which a fire was lit to get the water boiling. Clothes were sorted the night before and then put in the dolly tub with a wooden poncher which would be used to loosen the dirt.

Whites would be boiled and then mangled and rinsed and mangled again and then put out to dry. The process took all day – it was always cold meat on Monday washday – the meat left over from the Sunday joint.

 Like most of the Estate houses, Holly Cottage had a 2 hole bucket loo in an outhouse and a tin bath which was brought inside to have a bath by the open fire. In the mid 50s a lot of the Estate Cottages had one of the bedrooms converted into an inside bathroom."

Sir Ian Walker accepted that Monday was wash day, but it had been known that if washing was out on any other day, he would instruct his office staff to contact the offender and have the washing taken in.

MOTOR CYCLE RACING AT OSMASTON MANOR
(photographs and articles by kind permission of Mark Weston)

1951-1957 The Track was a 0.75 miles Circuit on Estate Roads.

"I cycled to a motorcycle road race in Derbyshire with a mate at a place called Osmaston Manor. It was the 1950s and at that time road races happened in the grounds of country estates. To be honest, I had no interest in going but my mate was very keen. I can't describe the atmosphere when we got there, the smell of fuel and Castrol R oil, the noises and the sights. I was hooked from that moment onwards".

128

Osmaston Manor Racing

Exciting Meeting on New Short Circuit : P. A. Davey
Wins Derby Cup

ONE of the most exciting race meetings to be seen in this country since the war was held on a small road circuit at Osmaston Manor, near Ashbourne, last Saturday. The ¾-mile circuit writhes through a classic example of an English country house estate, the property of Lt. Col. Sir Ian Walker, Bart. D.S.O., Lord Lieutenant of Derbyshire. The lap is of varying width—12ft along the straight past the start and maybe 15ft on other sections. There are tricky left and right corners, and one section, where the track is narrow, is so sinuous that in it, overtaking was prohibited. The surface is tar-macadam.

It is the sort of circuit almost ideally suited to engines with straight-through, rather than megaphone exhausts, and which produce crashing acceleration. Last Saturday, J.A.P.-engined machines were unassailable. The stars were the local grass-track and scramble kings, A. G. Briggs (husband of Mrs. Mollie Briggs, the trials rider), F. Wallis and P. A. Davey, and a newcomer in his first road race, V Parker.

Parker rode W. A. Lomas's 197 c.c. James, which had been converted to run on alcohol fuel. In the 200 c.c. race he felt his way round for the first few laps riding steadily behind A. G. Briggs, who was on his wife's James, and A. A. Fenn (197 Dot). On the fourth lap he dug in his spurs and overtook Fenn. On the fifth he took the lead and thereafter was unbeatable. In the 250 c.c. race, Parker, again on the James, astounded everybody

by leading on the first lap, and running second, between P. M. Doncaster (248 B.S.A.) and A. A. Fenn (248 Excelsior), for a further four laps. Then Fenn overtook. Parker was third until F. G. Smith (249 Norton), rashly trying to overtake on a corner, ran him down. With a display of the utmost pluck he was up in a flash—and finished third, to the vociferous plaudits of the crowd. His riding style and line on corners were exemplary.

All other finals were really hotly contested. That for the 350 c.c. race was fought out among nine riders who had proved fastest in four eliminating heats. There was throughout grass-cutting and "ear-'oling "—by A. G. Briggs (349 Triumph). A. A. Fenn (348 Norton), F. Wallis (347 A.J.S.), C. H. Francis (348 Triumph) and E. Houseley (347 Matchless)—of the type that stirred the crowd as probably no other sport could. Fenn led on Lap 1; Briggs on Lap 2; and, until Lap 9, they remained thus, with Wallis third. Then Wallis displaced Fenn and pressed Briggs so hard that the Triumph rider overdid things and came off. He did no serious damage Wallis won, Fenn was second and Francis third.

The 500 c.c. final was led throughout by P. A. Davey, who built up a lead that kept on increasing so long as he held the taps wide. Behind him F. Wallis (497 A.J.S.) and J. Hunt (498 Triumph) scrapped like wild cats for second place and, behind them, there was an exciting three-cornered scrap

150

John Cooper's first race was in 1955 at Osmaston Manor when he was 17 – he won the race and was carried shoulder high to collect his prize of £8.   At the time, he was working at Wileman's bike shop in Siddals Road, Derby.   After this race he never looked back, retiring in 1971.

(All photographs and articles by kind permission of Mark Weston)

John Teasdale remembers the Derby Pathfinders motor cycle club raced at the Manor on Spring Bank Holidays and Whitsun until the cattle grids were put in and the racing ceased.

FERBRACHE STARS AT OSMASTON

Wet Track Drops speeds in Derbyshire

HEAVY and continuous rain throughout the night and well into the early hours of Saturday morning gave rise to serious doubts whether or not the Derby Phœnix M.C.C.'s open to East Midland Centre road races at Osmaston Manor would be held. However, in the astonishing way in which the English climate can behave, brilliant sunshine greeted mid-day visitors to the Manor grounds.

Peter Ferbrache's journey, with his Ariels, from Enfield to Osmaston-by-Ashbourne proved to be thoroughly worthwhile. Annexing first place in the 350 c.c. Final, the Middlesex man took third place in the 500 c.c. event and then proceeded to win, for the second successive year, the Derby Cup—awarded to the winner of the gruelling 20-lap race with which the meeting concluded. F. Wallis (A.J.S.-J.A.P.) provided Ferbrache with his strongest opposition, chasing the Ariel rider hard.

In the 500 c.c. Final, Wallis and A. G. Briggs (498 Triumph) made good use of their scramble experience in negotiating a course which was decidedly slippery in parts, Wallis' winning speed was over 9 m.p.h. slower than the 55.8 m.p.h. race record which is held by Ferbrache.

P. Reed (122 Excelsior) had virtually no opposition in the 200 c.c. Final. The 250 c.c. event provided Briggs with a win. And he annexed second and third places in the 500 c.c. and Derby Cup races respectively.

Wallis repeated his 1953 success of winning the Underwood Memorial Cup, which is presented to the rider who makes the best aggregate performance in the larger capacity races during the season.

Provisional Results

200 c.c. Race (8 laps): 1, P. Reed (122 Excelsior); **2,** J. H. Allen (197 Dot); **3,** Mrs. M. A. Briggs (197 D.M.W.). **Winner's time:** 8 min. 34 sec. (42.02 m.p.h.)

250 c.c. Race (12 laps): 1, A. G. Briggs (249 Triumph); **2,** F. Wallis (246 A.J.S.-J.A.P.); **3,** N. H. Storer (248 Velocette). **Winner's time:** 12 min. 24.6 sec. (43.5 m.p.h.)

350 c.c. Race (12 laps): 1, P. Ferbrache (344 Ariel-J.A.P.); **2,** F. Wallis (344 A.J.S.-J.A.P.); **3,** T. E. Hutchinson (348 Velocette). **Winner's time:** 10 min. 14.4 sec. (52.8 m.p.h.)

500 c.c. Race (12 laps): 1, F. Wallis (497 A.J.S.-J.A.P.); **2,** A. G. Briggs (498 Triumph); **3,** P. Ferbrache (499 Ariel). **Winner's time:** 11 min. 42.4 sec. (46.1 m.p.h.)

Derby Cup Race (20 laps): 1, P. Ferbrache (499 Ariel); **2,** F. Wallis (497 A.J.S.-J.A.P.); **3,** A. G. Briggs (498 Triumph). **Winner's time:** 19 min. 39.2 sec. (48.2 m.p.h.)

MEMOIRS OF ANNE MORLEY-daughter of the village bobby

Memoirs of Anne Morley. *"My Father, Frederick George Morley used to work on Osmaston Estate as a Groom but Joined as a special constable in 1939 and the regular force in 1957 – until he retired. On his bike, he covered the villages of Osmaston, Yeldersley, Wyaston, Yeaveley, Shirley, Rodsley, Ednaston, Bradley & Edlaston. If there was any trouble with the children he told the parents – they got into more trouble that way than reporting them!"*

Photograph courtesy of Anne Redfern (nee Morley)

Osmaston's police constable to retire

With the retirement next week of P.c. Frederick George Morley of Stone Cottages. Osmaston will come the end of a never to be repeated era in local police work.

A happy and respected by young and old P.c. Morley has for many years been the epitome of that dying race of 'village bobby'. He has been what everyone considered a village policeman should be. A font of wise words and advice and an officer generous with words of caution.

In these days of Z-cars and Panda cars which pass in a flash it has always been a comfortable feeling to see the old means of transport still used by at least one member of the Constabulary.

The bicycle and P.c. Morley could in an affectionate kind of way even be regarded as synonymous for one was seldom seen without the other. and over the years he had become a popular figure riding along the country lanes in the course of his duty.

P.c. Morley joined the police in 1939 with the specials. the following year becoming a member of the War Reserve. When the time came for him to finish with the Reserve he decided to continue in police work and joined the regular force in July 1957.

Although he hates publicity P.c. Morley did tell the 'News Telegraph' he had always tried to meet people on the same level to be amiable towards them and to offer what advice he could.

Memoirs of Keith Davis "P.C. Morley lived at No.4 Stone Row. He looked like a typical village bobby, large to us lads, and rotund and rode a large black bike. In the summer holidays, the boys of the village would meet by the pond to plan their next adventure – it usually amounted to nothing more than stealing the odd apple from someone's garden or lighting a fire in the woods or playing around in the various streams and ponds. We would mess around at the pond and on the seat until we saw P.C. Morley ride off on his rounds, then we would be off to cause mayhem and mischief.

P.C. Morley had the uncanny instinct of knowing what we were up to and suddenly his face would appear over the hedge or garden wall with "Hey Lads – what are you up to then" at which we all ran off because we knew he couldn't catch us. He didn't need to – he knew who we were."

K Davis Australia

152

1953-CORONATION CELEBRATIONS John Teasdale remembers the tea served in the Hall after sports were played on the polo field and also winning a book as second prize in the sackbag race.

TEA IN OSMASTON CORONATION HALL

Left side from front: John Teasdale, David Mawbey, Roger Silcock, Robert Jones, David Jones, Graham Bond, Kenneth Bull, Tony Nash, Brian Chadwick

Right side from front: Jean Dawson, Margaret Teasdale, ?,?, ?, Susan Silcock, Margaret Goodall, Peggy Thompson.

Miss Grindey at the back with Mrs Batley   Photograph courtesy of John Teasdale

NEW BUS SHELTER
A Coronation Committee that had been formed for raising funds, built a Bus Shelter at the Osmaston Lane End which is still there today.

ROYAL CONNECTIONS

Miss Jane Walker-Okeover had known the Queen Mother for most of her life as the Walker's family home "Glenmuick" in Scotland was next door to Balmoral. Miss Jane first met Her Majesty, the Queen Mother, when she was aged 7 at Glenmuick when she came to tea accompanied by Princess Margaret. She also met King George VII when he came to shoot with her father.

Osmaston Manor and Yeldersley Hall also have a royal connection as Sarah Ferguson married Prince Andrew. Sarah Ferguson's mother was a Susan Wright (from the Fitzherbert Wright's of Yeldersley). Fitzherbert Wright 1841-1910 was the 9th child of Frances and Selina Wright and they were the great, great, great grandparents of Sarah Ferguson.

OSMASTON MANOR GARDENS IN THE 1950s MEMOIRS OF JERRY SHENTON GARDENER

Left to Right

Jerry Shenton,
Maurice Beeston,
Arthur Northledge,
Cliff Brown
2 casual labourers

Photograph Osmaston
History Group

Kitchen Gardens
with
Head Gardener's
house in the
background

Photograph Osmaston
History Group

Memoirs of Jerry Shenton –"The bothy which housed boilers for the adjoining glasshouses as well as providing accommodation for itinerant workers, is the building in the centre of the picture. The stove used for growing cucurbits such as cucumbers, melons and orchids, is the glasshouse closest to the Bothy. Peaches of many varieties were ripened on the long south facing glasshouses seen in the foreground. A profusion of raspberries and other soft fruits are to the left of the picture behind the Bothy.

High standards naturally encouraged entries in county and other shows and the potting sheds were full of rosettes. Competition was fierce, with Osmaston pitted against Derby Parks Department (managed by Percy Thrower who later became a TV legend) to the East and Lord Burton's Rangemore Estate away to the South West. Jerry remembers the drive for perfection – e.g. using ivory tweezers to manipulate the individual petals of prize chrysanthemums".

Bert Hodgkinson was Chauffeur to Sir Ian. His wife, Annie Hodgkinson, was the organist in the church. Bert continued to work for Sir Ian when he moved to Okeover and continued living in the same cottage on Painters Lane.
Photograph Osmaston History Grouop

MEMOIRS OF JOHN TEASDALE of Stud House from 1952 - 1960

"I count myself very blessed in being able to recall what was ostensibly an idyllic childhood living the first fourteen years of it in Osmaston. I had a sister, Margaret, who was 3 years older and my immediate playmate was Michael Harrison who lived in the flat above the Polo Stables, next to Stud House. The majority of the Stud buildings were left empty after Sir Ian sold off his polo ponies and were used as a paint shop, glazing store and storage for bricks, tiles, pipes etc. and sand and gravel with one area used as a garage.

There were occasional visits by the Estate workmen to the yard – Charlie Leach, Ossie Morley, Jim Elkerton, Albert Harrison, Arthur and Harry Stubbs etc. Apart from delivering our milk, Reg Bull and his lorry were often around and before that Harry Matkin used to bring our milk on a trap with a white horse. Mr Bates and his bread van used to come into the village from Ashbourne and Mr Wibberley with his greengrocers van from Kirk Langley.

The Estate joinery work was carried out at the then, very active sawmill, which I often visited with my father, where George Mawbey and Laurie Green were based and I still have the sledge that Mr Green made for me.

The pond in the rock garden was excellent for collecting frogspawn and catching newts. We were careful not to fall foul of Mr Peffers, Head Gardener, but they were long suffering and rarely brought us to task.

On one occasion, my father and I walked along the tunnel that linked the Manor with its famous smoke tower. For one year at least, in a field near the Manor reservoir and icehouse, the Home Farm planted potatoes for estate employees and I can remember early one morning going to dig up our row of lovely potatoes."

1954- POST WAR BALL DERBYSHIRE YEOMANRY OFFICERS AT OSMASTON MANOR – "Officers of the Derbyshire Yeomanry had every reason to be pleased with the success of their first post war ball, given at Osmaston Manor, the beautiful home of their Honorary Colonel. Leading Derbyshire residents and many members of the 12th Lancers of the Yeomanry's "sister regiment" were among the 250 guests" The Tatler 24 11 1954

1956-PLANS FOR THE FUTURE –LEAVING OSMASTON AND FORMAL NAME CHANGE

By royal licence, on inheriting property at Okeover Hall through his mother, Sir Ian's name was legally changed to Sir Ian Peter Monro Walker-Okeover. The decision was also made to leave Osmaston Manor and move to Okeover Hall which was a much smaller and compact hall. Plans were put into place to put Okeover Hall back into a state of good repair.

The Walker-Okeover coat of arms bears the motto "Esto Vigilans" which translates to "be watchful".

Coat of Arms courtesy of Sir Andrew Walker-Okeover

Village Concerns-Rumours were rife within the village as to what would happen to the Estate which had such an influence on village life. Had a Hotel Chain taken it over? Was it going to be a Girls School? There was, however, no need for initial worry as there was very little interest in large country houses at this time.

1956-57 Osmaston Village at this time consisted of:-

9 farms, let to 6 tenants

2 small holdings

Sir Ian's Home Farm of 272 acres

46 cottages – 19 occupied by Estate Workers

9 rent free, 18 tenants paying rent

12 cottages built before 1890

26 built between 1850 and 1914

4 built during the war (Coronation Cottages)

4 built since 1946 (New Cottages)

The Osmaston Shoot-Regular shoots continued in season. Sir Ian ran the Osmaston Shoot from the Estate Office within Osmaston Manor. His Head Keeper planned and reared stock and organised the events. Beaters were found from the local community. Shoots continue on the estate to a current date but are Leased out.

1955 TO 1960 STREET MAP OF OSMASTON. DRAWN BY JOHN TEASDALE AS A SCHOOLBOY.

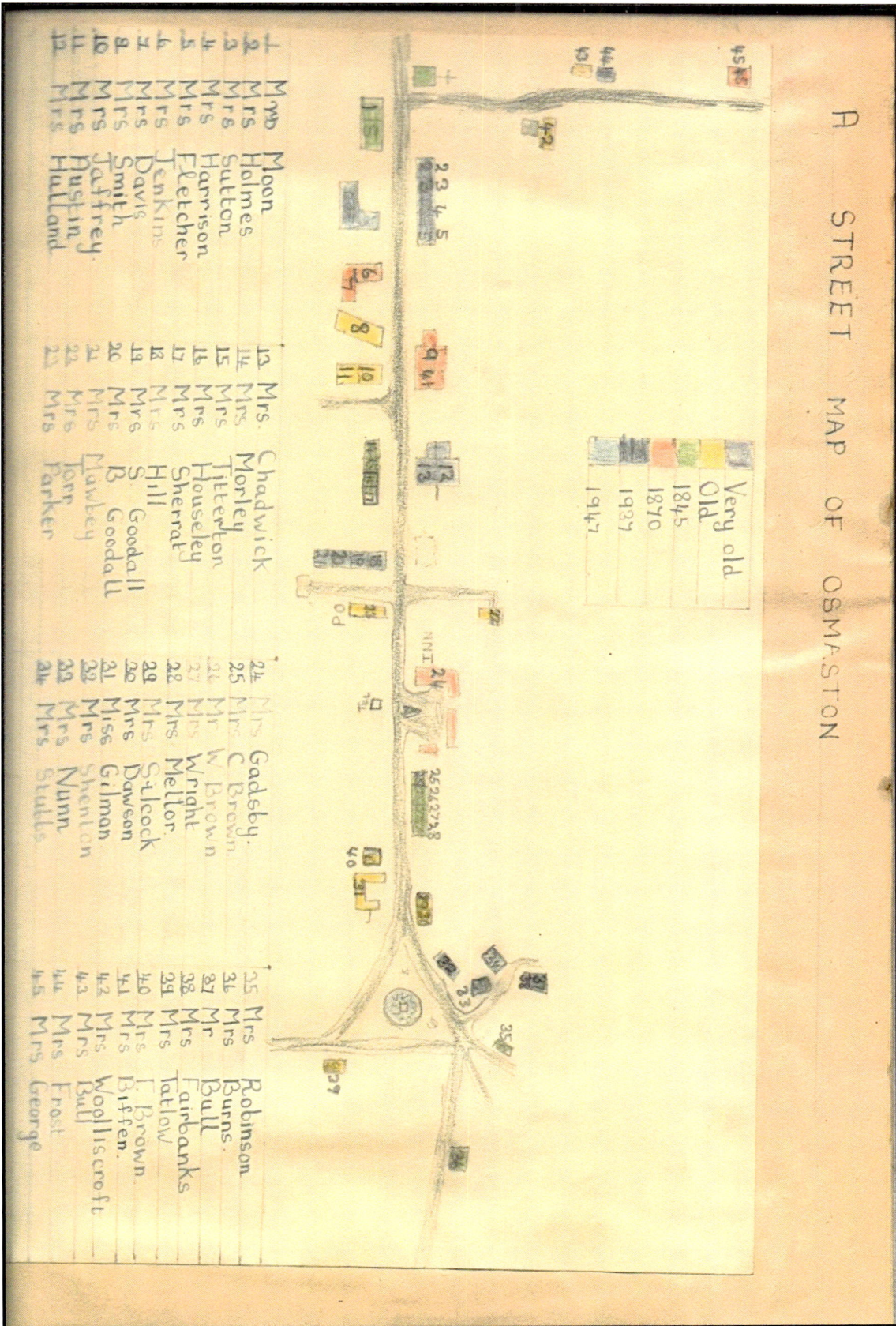

A STREET MAP OF OSMASTON

Legend:
- Very old
- Old
- 1845
- 1870
- 1937
- 1947

1 Mrs. Moon
2 Mrs Holmes
3 Mrs Sutton
4 Mrs Harrison
5 Mrs Fletcher
6 Mrs Jenkins
8 Mrs Davis
9 Mrs Smith
10 Mrs Jaffrey
11 Mrs Austin
12 Mrs Holland

13 Mrs. Chadwick
14 Mrs Morley
15 Mrs Titterton
16 Mrs Houseley
17 Mrs Sherratt
18 Mrs Hill
19 Mrs S Goodall
20 Mrs B Goodall
21 Mrs Mawbey
22 Mrs Torr
23 Mrs Parker

24 Mrs Gadsby
25 Mrs C Brown
26 Mr W Brown
27 Mrs Wright
28 Mrs Mellor
29 Mrs Silcock
30 Mrs Dawson
31 Miss Gilman
32 Mrs Shenton
33 Mrs Nunn
34 Mrs Stubbs

35 Mrs Robinson
36 Mrs Burns
37 Mr Bull
38 Mrs Fairbanks
39 Mrs Tatlow
40 Mrs L Brown
41 Mrs Biffen
42 Mrs Woolliscroft
43 Mrs Bull
44 Mrs Frost
45 Mrs George

1951-1957 JOHN TEASDALE MEMOIRS OF OSMASTON SCHOOL
Extracts from an account written by John Teasdale happily recalling village life in the 1950s and provides much detail of the school.

"Between Easter 1951 and July 1957, I attended Osmaston School, firstly in Miss Grindey's infant class before moving up to Miss Prince's primary class. I only have really positive memories of both teachers. When I left, there were only six pupils in my year and throughout those years, there were not many in excess of forty in total in any one year. I can still picture Miss Grindey's classroom, which was to the right of the central porch area of the old stone building, very clearly. There was a sand pit, Wendy House, large metal radiators that defrosted many a third of a pint bottle of milk and a smell of plasticine. The pictures included the "Temptation of Jesus" and the" Light of the World" by Holman Hunt.

The playground at the front was divided into sections for infants and juniors and to the rear of the two classrooms were two separate cloakrooms. I remember a rather lethal looking wheeled trolley on tracks that descended an incline and filled me with dread having recently fallen from my father's car and broken my leg. It was known as "the slide". Playing with Dinky toys was a major playtime activity for boys in my age group. The toilets were outside and of the non-flush bucket variety. Mr & Mrs Moon lived at the attached, former schoolhouse, and to a four year old they seemed very, very, old!

In Miss Prince's classroom we had "proper" desks with knibbed pens, inkwells, and blotting paper. We would sing a hymn every morning and every evening whilst Miss Prince played the piano. We also seemed to do a lot of nature related activities sticking leaves, flowers and berries to brown sheets of wrapping paper! PE was called "drill" and we changed in the "Reading Room" which was attached to the rear of Miss Prince's classroom and used largely for storage for drill and games equipment as well as the Maypole and a windup record player used for all dancing."

Maypole dancing, particularly on May Day, weather permitting, was great fun if not always as co-ordinated as it should have been!

Photograph courtesy of Anne Redfern (nee Morley)

Sports days were held on the Polo Field and I recall two, "boys' only", unsupervised cross-country runs. On Ascension Day, we would all attend church and then have the rest of the day as holiday. In summer months, senior children would go swimming with Miss Prince, via Trent bus, to the outdoor pool in Ashbourne. There were two special school day trips both by train from Ashbourne Station, one to Chester including the Zoo and another to Liverpool including the docks. Both seemed long and thirsty days!"

1958-FAREWELL TO THE MANOR Miss Anne Walker-Okeover remembers there being several Hunt and Yeomanry balls at the Manor and the last dance in 1958 as their swansong. The House was floodlit from the drive and looked quite splendid on a very sad day.

Photograph Osmaston History Group

1958-Staff Changes Jerry Shenton was appointed Head Gardener for Okeover Hall and although he was still living at The Thatched Cottage by the duck pond at Osmaston, he commuted to Okeover to supervise the development of the new garden.

1959-The Cottage, Also Known As Park Cottage Is Extended Park Cottage had been inherited by Francis Wright from the Beresfords and was part of the Osmaston Estate. Various people lived there over the years. In 1959, it was extended and redecorated for Col. Clarke, agent for the Estate who, having known Sir Ian through the Derbyshire Yeomanry, continued to live on the Estate following his retirement.

LEAVING OSMASTON AND MOVING TO OKEOVER HALL.

Memoirs of Miss Jane Walker-Okeover
"Sir Ian's Okeover uncle died childless and his unmarried niece passed the inheritance to him. Okeover Hall was in a very bad state after the war, having been successively a prep school, then housing American troops and finally storing Nestlé's tinned milk. With a very long family history and the possibility of making the best part of the house into a manageable home, it was decided with great regret to leave Osmaston"

1960s-Okeover Hall Alterations and extensions were made to the Hall and in the early 1960s, the Walker-Okeover family took up residence at the Hall, together with Miss Jane Walker-Okeover and her mother. The Coach House/Garages at Okeover Hall were altered to provide upstairs accommodation for the Osmaston and Okeover Estate Office. The downstairs was used by the gardening and maintenance staff.

1961-SUNDAY SCHOOL OUTING TO TRENTHAM GARDENS

Photograph Osmaston History Group

Back row Left to Right: Mrs Silcock, Ruth Chadwick, Anne Morley, Pat Jaffrey, Roger Silcock, Jean Dawson, Richard Owen, Robert Jones, Mrs T Archer, Renee Brown, Sheila Wooliscroft
2nd row from back: Mrs Jones, Susan Silcock, Doreen Mellor, Phyllis Torr, Phylis Torr Senior, Mrs Price, Rev Price.
3rd row from back: Mrs Dawson, Mrs Foster, Mrs Gilman, Mrs Hill, Hazel Wright, Betty Wright, Mrs Harrison, Mrs Harrison (their husbands worked for Tom Archer)
4th row from back: Mrs Guild, Mrs Duffield, Mrs Mellor, Miss Stanley, Linda Dawson, Ann Gilman, Jennifer Jones, Susan Walker, David Foster, Stephen Hill, Colin Duffield, David Mellor, Stephen Torr, Mrs Walker & Douglas.
Front Row: Alan Dawson, Phillip Harrison, Anthony Swinscoe, Leslie Harrison, Grant Guild, Gail Swinscoe, Wendy Walker, Jennifer Archer, Kathleen Harrison, Michael Archer, Graham Wolliscroft.

JUNE 28th-30th 1961 OSMASTON MANOR–
SALE OF CONTENTS

Henry Spencer & Sons, Auctioneers, advertised that the contents of Osmaston Manor would be sold during a three day sale.

Extracts from the Catalogue-"Fine Furniture", " Magnificent Garden Statuary", " Georgian & Modern English Silver and Pewter", "English, Continental, Oriental Porcelain & China", " Sporting Prints & Oil Paintings", " Books", " Hunting Saddlery" and "Conservatory Furniture" etc. etc.

The sale also included some Polo Helmets, Furs, a Collection of Walking Sticks, Carpets and many pairs of Curtains with drops of 17 feet which indicates the vast height of some of the Manor rooms.

Sir Ian advertised the property for Lease, suggesting its suitability as a potential Headquarters, Hospital, Public School, Offices or Institutional use.

OSMASTON MANOR LEFT STANDING EMPTY

Winter Garden at Osmaston   Photograph Osmaston History Group

1962-Osmaston Nurseries Mr Hartwig Bertleson took over the gardens at Osmaston Manor as Nurseries, maintaining the greenhouses etc. Their construction is thought to have been supervised by Joseph Paxton. He continued running a small market garden business from the property and many village children worked in the nursery pricking out plants to earn extra pocket money.

1962-Storm Damage to Limes There was a great storm in Osmaston and surrounding villages. One row of Lime Trees on the Manor Drive came down, together with damage to other village properties.

Although interest was shown in the Manor by various organisations no-one wanted to lease it and the decision was made to demolish the Manor.

One of the fireplaces went to the Shire Horse at Wyaston. Bricks from the Manor were used to build Greystones, a bungalow at Bradley and a staircase went to Wootton Lodge. Some of the stone also went to build a bar in The Shoulder of of Mutton and some double internal doors were bought by Mrs Leaf (nee Wright). A local architect recalls surveying the Staircase in the Winter Garden for potential use elsewhere.

A Unicorn's head (the symbol of the Butterley Company) was found above the Main Entrance Door to the Manor and on the Hopper Heads.

1964-A FINAL GOODBYE TO OSMASTON MANOR – DEMOLITION BEGINS

The Manor had been a major influence on the village for over a hundred years.

When the demolition contractor was asked how he felt about the demolition, he looked up at the towers and turrets and said "Osmaston doesn't want to go", "she is struggling every inch of the way" "I've called her a "She" all along – perhaps its because the building is as obstinate as an old woman".

DEMOLITION

Between 1964 and 1965, the Manor was gradually demolished.

Picture and information from Derbyshire Countryside Oct/Nov 1964 Volume 29

Architectural Salvage-"Staircases, doors, panelling, lead gutters and down-pipes, and all such things as can be used elsewhere, were being carefully dismantled. The main staircase, intricate panelling and mouldings and other fittings were dismantled so that their re-assembly elsewhere is facilitated.

Acres of floor tiles and stones lay in neat stacks in the courtyard. Mr Beadle, the demolition contractor, remarked that Osmaston Manor was imposing in size, magnificently sited and impeccably built, it was certainly one of H I Stevens best works."

"The Manor was built in the years 1846 to 1849. Domestic labour was plentiful and cheap, maintenance and material costs were low.

New standards of comfort and efficiency, and many economic factors have now robbed such houses of their charm." Picture shows demolition of Stud Farm.

1966 OSMASTON MANOR GROUNDS & POLO FIELD CONTINUE TO BE USED
Although the Manor had gone, the grounds continued to be used by various organisations.

1966–Osmaston Cricket Club

Back L to R : F Johnson, K Brown, R Silcock, P Watson G Oldfield ,R Leonard umpire
Seated L to R: (Scorer)Ted Mellor, R Calladine, M Fearn, C Grime, W Fearn, C Hill, G Parker.

Meynell & South Staffordshire Hunt

LATE SUMMER BALL

At the Polo Ground, Osmaston on

23rd September Ticket Price £38

(tickets including dinner, are available from Mrs Bridget Noakes of Abbots Bromley).

ASHBOURNE ROUND TABLE
DONKEY DERBY

Osmaston Polo Ground
WHIT MONDAY
30th MAY 1966
Open 1.30 p.m. First Race 2 p.m.

1968-Col. Peter Walker-Okeover (Son of Sir Ian)
He was Commissioned an Officer of The Blues and Royals and served in Germany and Northern Ireland.
21st Birthday -the very large photograph below was taken of the tenants and family in Okeover park from the church tower.

Reg Brown, Sir Ian's private secretary presenting Peter Walker-Okeover with a silver cigarette case.

A plaque from estate employees past and present was also presented.

Sir Ian and Lady Walker-Okeover entertained over 400 tenants and employees together with their families at Okeover Hall to celebrate the coming of age of their Son and Heir, Peter. Mr Peter Walker- Okeover was educated at Eton and Sandhurst and had served with the Royal Horse Guards (The Blues). Presentations to Mr Walker-Okeover were made by Mr William Goodall on behalf of the tenants and by Mr Reginald Brown on behalf of the household staff. After expressing his thanks for the presentation, he planted a commemorative tree. Mr S H Clowes proposed the Toast.

OSMASTON VILLAGE LIFE 1960s/70s
1967-Osmaston School - Margaret Marsden - Infant Teacher, Miss Grindey - Junior Teacher and Miss Prince was now the Head Teacher. Mr David Newberry took over as Head Teacher in 1969. Other teachers around this time were Miss Jones, Miss Smith and Mrs Hopewell.
1972-Osmaston Village Designated a Conservation Area. There were 53 buildings including 11 Grade 2 listed buildings.
1972-W.I. and New Over 60s Club. A new over 60s club was formed in Osmaston which resulted in the W.I. discontinuing their organised old persons' parties and outings. The WI continued to thrive with visits to Port Sunlight, Brighton, Weston Super Mare, The Ideal Home Exhibition, Buckingham Palace, Geoff Hamilton's Garden, Kew Gardens and the Garter Ceremony at Windsor Castle. They also organised theatre and shopping trips and of course, regular entries into the various shows.

1972 PETER WALKER-OKEOVER MARRIES

1972-Marriage Cptn. Peter Walker-Okeover, Sir Ian's eldest son and heir, married Catherine Mary Maule Ramsay, descended from the Earls of Dalhousie. They continued to live in London as he was still a serving officer. The Queen Mother was a guest at their Wedding. Cptn. Peter Walker-Okeover would eventually inherit Osmaston Estate.

1975 NEW VILLAGE HORSESHOE SEAT BY MR GRAHAM SUTTON

1975 Sir Ian Walker-Okeover who is pictured trying the seat, with his wife and Mr C A Robinson who has served on the Village Committee for 18 years. The village pond at Osmaston presented a beautiful setting for a unique presentation carried out by Sir Ian Walker Okeover before a large crowd of villagers.

VILLAGE HORSESHOE SEAT PRESENTATION CONTINUED

Introduced by Mr S Clowes, Sir Ian was at Osmaston for the dedication of a seat made of horseshoes by the village blacksmith, Mr Graham Sutton, which he had given to the village. Sir Ian went on to perform the unveiling ceremony.

The second duty was to present Mr C A Robinson, affectionately known as Robbo, with a book token in recognition of his 18 years as secretary to the Village Committee. The gift was on behalf of fellow members. The new secretary was Mrs Muriel Hill.

The Shoulder of Mutton Pub continued to be the hub of the Village for socialising and village life. It changed hands on quite a regular basis. Gerald Parker remembers that at some stage monkeys were kept in cages in the outbuildings on the forecourt.

Listed below are the Inn Keepers from 1949

1949-1956	**Charles Alfred Robinson**
1956-1960	**Francis Gadsby**
1960-Jan	**Leonard Alfred Andrews**
1960-1967	**John Maldwyn Owen**
1967-1972	**Stanley Claude Chubb**

MEMOIRS OF ASHBOURNE RUGBY UNION FOOTBALL CLUB 1934-1976

A short history of the Club.

Ashbourne Rugby Club has a longstanding connection with Osmaston. The club originally played on Osmaston Polo field until 1976 when the Rugby Club moved to the Ashbourne Recreation Ground. This short history outlines the background of the club and its links with Osmaston.

1931-The game of rugby was introduced to Ashbourne by Major C F Ball, the Headmaster of Queen Elizabeth's Grammar School. His enthusiasm brought much success and in 1932-1934 the Club played its first games on the Grammar School Grounds.

1934-35 Ashbourne Rugby Club began playing on Osmaston Polo Ground. Sir Ian Walker gave the Club the use of part of the Polo Ground from the start of the season as Polo matches continued to be played on the rest of the ground. The first rugby game in Osmaston was against the Old Mannerians on September 15th 1934 when they lost 3 – 8.

The Club's HQ was at The Shoulder of Mutton, Osmaston, then run by Mr and Mrs Jones. The loft over the pub stables was made into a changing room with a bath house built below which had two enamelled cast iron baths, one of which was recovered from a field off Derby Road. At first, the landlady would carry jugs of beer up from the cellar which limited the amount of beer sold. The team were eventually allowed to get their own jugs of beer and "settle up" later! A Dinner or Buffet dance was held annually.

> Annual Dance held on March 5th 1937
> at the New Inns Hotel
> Dancing 8.30 pm to 2.30 am
> Music supplied by The Belmont Dance Band
> 6 shillings including supper
>
> Carriages 2.30 am

Rugby Club Continued

1939-Play ceased with WW2 and resumed in 1946, when players returned from the services. Games were held at the Grammar School as Osmaston Polo Ground was still in use by the Army. Amongst those who appeared in the Forties team lists were :

Allen Harries, Vernon Howard, Laurie Clifford, Ken Pearson, Jack Spencer, Nick Miller, Arthur Birch, Alan Woolley, Ray Etherington, Noel Colwell, Peter Wright, Ken Beardmore, Bob Warner, Harry Ginnis, Roy Bennett, Charles Forgan, Mick Partridge, Eric Regnauld, Roy Simmonds, Ernie Simmonds, Ken Burton, Bill Clay, John Frearson, Warwick Dunn, Philip Frearson and Philip Thorpe.

1958-Play returned to the Polo Ground in October. The Club then had use of the pavilion. Club members, with F P Birch & Son (and Arthur Birch) refurbished the building and built on a bath house.

Bath Time!

"The bath holds thirty men and is behind the kitchen and they had to walk through the kitchen to get to it. As this is where the ladies prepared tea, the players had to keep a towel wrapped around them to protect their modesty. A member of one visiting team decided to put his towel around his head so the ladies couldn't recognise him!"

1960s-The Rugby Bar A bar licence was granted for the Polo Ground Pavilion.
The players would have a drink after the game and then move over to the Shoulder of Mutton. They very often played touring teams from Wales but unfortunately one young man decided to dance naked on the bar at the Shoulder of Mutton so that team was not invited back again!

Money saved by the Rugby Club was spent on improving the Pavilion in conjunction with the Village Committee.

1969-Ashbourne Rugby Union Football Club taken on Polo Ground in March 1969
Photograph taken by Lawrence Avery, a well-known figure in Ashbourne at the time.

Back Row L-R – Alan Gilman, Norman Whyte, Colin Burton, Andy Birch, Derek Griffiths, Ian Campbell, Mick Flather, Geoff Nadin, George McCabe.**Front Row** L-R – Roy Johnson, Pete Sandall, Andy Haslam, Alan Hirst, Richard Forrester, Chris Flather, Unknown.

Rugby Club Continued

Ashbourne Rugby Club used the Polo Field and Pavilion as their headquarters for many years and this meant that they had, in fact, a full sized Rugby Pitch on which Derbyshire played some of their County matches.

The Club which is still going strong today, played on the polo ground until 1976 when it moved to Ashbourne Recreation Ground.

Tim Sadler provided the history of the club celebrated in the late Mr P A Harries' book "50 Years of Rugby- Ashbourne Rugby Union Football Club-Golden Jubilee 1933-1983.

Memories of Ashbourne Rugby Club Many people will remember the float entered each year by Ashbourne Rugby Club in Ashbourne's Carnival Parade. Their strong presence was only realised by the Spectators when they found themselves covered in bags of flour thrown from the Rugby float.

1976-77 Captain Peter Walker-Okeover leaves the army Captain Peter Walker Okeover's first child was born, Georgina Elizabeth and the family were still living in London.   In 1977, he left the army with the rank of Captain after serving in Germany and Northern Ireland.

1977-"FANCY DRESS SILVER JUBILEE CELEBRATIONS IN THE VILLAGE HALL"

Ashbourne News Telegraph June 16th 1977

A FEW of the many who took part in the fancy dress competition at Osmaston and Yeldersley Jubilee party which was held in the hall due to rain.

1977-The Church Clock was restored by Churchwarden, Lawrence Green and his wife Amy, and on 8th July an electric motor was installed which now winds the clock and ensures the bell is still struck on the hour.

ARRIVAL OF SON AND HEIR

1978-22nd May Captain Peter Walker-Okeover and his wife announced the arrival of their son and heir to the Okeover/Osmaston and Glenmuick Estates, Andrew Peter Monro Walker-Okeover.

1978-SHROVETIDE Captain Peter Walker-Okeover is given the honour of turning up the Shrovetide Ball in Ashbourne on Shrove Tuesday as his father had before him.

1980s-OSMASTON WIND BAND – MR REG BULL RETIRES

Hanging up the baton

Photograph Osmaston History Group

Mr Reg Bull, aged 82, of Church Cottage retired after 74 years. He joined the Band as a lad and played the euphonium and bass before taking over the baton 30 years ago. Cllr. Ted Hill presented Mr Bull with a bottle of whisky for his service and £25 for Band funds.

CHANGES IN OSMASTON VILLAGE

1970-80s The Walker-Okeover Estate sells off land. In 1978, a new private house - Roag House was built in Osmaston, almost opposite The Shoulder of Mutton. Other new private houses were also built, Croft House at the far end of the village, Osmaston House and Stagsfell House near the duck pond.

1980-Park Cottage occupied. Captain Peter Walker-Okeover returned from London with his family to live in Park Cottage on Osmaston Park whilst at the same time attending Cirencester Agricultural College to study estate management.

1980-Osmaston Cricket Club folded after the 1980 season. Cricket matches had been played at Osmaston since 1907.

1980s-Osmaston School. Mr Newbury was still Headmaster with Miss Grindey, Junior Teacher, and Mrs Marsden, Infant Teacher. Other Teachers during this period were Mrs Hopewell, Mrs Oliver and Alison Turnbull.

1981-Planning Permission Request for Caravan Site On Former RAF Site

Plans for a caravan site were submitted by Col. Peter Walker-Okeover in partnership with a Mr Massey, on the land that had been previously occupied by the RAF Station.

The majority of the buildings were temporary and had already been removed but some buildings remained and traces of others such as air raid shelters and hut bases, can still be seen close to the local footpaths. Buildings such as the Officers' Mess, Squash Court, Gymnasium and Water Tower still remained.

169

1982-ANNOUNCEMENT OF THE DEATH OF SIR IAN WALKER-OKEOVER

On the 20th February, the death of Sir Ian Walker-Okeover aged 79 was reported. His many obituaries listed the many diverse roles he fulfilled. He was a member of Royal County Archers, Officer Most Venerable Order of the Hospital of St. John of Jerusalem (O.St.J.) in 1974. Former Col. Commandant of the Yeomanry regiments of the Royal Armoured Corps, and a former Derbyshire County Councillor. He was a JP and one time president of Derbyshire Boys Clubs, a former governor of Abbotsholme School, Chairman of the Governors of Ashbourne Secondary School and a prominent member of the Derbyshire branch of the Landowners Association. He was a prominent member of the council for Preservation of Rural England and of the Royal Agricultural Society. He was also a Joint Master of the Meynell Hunt.

dies after short illness

DISTINGUISHED Derbyshire soldier and baronet Sir Ian Walker-Okeover, former Lord Lieutenant of Derbyshire, died at St Mary's Nursing Home, Ednaston, at the weekend at the age of 79.

Sir Ian who commanded the Derbyshire Yeomanry in North Africa and Italy in the Second World War was awarded the DSO and bar.

For more than 60 years, he was a significant figure in the life of the county.

Sir Ian, who was born in London, died after a short illness in the early hours of Saturday morning. A private family funeral will be held at St Martin's Church, Osmaston, near Ashbourne, on Thursday, before his burial in the family grave.

County councillor

He leaves a widow, Lady Elizabeth Walker-Okeover, three children and four grandchildren. His heir Sir Peter Walker-Okeover a former captain in the Household Cavalry, will become head of the two family estates at Okeover and Osmaston which span 7,800 acres and 36 farms. Sir Ian also had a personal sporting estate, Glenmuick at Ballater, Aberdeenshire.

Former Colonel Commandant of the Yeomanry Regiments of the Royal Armoured Corps, Sir Ian was a Derbyshire County councillor for many years and served with many diverse organisations.

He was a J.P., a one-time president of Derbyshire Association of Boys Clubs, a former governor of Abbotsholme School, former chairman of the governors of Ashbourne Secondary School, a prominent member of the Derbyshire branch of the County Landowners Associa-

tion and chairman of the body for many years, a prominent member and former president of the local branch of the Council for Preservation of Rural England and a former governor of the Royal Agricultural Society.

It was in 1915, at the age of 13, that he succeeded to the Walker baronetcy, and to the spacious estate of Osmaston, near Ashbourne.

The estate included the huge 19th century Osmaston Manor, which between the wars was the focus for a social scene reminiscent of traditional English country life in its most picturesque form.

But more than 30 years after moving to Osmaston rising costs made Osmaston Manor uninhabitable.

When Sir Ian inherited the

Okeover estate from an uncle he saw where his future lay.

In 1956 by royal licence he added the name of Okeover to that of Walker and exchanged the Walker arms with the motto Cura et Industria (by care and hard work) for Okeover's Esto Vigilans (always vigilandt). He did this to stop the name dying out — the Okeover family owned land at Okeover since the Norman Conquest.

His new home was, in fact, in Staffordshire — but only by some 300 yards across the River Dove.

The sad side of this great merger was that Osmaston Manor had to go. Sir Ian unsuccessfully tried to let it. "I could have sold the house and the estate but this I was not prepared to do," he said at the time.

The manor fell to he

demolition men in 1964, five years after Sir Ian had moved to Okeover.

Keen on game shooting, and acknowledged as one of "the best shots" in Britain, the Derbyshire landowner, farmer and country gentleman also excelled as joint master of the Meynell Hunt for many years.

Mr Simon Clowes, Sir Ian's agent, said yesterday: "He was a much loved and respected character of great integrity."

Sir Ian Walker-Okeover seen at his desk in 1977

Sir Ian Walker-Okeover's Funeral was held at St Martin's Church, Osmaston and he was interred in the Family Vault.

After Sir Ian died, his son, Sir Peter Walker-Okeover became the 4th Baronet and moved with his family into Okeover Hall.

Miss Jane Walker-Okeover, his aunt and her mother Lady Elizabeth moved out of Okeover Hall into Park Cottage at Osmaston which she adored.

Chapter 7. OSMASTON AFTER THE MANOR

SIR PETER RALPH LEOPOLD WALKER-OKEOVER 4TH BARONET (1947- 2003) INHERITS OSMASTON ESTATE

Peter Walker-Okeover is pictured in uniform with his father, Sir Ian Monro Walker- Okeover Bt.
Sir Peter Walker-Okeover Bt. inherited the Osmaston estate at the age of 35 in 1982.
He was educated at Eton, then at Sandhurst Royal Military College and he was later Adjutant in the Household Cavalry.

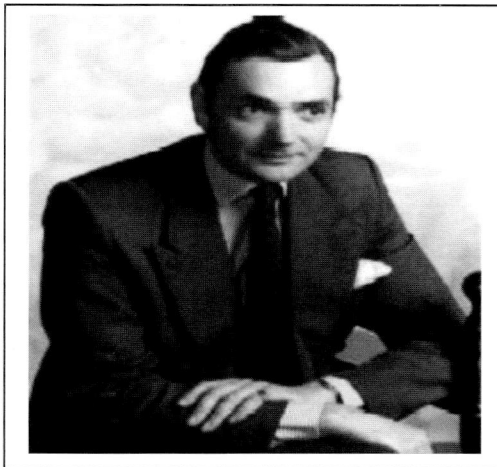

Photograph Osmaston History Group

Sir Peter Walker-Okeover Bt.
Photograph Osmaston History Group

1982-Sir Peter, Lady Walker and family moved into Okeover Hall and shortly afterwards, on May 6th, they announce the arrival of their third child, Patrick Ralph Walker-Okeover. Sir Peter now has three children, Georgina, Andrew and Ralph. Sir Peter is involved with the Estate management and, together with the Game Keepers, the running of the Okeover and Osmaston Shoots.

1983-Caravan Site Mr Massey signed the Lease for the Osmaston Caravan Site. Sir Peter was then involved with it until 1995.

Inn keepers at The Shoulder of Mutton
1972-1990	Hubert Mountford
1990-1993	Ian & Shirley Dorothy Gray
1995-present	Paul Brian Cranstone & Alison Tina Peach

171

1980-1990 OSMASTON VILLAGE

1980s-Boys Camps Each year, during the summer months, the Estate continued the tradition of boys' camps on the park. Ashbourne Cubs and Boy Scouts camped in the woods at Osmaston and many local men will remember their time at the "Lads and Dads Camp".

1984-Fighter Pilot at Ashbourne Royal Shrovetide. Mr. Karel Zouhar, a former Czechoslovakian fighter pilot was accorded the greatest honour Ashbourne could bestow by turning up the ball to start the Ashbourne Royal Shrovetide football game in 1984.
He had been a member of the Czech Airforce and was then able, in 1938, to join the Royal Air Force. As an RAF officer, he flew Hurricanes and Spitfires during WW2. Mr Zouhar went on to establish Tyremiles Ltd of Moor Lane, Osmaston with Mr Gordon Wheatcroft. Sadly in March 1985, Mr Zouhar died. Ashbourne News Telegraph 1985

1985-Gathering Chieftain at Highland Gathering. The first Ashbourne Highland Gathering was held, organised by members of the Ashbourne Pipe Band committee. Sir Peter was invited to act as the first Gathering Chieftain and held the appointment of President until 2003.

1985-Lady in Waiting. Miss Jane Walker-Okeover was appointed Lady in Waiting to HM Queen Elizabeth, the Queen Mother.

1987-Vicarage-Sale. The Vicarage, which was built in 1881, was put up for sale by the Church Authorities and was bought by Mr & Mrs Thorpe at Auction and included the Coach House building and land. They immediately sold the Vicarage and some of the land to Mr Peter Gadsby and began making plans for the restoration of the Coach House into a dwelling. They moved into the Coach House in 1989.

1988-New Church Gates were presented to St Martin's Church by the Gilman family in memory of John Gilman. The gates were made and erected by Mr Laurie Green.

Photograph Osmaston History Group

1990s OSMASTON VILLAGE CONTINUED

OSMASTON & DISTRICT WI continued to thrive with monthly meetings and visits to places of interest together with theatre and shopping trips and, of course, regular entries in Ashbourne Shows. The picture below shows them celebrating Christmas.

L-R Front row kneeling: Marion Pattinson, Anne Redfern, Susan Cresswell, Peggy Yeomans, Betty Hardie.
1st row seated: Nancy Mellor, Mary Tomlinson, Dot Pattinson, Amy Green
Standing; Anne Weston, Hazel Taylor, Ms Tomkinson, Anne Salt, Sheila Coxon, Joyce Harrison , Heather Kitchen, Jennifer Kitchen, Sue Aspbry, Sheila Dawson, Hazel Swinscoe, Joyce Keys and in front of her is Molly Beer.

1990-92 Changes at Osmaston School. Mr Newbury retired after being at the School since 1969 and Mr Tim Dutton was the new Headmaster. In 1992 Mrs Marsden (1967-92) and Miss Grindey left and Mrs Robinson was the Infant Teacher. It is believed that Miss Grindey was originally a pupil at Osmaston School and then returned as a Teacher and remained for all of her working life.

1991-92 Sir Peter and Lady Walker were divorced in 1991 and Sir Peter was appointed Deputy Lieutenant for Staffordshire, 1992.

1993-Remarriage Sir Peter married Mrs Patricia Margaret Sanderson and he became step-father to Laura, James and Harry.

MISS JANE WALKER-OKEOVER- In the late 1990s, the Queen Mother invited Miss Jane to become an Extra Woman of the Bed Chamber. This entailed serving Her Majesty for two weeks on two separate occasions each year, one in Spring in London and one in Summer in Scotland.

Her duties would include helping with Her Majesty's correspondence or accompanying her on engagements. In Scotland, Miss Jane frequently visited Birkhall on the Balmoral Estate and also the Castle of Mey.

1995

Shoulder of Mutton Paul Cranstone and Tina Peach took over the tenancy as Innkeepers of the Shoulder of Mutton and have continued to improve the premises with a new kitchen, toilets and lounge/dining room extensions. They are very involved with the village and fund raising events, supporting both the football and cricket clubs and other local organisations. The back room now houses a snooker table and other traditional pub games are enjoyed. There are welcoming log fires in the bar and dining room. They also opened a Post Office in one of the outbuildings to serve Osmaston and surrounding villages.

Caravan Site Paul Cranstone (of The Shoulder of Mutton) and Karen Peach took over the tenancy of the Caravan Site. Surviving RAF buildings on the site had been adapted and renovated with the former Officers Mess now serving as the restaurant and bar. It was at that time, called "Gateway Caravan Park".

Osmaston Manor Site At the beginning of the 20th century, there were 46 full time gardeners. After World War I, there were 26 and by the outbreak of the last war this figure had fallen to 14. Eventually, this reduced to 5 with a little extra seasonal help employed as needed. Today, the staff from Okeover Hall carry out any necessary care of Osmaston Grounds.

The Manor is used on few occasions. In the late 1990s, Lady Patricia Walker-Okeover, Sir Peter's second wife, became involved with the organisation of Osmaston Horse Trials which were held on the old Manor site. Although they were well supported events, they only survived for two years. Mr Dallas Burston was the main sponsor and Ann Sheldon helped with the Horse Trials.

1996-Miss Jane Walker-Okeover in Queen's Birthday Honours. Miss Jane was awarded Lieutenant of the Royal Victorian Order (LVO).

The Greenfields Club The club, originally formed, in 1972 for the over 60s in the area continued to thrive. Gerald Parker who has lived in Osmaston for most of his life, and has been a member since its formation, is very involved in the Club which meets every month. Gerald has been involved in organising speakers and outings to stately homes and gardens, lunches out and general entertainment for the group.

Greenfields
Over 60s
Club In 1999

1999-Mrs Jeanette Hart is appointed Headmistress of Osmaston C of E School.

2001-2003 OSMASTON VILLAGE

Foot and Mouth Disease is reported in Derbyshire and the farming community in Osmaston are on high alert. During the Foot and Mouth epidemic, Osmaston Coronation Hall was closed. The Osmaston and District WI meetings and the Greenfields Club moved to Wyaston Village Hall and in 2001, it was decided to move the meetings there permanently.

Photograph of Miss Jane Walker-Okeover

2001/2-April Miss Jane Walker-Okeover (LVO) was appointed High Sheriff of Derbyshire.
Miss Jane thoroughly enjoyed all that it entailed.
At her legal High Sheriff's Service in Derby Cathedral, she spoke of "the time to value our Freedom".

A solo was sung by former Osmaston man, Stephen Hill.

Ashbourne News Telegraph 17 10 2001
Photograph Osmaston History Group

2002-Miss Jane Walker-Okeover was appointed as Deputy Lieutenant (D.L.) (Derbys 2002).
Miss Jane continued living in Park Cottage at Osmaston with her mother. She was very involved with St Martin's Church, and worked hard helping with flower festivals and fund raising. She welcomed newcomers to the village and made sure standards were maintained in everything she did. Miss Jane enjoyed stalking on the Glenmuick Estate in Scotland and would visit with her sister, Anne and family, staying in either The House of Glenmuick or one of the cottages. Miss Jane and her sister also enjoyed "picking up" at either the Osmaston or Okeover Shoots.

A metal stag which had previously been used for target practice was put in the woods at Osmaston opposite Home Farm and Park Cottage where Miss Jane lived. It continues to be a source of amusement.

Photograph Osmaston History Group

2003-6th NOVEMBER - THE DEATH OF CAPTAIN SIR PETER WALKER-OKEOVER Bt.

"Sir Peter Walker-Okeover Bt. had lost his three-year fight against cancer. He was aged 56, and was the 4th Baronet of Okeover Hall, and the House of Glenmuick, Ballater, Scotland. He was survived by his second wife and two sons and a daughter. He also had 3 stepchildren, Laura, James and Harry from his second marriage.

The funeral took place at St Oswald's Parish Church, Ashbourne on 15th November and he was buried at Okeover Hall. The Bell in the bell tower of the small church next to Okeover Hall was tolled 56 times (one for each year of his life) by the Okeover staff. Sir Peter had already approached his Game Keepers on the Glenmuick and Osmaston Estates to be pall bearers and this they did with pride on the day."

"He was President of the Ashbourne Highland Gathering and president of many other Groups and Associations: Ashbourne Royal British Legion; Ashbourne Boy Scouts Association; Derbyshire Horticultural Society; Osmaston and District Wind Band; Ashbourne Cricket Club; Patron of Derbyshire Red Cross Society; church warden at St Mary's Church, Mappleton and chairman of the Meynell and South Staffordshire Hunt.

He was also a member of the Queen's Bodyguard for Scotland, President of the Ballater Highland Games and President of the Ballater Horticultural Society."

Extracts from Derby Evening Telegraph 11 11 2003

Sir Peter's eldest Son, Andrew Peter Monro Walker-Okeover then inherited the title and became the 5th Baronet.

Chapter 8.   OSMASTON TODAY

SIR ANDREW PETER MONRO WALKER-OKEOVER 5th Bt. BORN 1978

Andrew Peter Monro Walker -
Okeover pictured with his father
in uniform, continuing
the family tradition.

In 2003, Sir Andrew became the
5th Baronet at the age of 25.

A.P.M.W-O.   1983   P.R.L.W-O.

Photograph courtesy of Sir Andrew Walker-Okeover Bt.   Photograph Osmaston History Group

EARLY LIFE

1978-Andrew Walker-Okeover was born in London. Shortly after his birth, the family returned to this area and lived at Park Cottage, Osmaston. Sir Andrew's earliest memories of Osmaston were playing on the farm – discovering baby mice in hay bales, assisting with the milking and washing the cows – it was a little boy's dream and he loved it.

1982-Andrew, at the age of 4, moved from Osmaston into Okeover Hall when his father, then
Sir Peter Walker-Okeover, took up his position as 4th Baronet. His grandmother, Lady Elizabeth Walker-Okeover and his aunt, Jane Walker-Okeover moved to Park Cottage in Osmaston and Miss Jane became very involved with Osmaston Village.

EARLY EDUCATION AND CAREER

Andrew attended school in Ashbourne prior to leaving for boarding school in Northamptonshire aged 8. He then went on to Eton which was an experience he enjoyed and spent many summers in Scotland at Glenmuick. Glenmuick is very important to him and his mother, of course, was a "Ramsay" so he also has some Scottish blood.

1997-2000 It was at Manchester University, where he read Ancient History and Archaeology, that he met Miss Philippa L Swabey who would become his wife.   After university, one of his very early jobs when he first moved to London was working as a removal man.

OSMASTON ESTATE

Sir Peter had arranged for the Estate to be managed by a firm of Land Agents. Andrew was then working for Ogilvy Public Relations but he left Ogilvy's as his father was very ill and he wished to spend some time with him. His father died in 2003 and Sir Andrew inherited the title of 5th Baronet. The advice his father had given him was "not to move back to Okeover unmarried". After Sir Peter's death, Lady Patricia Walker-Okeover continued living at Okeover Hall for a few years. Sir Andrew returned to London and worked for Savills Country House Department until 2007.

2003-2006 OSMASTON VILLAGE LIFE

The Shoulder of Mutton - Paul Cranstone and Tina Peach continued as landlords, holding a variety of events at the pub. Their New Year's Eve fancy dress parties proved very successful. Regular Quiz nights and fund raising events were held for the various Clubs and Societies using the village and pub premises. The pub continues as the heart of the village and the Post Office and Shop proved an important part of the Community.

Caravan Site Bob Bowden took over the tenancy of the Caravan Site in 2004/5, changing its name to Peak Gateway Leisure Club. Various alterations and extensions were made to the site over the next few years, including the addition of a Ladies Beauty Salon, Dog Grooming Parlour and Fitness Centre. A function room was also made available for larger functions and parties and the Site would eventually accommodate up to 250 static and touring caravans and log cabins.

Lady Elizabeth Walker-Okeover, who had lived with her daughter, Miss Jane Walker-Okeover at Park Cottage, Osmaston, died in 2005 at the age of 91. Lady Elizabeth was the widow of Lieutenant-Colonel Sir Ian Peter Andrew Monro Walker-Okeover Bt. Lady Elizabeth was the last person to be interred in the Walker-Okeover family vault at St Martin's Church, Osmaston.

2005-Sir Andrew agreed to be the new president of the Ashbourne Highland Gathering. He then became the second ever president of the Gathering in its 21st year history, the first president being his father, who had been instrumental in getting the event off the ground. Sir Andrew was no stranger to Scottish heritage and the tradition of kilts and bagpipes due to his time spent at Glenmuick and the fact that he is also President of the Ballater Highland Games. (Information supplied by the Highland Gathering Committee).

Sir Andrew is also Patron of the Brailsford Hedge cutting Society and he loves country pursuits and second to his family, his passion is fly fishing on the River Dove as well as the Dee in Scotland.

2006-ENGAGEMENT AND WEDDING OF SIR ANDREW

The engagement was announced in November 2006, between Sir Andrew Peter Monro Walker-Okeover, 5th Baronet (b. 22 May 1978), eldest son of the late Sir Peter Walker-Okeover, 4th Baronet (1947-2003), of Ashbourne, Derbyshire by his wife Catherine Mary Maule Ramsay (now Mrs Andrew Lukas, of Wyck Rissington, Gloucestershire), scion of the Earls of Dalhousie, and Philippa L.M. Swabey, younger daughter of Lt Col (Ret'd) and Mrs Charles Swabey, of Tuscany, Italy.

Lt. Col. and Mrs Charles Swabey left Italy and moved into one of the cottages on the Osmaston Estate. Sir Andrew and Philippa decided to hold their wedding at St Martin's Church, Osmaston with the reception in a marquee on the site of the now demolished, Osmaston Manor. This entailed returning the Manor site back into its former glory – repairs to the grass areas, fountain, paths, pond, steps and balustrades took place. Osmaston tenants were delighted.

OSMASTON VILLAGE-MANOR SITE PLANS FOR WEDDING
2007 WEDDING IN OSMASTON

On 23rd June, Sir Andrew married Miss Philippa Swabey in St Martin's Church, Osmaston on a bright sunny day. A Scottish piper greeted their guests at the Manor site. The reception was in a Marquee on the site where Osmaston Manor had originally stood. The couple returned from their honeymoon to live at Okeover Hall.

Photograph courtesy of Sir Andrew Walker-Okeover Bt.

Wedding Venue Plans

From the success of Sir Andrew and Lady Walker-Okeover's own wedding on the old Manor site, came the recognition of the potential of the venue. Plans were then put in place to fully restore the estate grounds at Osmaston and to market the site as a Wedding Venue. Advice was sought and it was decided to use an extendable marquee that could cater for up to 500 guests. Their first weddings were in 2009.

Photograph courtesy of Sir Andrew Walker-Okecver

Many couples have been delighted to marry in St Martin's Church in Osmaston Village.
Miss Jane Walker-Okeover, along with village ladies, would decorate the Church for the weddings.
St Martin's Church regularly ran fund raising events with quizzes, talks and visiting choirs including the Derbyshire Police Male Voice Choir who returned on a regular basis.

2009-Highland Gathering Sir Andrew was invited to be Gathering Chieftain for the 25th Anniversary of the Highland Gathering. This year's Gathering was unfortunately cancelled due to poor weather conditions. It resumed in 2010 when Sir Andrew was again Chieftain.
(Information from Highland Gathering committee).

FIRST SON AND HEIR

2010-2011 Sir Andrew and Lady Walker-Okeover announced the arrival, at Okeover Hall, of their first son and heir, Peter Charles Monro Walker-Okeover and, again in 2011, the arrival of their second son, Edward Donald Ian Walker-Okeover.

2011-Osmaston Parish Census The population of the civil parish of Osmaston in the 2011 Census was recorded as 140 people.

2012-Queen's Diamond Jubilee Year In celebration, a barn dance and BBQ was held in a Marquee on the Polo Field which proved to be fun with lots of red, white and blue flags.

2012-DEATH OF MISS JANE WALKER-OKEOVER

Miss Jane Walker-Okeover (LVO) sadly had known she was terminally ill for the last 4/5 months of her life. She spent that time bravely putting things in order and she personally thanked the tradesmen of the town for the wonderful service they had given her over the years. Miss Jane died on 28th October 2012. The service was at St Martin's Church with an overflow in the Village Hall. Mr Rupert Turner D.L was there as a representative for HRH The Prince of Wales. As requested by Miss Jane, her ashes were scattered on Osmaston Park. She is sadly missed by the village of Osmaston.
Miss Jane was involved with numerous organisations including St. Oswald's Hospital League of Friends, the Red Cross in Derbyshire and Ashbourne Show etc.

2014-Temporary Return to Osmaston. Sir Andrew and his family moved back to Osmaston as a temporary measure whilst work was being done at Okeover Hall. He was delighted that his children would have the opportunity to live at Park Cottage, Osmaston and experience some of the memories he remembered from his childhood at the cottage.

2015-X-runner took place for the first time on the Osmaston Manor Estate. Both Sir Andrew and Lady Walker-Okeover have taken part themselves and the event now takes place regularly in March each year.

> **Advertisement literature - Osmaston X Runner Event**
> This adventure race and fun run will be in the usual 5k and 10k formats, a trail and mud run with over sixty challenging obstacles in the full race distance.
> You can expect to encounter mud, water, tunnels, monkey bars, fire, giant walls, cargo nets, balance beams, hurdles, jacobs ladders, tightropes and the amazing cresta run.

2015–The formation of Osmaston History Group There were numerous people in the village who had collected photographs, newspaper cuttings etc. and who all had stories to tell. The idea was to record these memories before they were forgotten.

OSMASTON CELEBRATES THE QUEENS 90TH BIRTHDAY
MAY 2016 PICNIC IN THE PARK

Picnic in the Park

You are cordially invited to attend the Osmaston and Yeldersley celebration of the Queen's 90th Birthday

Sunday 15th May 2pm-6pm (closing ceremony from 5.30pm)

FREE Entry for all

THE QUEEN'S 90TH BIRTHDAY CELEBRATION

On the site of the Old Osmaston Manor, Osmaston.

Bring your own Picnic

Free Gift for ALL children aged up to 11

Geoffrey Jumper Children's Entertainer   Bouncy Castle   Maypole Dancing

Souvenir Programme - £1   Cake, Tea & Coffee Stall   Bird Display

R.S.V.P.: Phone 01335 342371, Text 07742 693 764 OR Email oy.picnicinthepark@gmail.com

The Picnic in the Park is for all residents (and their family and friends) of Osmaston and Yeldersley and the parents, family and friends of all pupils attending Osmaston CE Primary School.

Tenants from Osmaston and Yeldersley, school children and friends gathered to celebrate the Queens 90th Birthday in style with a picnic on the Manor site by kind permission of Sir Andrew Walker-Okeover Bt.

Photograph Osmaston History Group

Lt. Col and Mrs Swabey and a committee made arrangements which included the Osmaston Band, the School Maypole dancing, a Falconry display, cakes and refreshments, a Treasure Hunt and the History Group had a display of their photographs and memorabilia.

Photograph Osmaston History Group

Each child was presented with a coin by Lady Walker-Okeover and Mrs Anne Clowes (daughter of Sir Ian Walker-Okeover) to remember the day. The sun shone and the day ended with singing God Save the Queen and lots of flag waving. A perfect end to a perfect day.

BIRTH OF FIRST DAUGHTER

In May 2016 Sir Andrew & Lady Walker-Okeover announced the arrival of their first daughter, Henrietta Evelyn Rose Walker-Okeover at Okeover Hall.

2016-Osmaston Manor Site The Osmaston Manor Site was busy with weddings on most summer weekends. Each year, at the beginning and end of the wedding season, a Wedding Fayre is usually held and the Marquee is also used for occasional Charity fund raising events.

Osmaston Polo Field-Ongoing Use
The Polo field continues to be used on a regular basis by numerous clubs and societies:

- The Caravan Club and Societies regularly visit the Polo Field
- The Sunbeam Motor Bike Club hold a rally for a weekend every year
- Dog Agility competitions
- The Toc H Camp visit annually with about 100 children for 2 weeks in the summer holidays.
- Cricket matches
- Ladies football. Junior Football practice on a Sunday morning
- Ashbourne Agricultural Show is held the 3rd Saturday in August every year. The show continues to grow and St Martin's Church regularly has a fund raising "Granny's Attic" stall.

Osmaston Shoot-The Osmaston Shoots are no longer managed by the Estate but are leased out and the Shoot lunches are held in the Gardeners Old Bothy.

ASHBOURNE SHOW

Photograph courtesy of Derbyshire Life

The Show continues each year on the Polo Ground. Rohan and Joy Yeomans received the prize for the best Agricultural Stand from Sir Andrew Walker-Okeover Bt. (Derbyshire Life)

2016 OSMASTON VILLAGE

VILLAGE CHRISTMAS DINNER

WE ARE HOLDING A VILLAGE CHRISTMAS DINNER ON

Sunday 10th December at 7pm

IF YOU WOULD LIKE TO ATTEND PLEASE FILL IN THE ATTACHED SLIP AND RETURN IT TO THE SHOULDER OF MUTTON BY 24TH NOVEMBER

THE SHOULDER OF MUTTON

PRICES
Adults £15
Children (U16) £7.50
Children U3 Free

MENU
Homemade Soup of the Day
...
Traditional Christmas Dinner
...
Homemade Christmas Pudding or Gateau

To encourage the village to meet together, Paul and Tina held a "Village Christmas Dinner" at The Shoulder of Mutton. Last year, the event was full to bursting and a great success, enjoyed by all.

OSMASTON HISTORY GROUP

The History Group have continued to meet but realised that fund raising was a high priority if they were going to achieve their aim of producing a book.

Lt.Col. and Mrs Charles Swabey helped the History Group get started with a fund raising Coffee Morning. The response and information received was very encouraging. Further events followed with Village Breakfasts at The Shoulder of Mutton, a Car Boot Sale, a Snail Race and a talk by Charles Wright, a descendent of Francis Wright, which all helped raise funds. Research continued and an application for a grant from Foundation Derbyshire was approved and was greatly appreciated.

OSMASTON C OF E SCHOOL PRIMARY SCHOOL

2017-Gerald Parker, a former pupil of Osmaston School, had been invited to the School to talk about his memories of "WW2 and what it would be like to be an evacuee ". The History Group provided a prize of £10, for the best piece of work based on Gerald's memories. Louie Goldberg was awarded the prize for his article, written in the form of a letter home from an evacuee. The presentation was photographed and appeared in the Ashbourne News Telegraph.

LOUIE GOLDBERG'S WINNING LETTER ON LIFE OF AN EVACUEE

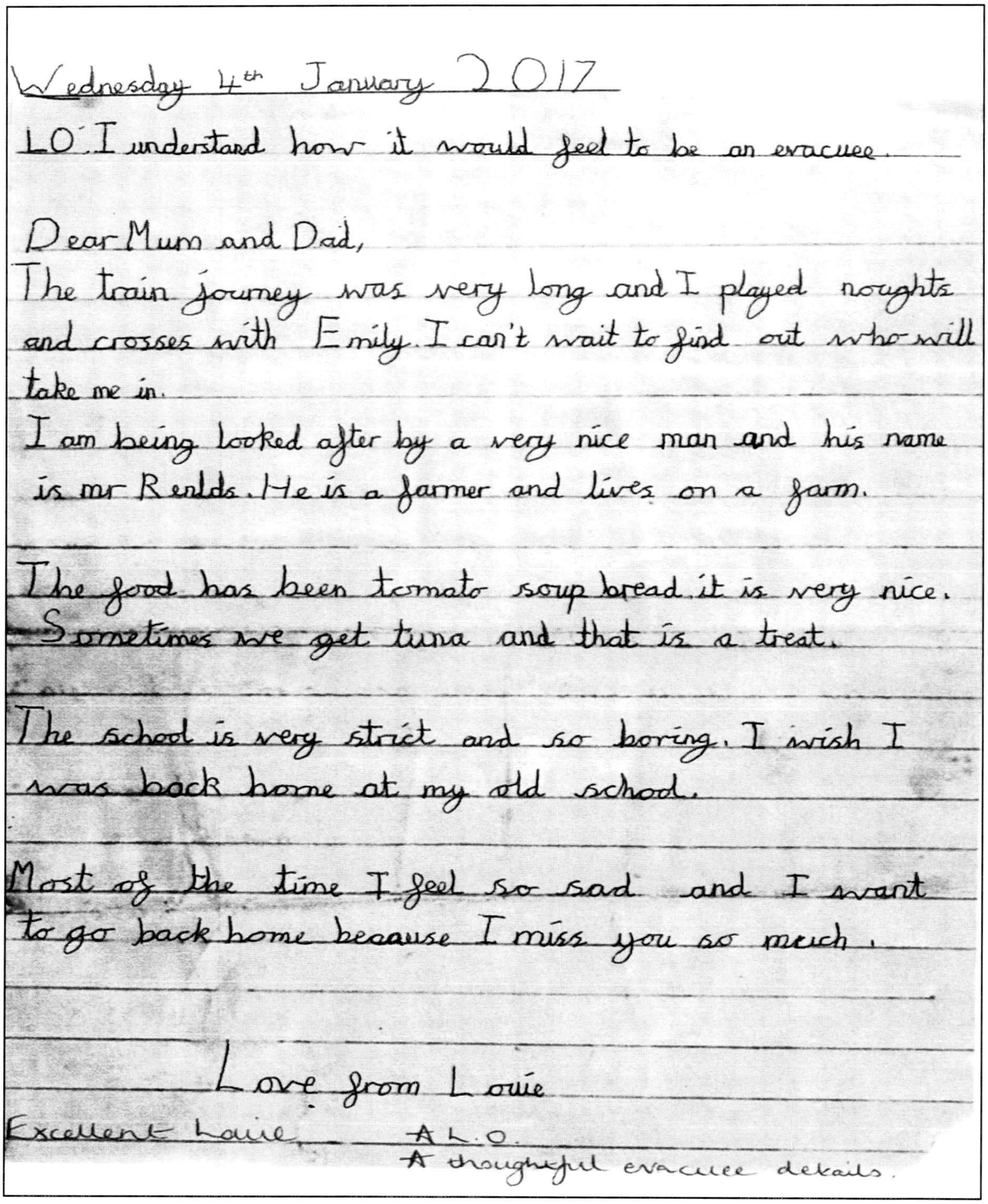

Wednesday 4th January 2017

LO: I understand how it would feel to be an evacuee.

Dear Mum and Dad,

The train journey was very long and I played noughts and crosses with Emily. I can't wait to find out who will take me in.

I am being looked after by a very nice man and his name is mr Renlds. He is a farmer and lives on a farm.

The food has been tomato soup bread it is very nice. Sometimes we get tuna and that is a treat.

The school is very strict and so boring. I wish I was back home at my old school.

Most of the time I feel so sad and I want to go back home because I miss you so much.

Love from Louie

Excellent Louie, A L.O. A thoughtful evacuee details.

Mrs Jeanette Hart has been Head at Osmaston C of E Primary School since 1999 and runs a very successful school.

2017-New Plans were submitted to demolish Church Cottage, a small house next to the Church, and build a much larger house but the plans were not approved. New plans were submitted incorporating extensions onto the existing cottage and a young family already living in the village, moved in.

Church Cottage originally had a thatched roof which had been replaced with tiles many years ago.

Church Cottage after 2017 renovations. A new extension was built on the back and a small extension on the side. Everyone was delighted with the result.

OSMASTON LOOKING TO THE FUTURE

There are several small and large businesses that operate from Osmaston Village and Osmaston takes it all in her stride. The Wedding Venue, during the summer months, can bring in large wedding parties and guests. The Peak Gateway Leisure Caravan Club has a Beauty Salon, Dog Grooming and Fitness Centre and again brings visitors into the village and trade to the Shoulder of Mutton. Opposite Church Cottage is Church Farm which has undergone careful alterations and created Sunshine Barn Therapy Centre. Sunshine Barn, is a peaceful, private and cosy sanctuary for adult counselling/coaching and a children's therapy Centre. There is also a Photographer; Decorator/Handyman; Garden Services; Bed and Breakfast; Dog Boarding Kennels; Tyremiles; a Tennis Club and the Shoot operates in the Winter months.

Some things in Osmaston have been recycled – the red telephone box is now an Information Centre where Posters, Advertisements etc. are displayed

MEMBERS OF OSMASTON HISTORY GROUP

L to R-
Keith Tucker,
Ann Plant,
Gerald Parker,
Maggie Silcock

OSMASTON VILLAGE TODAY

Life in Osmaston village has changed a great deal since the time of Francis Wright, Sir Andrew Barclay Walker and Sir Peter Carlaw Walker. At one time, most of the people living in the village would have worked for the Estate and a cottage would have gone with the job. Over the years, times have changed and the Estate now employs about 5 people based at Okeover, and of course, there is no Manor.

The school has an excellent reputation and is very sport orientated. Gerald Parker on a regular basis has been invited into the school to talk about the part Osmaston played in the War, the Evacuees, the War Horses and Indian army. Sir Andrew and Lady Walker-Okeover have taken the School children on nature walks around the Estate and Lady Walker-Okeover is one of the School Governors.

Sir Andrew is a daily visitor to Osmaston, showing couples around the Wedding Venue and attending to wider estate matters. Although the village farms usually have long term tenancies, many of the cottages now change tenants fairly regularly. This has had an effect on the village community, however the History Group has been astounded by the interest shown by families and tenants who previously lived in the village, newcomers to Osmaston and visitors to the area. It is hoped that this book "The Story of Osmaston by Ashbourne" expresses, a sense of the life, events and people who are living, or who have lived, in Osmaston and are part of its heritage.

Since the formation of the Osmaston History Group, Miss Jane Walker-Okeover, Mr Jack Wright and Mr Jerry Shenton have all contributed a great deal of material which we have used in our book. We are sad to announce that Miss Jane Walker-Okeover died in 2012, Jack Wright died in 2017 and Jerry Shenton died in May 2018. We are grateful to all the families for giving their consent for the material they contributed, to be used.